# Complete Handbook
# of All-Purpose
# Telemarketing Scripts

## Barry Z. Masser

**PRENTICE HALL**
Englewood Cliffs, New Jersey 07632

Prentice-Hall International (UK) Limited, *London*
Prentice-Hall of Australia Pty. Limited, *Syndey*
Prentice-Hall Canada, Inc., *Toronto*
Prentice-Hall Hispanoamericana, S.A., *Mexico*
Prentice-Hall of India Private Limited, *New Delhi*
Prentice-Hall of Japan, Inc., *Toyko*
Simon & Schuster Asia Pte. Ltd., *Singapore*
Editora Prentice-Hall do Brasil, Ltda., *Rio de Janeiro*

© 1990 *by*

PRENTICE-HALL, Inc.

Englewood Cliffs, NJ

10 9 8 7 6 5 4 3 2

**Library of Congress Cataloging-in-Publication Data**

Masser, Barry Z.
    Complete handbook of all-purpose telemarketing scripts / by Barry Z. Masser.

      p.   cm.
    ISBN 0-13-161068-6
    1. Telephone selling—Handbooks, manuals, etc.  2. Telemarketing-
-Handbooks, manuals, etc.  I. Title.  II. Title:  Telemarketing
scripts.  III. Title: Scripts.
HF5438.3.M368  1990
658.8′4—dc20                             90-36937
                                                         CIP

ISBN 0-13-161068-6

**PRENTICE HALL**
**BUSINESS & PROFESSIONAL DIVISION**
A division of Simon & Schuster
Englewood Cliffs, New Jersey 07632

PRINTED IN THE UNITED STATES OF AMERICA

# PREFACE

## WHY TELEMARKETING SCRIPTS GET THE
## JOB DONE FASTER AND BETTER

When a tough sale is closed, it is because the right words were spoken by the salesperson. When a difficult customer-service problem is resolved, it is because an appropriate response came from the service rep. When a credit predicament is settled, it is because the best possible dialogue was delivered by an accounting employee.

When winning performances like these are documented, tested, and further refined, the results are segments of dialogue that *work* in the most challenging business situations. Tests show that these optimized techniques consistently provide better outcomes than spur-of-the-moment responses.

One top marketing strategist put it this way:

> Why would *any* telemarketer or sales rep want to reinvent the wheel every time a tricky situation comes up with a prospect or customer? In our company, we stopped improvising. We started to write down exactly what was said when a situation worked out well. Now every time our people discover words and phrases that work, we "bottle" and save them so they're ready to use when needed.

That is *exactly* what this handbook brings you. It's packed with telemarketing scripts and letters that have been proved effective and are suitable for a wide range of purposes. Taken from leading telemarketing operations, they are ready for use in virtually any set of circumstances you are likely to encounter while selling and servicing your market—no matter *what* kind of business you're involved in.

## WHO SHOULD READ AND USE THIS HANDBOOK

A sales or telemarketing manager can conduct enormously effective training sessions with this handbook as an information source. Every chapter will contribute to the skill of telemarketers or outside sales reps.

The chapter on interviewing telemarketing candidates is of special value in helping recruiters and managers select the best personnel for a variety of jobs. This four-step screening program was created by managers in a national equipment-leasing company. They use it to keep caller turnover under a remarkable seven percent per year.

A busy entrepreneur running a new or start-up business can immediately begin using proven approaches in *every operating facet* of an enterprise. When there is simply not enough time to sit down and create presentations or devise vital new programs, this volume can certainly be the answer.

Telemarketers who need extra punch and an expanded array of tools to reach top productivity will find this information not only valuable, but very possibly the best ever offered in the field. Most books on telemarketing do a good job of laying out the how-to's of script-building; but few, if any, actually supply the *field-tested finished product* as this one does.

Marketing and sales strategists will find total integrated programs designed to either close by phone or gradually win major clients through a multicontact process. For example, the long-term account cultivation program in Chapter 10 was developed by a Fortune 500 company at a cost of many thousands of dollars.

*All* business readers will discover the means for economically servicing low-volume and distant accounts; tactics for reviving dormant customers; methods for neutralizing competition, and much more.

One chapter is completely devoted to nonselling scripts that build revenue and cut costs. Almost any administrative executive could make quick, profitable use of that unique section.

Retailers, manufacturers, and wholesalers—whether small or large—can start utilizing these approaches immediately. Whether you deal in products, services or both, this handbook will demonstrate its worth the first time you consult it.

## HOW TO USE THIS MATERIAL EFFECTIVELY

In the earliest days of telemarketing, "script" was a dirty word. That reputation was deserved when dialogue was read verbatim. More often than not, those pitches came across canned and lacking in conviction. Worse, they usually did not encourage any kind of natural information exchange between the two parties.

This handbook essentially eliminates those old faults, but still preserves the positive and considerable impact of pretested scripts. This is how it's accomplished:

- While all of the scripts on these pages are used in a variety of industries that may not resemble yours, very few changes are needed to make them fit your needs as though they were custom-prepared for you. Typically, just a few minutes are required to change some key words in a script to make it right on target for you.

- Each chapter includes both a checklist and dialogue worksheets. These simplify the job of making changes to the scripts you select for use.

- Once desired changes have been made, a bit of practice with selected scripts will give *any* telemarketer the ability to deliver very strong presentations without trying to read the words during the call. The presentation rapidly becomes second nature and begins to sound as natural as spontaneous speech. Words or phrases that may not fit an individual's personal style or preference can be easily replaced.

- In almost every script, *sensitivity* is *built in*. Probing questions are strategically placed in order to get the other person's opinions and reactions. That provides maximum interaction and can be of enormous help to a telemarketer who tends to neglect qualifying or probing.

I am confident you will find this work a powerful device not only for today, but for years to come. As your business grows, new programs, and enhancements to existing ones, will almost certainly be created. This material should facilitate that important process and provide a rich source of ideas on how to best proceed.

*Barry Z. Masser*

# CONTENTS

# Chapter 1

# PROVEN OPENINGS FOR "COLD" TELEPHONE PROSPECTING

By far, the call that is considered most important by sales leaders is the *initial prospecting call*. This vital contact is the fastest and most economical way to add new customers and expand market share. It is also, however, the contact that most often runs into rejection.

The fact is, no matter how well a cold-call is constructed, it will inevitably meet with more resistance than, say, calls to active or dormant customers. This higher rejection factor is a natural outcome of brave pioneering in new and perhaps unknown territory.

Because of the higher rejection rate that goes hand in hand with the victories in cold telephone prospecting, many managers endlessly modify their cold-call approaches to improve the ratios. This fine-tuning process usually results in simpler, more concise presentations.

Getting to the point more crisply definitely *does* get more positive responses and cuts the rebuffs down—figures from leading telemarketing operations prove it. This chapter gives you the streamlined scripts and letters that can open many new accounts at low cost.

## PRECALLING TO VERIFY A PROSPECT LIST

One very effective way to get better results in your cold prospecting is to *precall* a prospect list before you turn that list over to a telemarketer. The underlying purpose of a precall is to maximize the time and impact of your telemarketer. Precalling takes a big step toward refining your list; thus, it saves valuable time and aggravation for the skilled caller. (Note: A precalling program is usually *not* used with large prospect lists. A list of thousands of firms is simply too much unless you have a staff of people who can do precalling or unless you yourself have the luxury of enough time to place all of the necessary calls.)

Here are the specific objectives of precalling:

- To verify the location and address of a *business* prospect. Precalling is almost never used in telemarketing to consumers.
- To verify or obtain the name and title of a buyer.
- If necessary, to find out what business the firm is in.
- To determine the size of the company.
- An optional step is to have the precaller set the stage for the regular telemarketer's contact.

Keep the precall down to about 60 seconds in length. Most important, *the precaller must not get into a selling situation!* He or she can usually confine basic questioning to a receptionist in the prospect company. No attempt is made to get in touch with a buyer in precalling.

Your precalling script is set up in modules. This enables you to structure either a very brief call that simply verifies address data or a longer one that probes rather deeply into the firm's buying patterns.

While receptionists are generally helpful and knowledgeable, they are often too busy to engage a precaller in extensive dialogue. This should be kept in mind when you set up your precall.

### SCRIPT 1.1a: PRECALL TO VERIFY BASIC PROSPECT FACTS

For example, to verify an address:

| | |
|---|---|
| *Receptionist:* | [Answers call in prospect company.] |
| *Precaller:* | *Hello. We're providing information to your company and I'd like to verify the accuracy of our records.* |
| | *What is your address, please? or Is your address 310 Main Street? (When verifying an address, also be sure to cover company name, city, state, and zip. Ask whether the mailing address is different from the street address.)* |

### SCRIPT 1.1b: IDENTIFY THE BUYER

One of the key pieces of information obtained through precalling is the *right buyer* and his or her *correct name.* Armed with this data, a telemarketer can operate much more effectively.

| | |
|---|---|
| *Precaller:* | *Can you tell me who in your company is responsible for purchasing janitorial supplies?* |
| *Receptionist:* | *I think that would be Joe Charles.* |
| *Precaller:* | [Verify spelling.] *Thank you. Do you know his title?* |
| *Receptionist:* | *Plant custodian.* |

| | |
|---|---|
| *Precaller:* | *Is there anyone else involved who might benefit from receiving our information?* |
| *Receptionist:* | *I believe that's it.* |

## SCRIPT 1.1c: GETTING BASIC QUALIFICATIONS

After the precaller succeeds in establishing good dialogue with the receptionist, the following additional information should be sought. It will be valuable to the telemarketer and others in the selling company.

| | |
|---|---|
| *Precaller:* | *What does your company do?* |
| *Receptionist:* | *We make plastic parts for small appliances.* |
| *Precaller:* | *If I may ask, how many people work there?* |
| *Receptionist:* | *About 75.* |
| *Precaller:* | *Do you have any other branches?* |
| *Receptionist:* | *We're a subsidiary of Elgee Corporation in Turner, Ohio.* |
| *Precaller:* | *But Joe Charles can make decisions on janitorial products. Is that correct?* |
| *Receptionist:* | *I'm pretty sure that's right.* |

## SCRIPT 1.1d: CHECK ON THE VIABILITY OF YOUR PRODUCT OR SERVICE

If at this point the precaller has not met with any resistance, basic product intelligence can be gathered. The receptionist may very well have the answers to questions like the ones here:

| | |
|---|---|
| *Precaller:* | *Do you use soap dispensers in the washrooms?* |
| *Receptionist:* | *Yes.* |
| *Precaller:* | *Do you use paper-towel dispensers or blowers?* |
| *Receptionist:* | *Blowers, but the shop uses paper towels.* |

## SCRIPT 1.1e: SETTING UP THE FIRST SALES ATTEMPT

In a further step toward assisting the telemarketer, a precaller can explore the contact's time availability. Again, this information could be known to the receptionist.

| | |
|---|---|
| *Precaller:* | *We'll be calling Mr. Charles for an appointment. When is the best time to reach him?* |
| *Receptionist:* | *He's in his office on Tuesdays and Fridays. Try in the afternoon on those days. Be sure to call him first.* |
| *Precaller:* | *Thank you, I appreciate your help.* |

## DOCUMENTING PROSPECT FACTS

Precalling can only be valuable when prospect data is recorded in an organized way, so that it can be retrieved and used later in the selling effort. A simple form is all it takes to capture the basic facts. This can quickly be completed by the precaller as contacts are being made. Each form takes just a few seconds to fill out.

The prospect facts are given to the regular telemarketer, who uses the precalling information to update prospect lists or inquiry cards. Form 1.1 can be changed to accommodate the information you seek from prospects in a precalling program.

---

### FORM 1.1:  PRECALLING INFORMATION

Date: _____ Call made by: _____

Prospect name: _____

New address information:

_____

_____

_____

Telephone number: (    ) _____

Buyer's name: _____ Title: _____

_____     _____

Best time to reach: _____

Nature of business: _____

_____

Number of employees: _____

Other locations: _____

_____

Presently use our product or similar product?

____ Yes     ____ No

---

## CONVINCING PRETEXTS FOR MAKING THE CALL

Many telemarketers feel more comfortable and confident when they can offer their contact a tangible reason why they have chosen to call that company in particular. When referrals, inquiries, and trade-show respondents are followed up, the reason for calling is evident; but calls to a cold list can be awkward to some telemarketers.

Does the average prospect care one way or another how their firm was selected as the target of a sales call? Apparently not to any major extent. Few contacts actually come right out and ask "Why did you pick *us* as a prospect?"

For those few instances when that question comes up, this section provides a variety of responses. If one fits the occasion, use it as needed.

### SCRIPT 1.2a: "I'M CALLING BECAUSE . . ."

A pretext for calling will immediately follow the telemarketer's introduction to a contact. This initial dialogue sets up the pretext itself.

| | |
|---|---|
| *Telemarketer:* | *Good afternoon, Mr. White. I'm Sherry Gibbs of Hansen Metal Corporation.* |
| | *I know how busy you are, and I appreciate the opportunity to spend a moment with you. Let me briefly fill you in on why I wanted to speak with you on behalf of Hansen.* |

After delivering these few words, which provide the foundation of the pretext, any of the following pretexts can be used by the telemarketer.

### SCRIPT 1.2b: "WE HAVE A MATCH"

This pretext is based on knowledge that the prospect *probably* has at least one application that fits the caller's product or service.

| | |
|---|---|
| *Telemarketer:* | *We understand that your engineering department is using light alloys on some projects. That area has been a specialty with Hansen, and we feel we have a lot to offer you.* |
| | *If you have another moment, I'd like to describe a few of our strongest capabilities.* |

### SCRIPT 1.2c: "_____ ASKED ME TO CONTACT YOU"

When a specific application in the prospect firm is not known to the telemarketer, a "blind referral" can be used as a pretext. The telemarketer mentions a name that very likely *is not known* to the prospect, but *sounds* important enough to command the contact's attention. Again, this pretext can follow Script 1.2a.

| | |
|---|---|
| *Telemarketer:* | *Herb Olsen, our chief metallurgist, feels that our work in light-alloy technology might be extremely valuable to you.* |
| | *I'm calling to find out if we should set up a high-level meeting to explore the possibilities.* |

Proceed to qualify and describe your company's basic capabilities.

SCRIPT 1.2d: "YOU'RE MAKING NEWS"

This pretext for calling takes the shape of a statement to the effect that the prospect company (or the contact) is being mentioned favorably by any of these sources:

- Competitors of the prospect
- Customers of the prospect
- Trade publications

In most instances, there *is* no specific source of positive gossip. So the telemarketer has to be vague if pressed to reveal it.

> *Telemarketer:*        *Some of the people here have heard good things about the growth of your organization and your excellent management team.*
>
> *Since we like to think we're the same kind of company, and our light alloy division may be tremendously useful to you, I felt it was important to establish communications between us.*

SCRIPT 1.2e: "WE'RE HELPING OTHERS LIKE YOU"

When contacting a group of companies in a similar industry (vertical marketing), this pretext puts a telemarketer on relatively safe ground, even when specific applications are unknown to the caller.

> *Telemarketer:*        *We're doing important work in light alloys with a number of other companies in your industry (or mention the industry by name).*
>
> *I don't know for sure whether our capabilities match your needs, but I believe there could be tremendous potential for both of us if there* is *a match.*

## HIGH-VOLUME COLD CALLING

Both business-to-business *and* direct-to-consumer marketers use the phone to do large-scale cold canvassing. The objective is to *identify likely buyers* hidden in a large population of companies or individuals.

This call is *not* used to gradually cultivate business. Instead, it's a quick contact designed to spotlight the apparent sales opportunities that exist at the moment. The underlying ideas are to deliver a clear but brief message and to make as many calls as possible in a short time—and still remain completely professional in the process.

The difference between a precall and a high-volume cold call is this: A precaller makes *no* attempt to sell, and does not make judgments on the quality of a prospect.

The cold-caller definitely *does* deliver a condensed "sales pitch," then makes a judgment of prospect quality. He or she will schedule interested prospects for a follow-up call.

### SCRIPT 1.3: CALLING PAST BUYERS

A major auto manufacturer urges its dealers to get in touch with consumers who purchased new or used cars or trucks years ago. These old buyers are considered to be cold prospects for two reasons: (1) Most dealers did poorly in following up after a vehicle was sold. Therefore, little or no goodwill had been built, and customer loyalty really did not exist. In fact, due to past quality-control problems, a previous buyer might well hold negative feelings for a particular vehicle make because of service hassles. (2) In businesses that suffer above-average turnover in the sales department, it is highly unlikely that the past salesperson would be around to place the new prospecting call. So it may be better to mention the old relationship somewhat cautiously.

These circumstances are by no means exclusive to the auto business. Old buyers in any industry are too often forgotten—and sometimes abused—by the original seller, so past customers will on occasion be handled as if they are new prospects.

Here's how aggressive dealers try to recapture prior buyers.

*Telemarketer:*          *Good morning, I'm Kent Diamond of McLain Chevrolet.*

*Is this Kate Moran?*

If yes, continue. If no, ask for correct contact.

*Our records show that most of our customers select new trucks about every three years. We have exciting new models in the showroom now that I think you'll really like.*

Although qualifying is covered thoroughly in Chapter 2, the key questions for this presentation are shown here:

- *If you have just a moment, can you tell me what you prefer in a new truck?*
- *Can you give me some idea about how soon you want to be in a vehicle like that?*
- *Do you mind telling me what other makes you've considered?*

If you determine that this is a qualified prospect, go directly to the close.

*As you may know, Ajax Motors now takes a much more personal interest in its customers. We've grown because of the service we provide.*

*I'd suggest we spend about a half hour at the dealership reviewing all of the possibilities open to you, such as financing options, cargo capacity, various engines available, comfort accessories, and other important areas.*

*Can you stop in with your husband tomorrow at 11:00 A.M., or is 5:00 P.M. better?*

## SCRIPT 1.4a: "ZAPSCRIPT" FOR QUICKLY REVEALING SALES OPPORTUNITIES

Here's a presentation that is typical of the type used to pluck the likely buyers from large lists. It gets right to the point to keep the time per call down to a minute or less. The people who express even mild interest are carefully set aside for later follow-up.

*Telemarketer:*          *Hello, this is Sylvia Eisenberg of Fletcher Insurance.*

*Have you been considering major medical coverage?*

A no response is further probed with . . .

*Would you be interested in information about coverage designed especially for small companies?*

No terminates the call. If yes, continue to next step.

*Do you carry major medical now? [If so, get information on size of group, ages, etc.] We're one of the oldest and most respected firms in America. Our plan provides excellent coverage for groups like yours—at competitive rates.*

## SCRIPT 1.4b: SETTING UP THE NEXT CONTACT

Here are alternative closings you can use with high-volume cold calls. The first one is used for situations in which the timing and method of follow-up activity is uncertain.

*Telemarketer:*          *There is no obligation to you in looking into this medical plan. I'll send an information package to you this afternoon, then check with you within a few days to answer any questions that might come up.*

This close is recommended when you *are* sure about the time and method of follow-up.

*Our representative, Mr. Lederer, is seeing people in your area on Thursday. Can I have him stop by to see you at 2:00 P.M., or would 4:00 P.M. be more convenient?*

When a cold-prospect list is especially large, you may not be able to follow up the promising leads as rapidly as you'd like to. If more than four days will elapse before you can call again, a letter is strongly recommended. This should be mailed on the *same day* the first call is made, if at all possible.

Letter 1.1 can be used to accompany the information you promised to mail or as an interim contact before you follow up again by telephone.

### LETTER 1.1: "WE UNDERSTAND YOUR NEEDS AND WE'LL BE IN TOUCH"

Dear Mr. Moyle:

We appreciate the interest you expressed today in our major medical health plan for small companies. As promised, I have enclosed a brochure that provides important facts about this extraordinary coverage.

We do understand your needs, and we'll be in touch soon to discuss them in more detail. In the meantime, please don't hesitate to call me at 000-0000 if questions come up. We look forward to serving you!

Sincerely,

Sylvia Eisenberg

## SUCCESSFULLY DEALING WITH SCREENS

One of the most vexing tasks encountered in any telemarketing program is getting past one or more screens to reach the decisionmaker. Most telemarketing managers agree that screens *can't* be intimidated or pushed aside if there is to be any hope of selling a new account. Today, many screens are trusted members of a management team, and they often have a say about which calls get through and which ones don't.

As a result, the very best method a telemarketer can use for getting through is to briefly explain the purpose of the call. In other words, handle the screen in much the same way you would handle the targeted contact.

Delivering a shortened presentation to the screen may require one or more callbacks, but the extra effort can pay off because it lays the first building blocks of a solid business relationship. It makes good sense to proceed in this way if the dollar value of your product or service warrants a cultivation process.

### SCRIPT 1.5a: THE "MINI" PRESENTATION

This is simply a condensed explanation of your offer. It must be complete and crystal clear to the screen, who may have to relate the story to a manager before you get the green light to contact a decisionmaker.

| | |
|---|---|
| *Telemarketer:* | [Introduction.] |
| *Screen:* | *Can you tell me about the nature of your call?* |
| *Telemarketer:* | *We make and install fiber optic cables for computer systems using terminals that are in different buildings. Among other advantages, fiber optics eliminate data transmission errors, and that can save your company lots of problems — especially when the data is critical.* |

> *Not every installation is right for fiber optics, so if I could ask your data processing manager a couple of questions, it would be a big help.*
>
> *Can you put me through?*

The screen will often put this call through. But if the response is "Send out literature and I'll see that he gets it," go to the next module.

### SCRIPT 1.5b: SET UP THE PAYOFF CALLBACK

An effective tactic rarely used by telemarketers is to get a solid commitment for the call-back. When the screen puts off a caller, it *certainly* doesn't mean contact with the buyer is banished for all eternity! Go for a definite future time this way:

| | |
|---|---|
| *Telemarketer:* | *I'll get a brochure in the mail today.* |

At this point, get the full name and title of the screen and the correct name and title of the decisionmaker.

> *Could you arrange to connect me with Ms. Hartt next Monday at about 2:00 P.M.? I'll need about ten minutes.*

### SCRIPT 1.5c: USING THE PRESIDENT'S OFFICE TO REACH THE BUYER

Reaching the correct decisionmaker in a large company can be accomplished by contacting the "office of the president." The screen in a top executive's office usually knows who the right contact is and will often redirect a telemarketer to that individual.

When you have the name of the executive secretary *and* the accurate identity of your targeted contact, an approach like the following should succeed:

| | |
|---|---|
| *Telemarketer:* | [Asks receptionist for office of the president.] |
| *Executive Secretary:* | [Picks up call.] |
| *Telemarketer:* | *Hello. I'm J. T. Allen of Cascade Plastics. I'm trying to get in touch with the person in your firm who is responsible for specifying and ordering the side panels you use on your machines.* |
| *Executive Secretary:* | *That would be Gil Trevors, extension 423.* |
| *Telemarketer:* | *Thank you. What is your name, please? (If not given earlier.)* |
| | *Can you connect me to extension 423, or should I call again?* |

Now the telemarketer is equipped to deal much more effectively with the decisionmaker's screen. This particular caller tells the buyer's screen *just enough* to make the introduction sound like a mandate from a top executive.

| | |
|---|---|
| *Buyer's Screen:* | *Good afternoon, Mr. Trevors's office. May I help you?* |
| *Telemarketer:* | *Hello. I'm J. T. Allen of Cascade Plastics. Mr. Shelton's office referred me to Mr. Trevors. Will you connect me please?* |

Under these circumstances, it is likely that the screen will put the call through to your contact. The secretary's name is mentioned only if necessary. The word "office" packs more punch because it infers that the president is behind the scenes.

## SCRIPT 1.5d: USING TESTIMONIALS TO BREAK THROUGH

A company that takes time to document the specific experiences of satisfied users can present a much stronger case to screens *and* buyers. Assume for a moment that the telemarketer encounters resistance from the buyer's screen.

| | |
|---|---|
| *Buyer's Screen:* | *May I tell Mr. Trevors what your call is about?* |
| *Telemarketer:* | *Yes. We supply plastic side panels for the machines of one of your competitors. We solved their cracking problems and saved them almost 15 percent on production costs.* |
| | *I think Mr. Trevors might be extremely interested in some of the things we discovered during our development work.* |

Few screens would block a call that carried that much impact.

## SCRIPT 1.5e: CREATING FIRM PRESSURE FOR A DECISION

Even the most promising strategies and presentations will sometimes fail to penetrate the more immovable screens. When the telemarketer senses that an especially tough screen is *not* sincere about presenting the offer to management, polite but firm pressure can be the best last resort.

| | |
|---|---|
| *Buyer's Screen:* | *I'll mention what you said to Mr. Trevors and get in touch with you if he's interested.* |
| *Telemarketer:* | *Good. Our feeling is that this information might bring your firm some significant manufacturing advantages. I think Mr. Trevors will want to pursue this.* |
| | *Will it work out for you if I call back tomorrow afternoon?* |

## SCRIPT 1.5f: EXPRESSING UNDERSTANDING FOR SCREEN'S RESPONSIBILITY IN ORDER TO GET SUPPORT

A screen might feel torn between a boss who demands protection from callers, and callers who are presenting logical and sometimes attractive offers. In such cases, a little understanding from the telemarketer can go a long way. Merely adding a statement like this can often make a big difference:

| | |
|---|---|
| *Buyer's Screen:* | *I'll tell Mr. Trevors what you said and get in touch with you if he's interested.* |
| *Telemarketer:* | *I'd really appreciate that. I know what you're up against in handling all the calls that you must get for Mr. Trevors. Deciding which ones are worthwhile must be tough.* |
| | *I want to assure you that I believe he'll be interested in what I have to tell him. If you need any other supporting facts, please call me.* |

This statement of understanding and support can be reinforced with a follow-up letter. The letter also serves to remind the screen to speak to the decisionmaker about your offer.

### LETTER 1.2: THANKING THE SCREEN FOR HELPING OUT

Dear Ms. d'Angelo:

Your patient guidance when I called Mr. Trevors on August 20 is appreciated.

As I mentioned to you, our work on the plastic machine components for a competitor of yours might help Mr. Trevors. When I speak to him, I can briefly highlight the cost savings and the technical improvements we achieved in that project.

When you mention my call to Mr. Trevors, please ask him to note any questions he would like to ask me about our work on the machine side panels.

Once again, your assistance is extremely valuable. I'll call you on Thursday morning at about 10:00 A.M.

Sincerely,

J. T. Allen

### LETTER 1.3: THE "INITIAL HERE" METHOD OF SPEEDING UP A DECISION

When repeated call backs do not result in contact with the decisionmaker, the following letter may sometimes get a positive response from the screen. By asking the screen to once and for all *initial* a turndown—or else put your call through—the transaction becomes a much more formal process, which may be the trigger that causes the screen to finally act in the telemarketer's favor.

Dear Ms. d'Angelo:

To save time for both of us, please initial the correct description below.

I have described your company's work on plastic side panels to Mr. Gil Trevors, and he . . .

_____ is interested in discussing it with you at your earliest convenience.

_____ is not interested in learning more about it.

For your convenience, return this note to me in the enclosed, stamped envelope.

I look forward to speaking with you again soon.

Best wishes,

J. T. Allen

# KEY STATEMENTS THAT ESTABLISH QUICK CREDIBILITY

Prospect time is guarded more jealously than ever today. A key person will not enter into discussion with a telemarketer unless the caller's opening words are clear, informational, and brief.

In creating effective telephone presentations, more hard work is spent on early key statements than on any other aspect of the sales story. Key statements represent the part of any presentation that has to be carefully worked out in advance, then further refined as contacts are made.

## SCRIPT 1.6a: CLEARING YOUR PROSPECT'S TIME

While some telemarketers feel that clearing time offers the prospect an opportunity to slip away, a majority agree that it demonstrates a caller's concern for the other person's time, thus getting the call off to a strong start.

|  |  |
|---|---|
| *Telemarketer:* | *Good morning, Mr. Harvey. I'm Carl Easter of Palmer Construction Company. We do a lot of the commercial building projects around the city and would like to briefly introduce you to our capabilities.* |
| | *Do you have just a moment? [or] Can we take a minute or two now? [or] Is this a convenient time for you?* |

If not, get agreement on a call-back time. If yes, proceed to the next step.

## SCRIPT 1.6b: KEY STATEMENT FOR A SERVICE

Openings for intangibles have to be worked and reworked until they deal with *specifics* instead of vague generalities. The approach used by a printing company is one example of how a service is described then highlighted by a resulting client benefit:

|  |  |
|---|---|
| *Telemarketer:* | *We're full-service, quality printers specializing in manufacturing companies like yours. If you have a moment, I'll briefly explain how we might fit in as a resource for you.* |
| | *We've been operating since 1963. Our strongest area is design and printing. That includes work up to three color, typesetting, embossing, binding, and every other step that takes the job from start to finish.* |
| | *That means your entire project can be completed under one roof, in one step.* |
| | *Major clients like Kuenstler's use us and find that all of their printing and graphic needs are taken care of at big savings in time, money, and hassle.* |

## SCRIPT 1.6c: PUTTING SPECIAL EMPHASIS ON THE BENEFITS

In the following key telephone statement used by a private paramedical school, it was determined that the main benefit and appeal should be for a job in a doctor's office in the near future. Prospects saw themselves as key members of the medical team, so the actual process of attending classes had to be downplayed if sales appointments were to be successfully set by phone.

*Telemarketer:*     *We get people like you ready to work with the doctor on procedures such as patient preparation, appointment scheduling, ordering supplies, and many of the other vital tasks so important to making a busy practice work. You can be ready for that in only 90 days.*

*These are areas the doctor handled himself in the past, but no longer has time for, so the people we train add tremendous efficiency to a medical practice. More patients can be seen than ever before thanks to medical assistants.*

*It's extremely demanding, but very rewarding. Do you feel you want to look into a career as challenging as the medical field?*

## SCRIPT 1.6d: KEY STATEMENT FOR A PRODUCT

This successful opening was developed by the manufacturer of a protection system for computer programs. Please notice that it does *not* get into the technical facts about how a disk wards off people who copy programs illegally. Instead, it goes right to the heart of how such protection can add to a user's profits.

*Telemarketer:*     *DiskGard appears to be revolutionizing the software industry. It's the only protection system available that's safe from program pirates or casual copiers. For example: The code embedded in the DiskGard disk can't be copied by nibble-and-bit devices, so all of the standard ways to pirate disks are obsolete against it.*

*Industry figures show that for every program licensed, up to ten are stolen. If you could recover just one of those thefts, you'd double your revenue.*

## SCRIPT 1.6e: DESCRIBING THE PURPOSE OF YOUR CALL

A surprisingly large number of prospects say that a majority of telemarketers do a good job of establishing trust and describing their offer but don't do well in explaining how to make the purchase or what is expected of the buyer.

Part of the opening can effectively deal with spelling out the *purpose* of the call.

*Telemarketer:*     *My purpose in calling is to introduce you to the basic concept of protecting your valuable programs and to learn more about what you do. Then we can see if there's a fit.*

### SCRIPT 1.6f: EXPLAINING WHAT ACTION
### IS EXPECTED OF THE PROSPECT

*Telemarketer:*     *If there is a fit, I can arrange for you to test a DiskGard disk on one of your programs at no charge or obligation.*

*When you receive that disk in the mail, copy your program onto it, then try to reproduce it using any copying method you can think of.*

### SCRIPT 1.6g: SETTING UP THE NEXT CONTACT

*Telemarketer:*     *I'll be in touch with you again about four days after you get the disk to find out how the test went. We can talk about your initial order at that point.*

or

*Telemarketer:*     *You'll get the test disk on Wednesday at the latest. Would you be able to review it by the close of business on Friday?*

*Prospect:*     *Monday would be better.*

*Telemarketer:*     *Okay, why don't I schedule a call to you on Monday, late afternoon. Does 4:00 P.M. sound good?*

Proceed to qualify prospect. Conclude call by confirming the call-back day and time.

### SCRIPT 1.6h: MAKING THE CALL LOOK
### EXTREMELY IMPORTANT

The paramedical school discussed earlier prefers a challenging approach, one that makes the telemarketer look like a judge who will be part of an admissions committee. The following script takes you through the reason for calling *and* setting up the next contact.

*Telemarketer:*     *Frankly, not all people can handle the fast pace and responsibilities of working with doctors and patients. By spending a few minutes talking on the telephone now, I'll get to know you a little better. In addition, you'll gain a better understanding about this field.*

*If we both decide that it makes sense for you to look further into a medical career, we'll arrange to have you come in for a personal interview. At that same time, you'll have a tour of the school for a firsthand look at what the work is like in a doctor's office. The school is set up just like a functioning medical practice.*

Now the telemarketer goes into deeper qualifying. If the telephone interview is still progressing well at the conclusion of qualifying, the caller sets up the personal interview and tour, at which time a close is attempted.

## REFINING YOUR COLD-CALL OPENINGS

Here are two tools that will help you continually strengthen your prospecting program: Form 1.2, the Cold-Call Checklist, helps assure that all vital components are included in both the overall calling program and in the telephone presentation to new prospects. Form 1.3, the Cold-Call Dialogue Worksheet, provides a convenient way to work out new sales dialogue—or modify existing presentations—so they better fit a specific product or service.

---

### FORM 1.2:  COLD-CALL CHECKLIST

1. Describe prospect list(s) to be used:

   *List Source*                          *Number of Prospects*

   _____     _____

   _____     _____

   _____     _____

   _____     _____

2. If contact names or titles are not provided on lists, who will be targeted by the telemarketer?

   _____

   _____

   _____

   _____

3. Describe desired outcome of the initial call: _____

   _____

   _____

   _____

   _____

4. Are follow-up letters, brochures, etc., ready to go?

   _____ Yes     _____ No

   If not, specify work that has to be done: _____

   _____

   _____

   _____

   _____

5. Is an adequate prospect-tracking system in operation?

____ Yes   ____ No

If so, does the tracking system

____ Pinpoint future call-back dates?

____ Provide space for notes about specific prospect situations?

____ Permit quick location of a prospect's records if that prospect calls in?

____ Allow sufficient recording of address information and other key data?

6. Does management have a system for tallying program results?

____ Yes   ____ No

7. Have adequate tactics been worked out for penetrating screens?

____ Yes   ____ No

8. Does the presentation opening capture attention?

____ Yes   ____ No

9. Does the opening *clearly* describe the offer?

____ Yes   ____ No

10. Does the opening explain what kind of action is requested of the prospect?

____ Yes   ____ No

11. Is the desired presentation in written form so it can be modified later?

____ Yes   ____ No

12. Has the presentation been role-played to assure smooth delivery?

____ Yes   ____ No

13. Does presentation length permit the desired number of daily calls?

____ Yes   ____ No

14. Have the following ratios been decided upon:

____ Total calling hours per day?

____ Average number of calls per hour?

____ Contacts with decisionmakers per hour?

____ Successful contacts per hour?

15. Have periodic progress meetings been set up with the telemarketer?

____ Yes   ____ No

Notes: _____

_____

_____

_____

_____

_____

_____

_____

_____

_____

_____

_____

## FORM 1.3:   COLD-CALL DIALOGUE WORKSHEET

1. Introduction: _____

_____

_____

_____

2. Request contact: _____

_____

_____

_____

3. Penetrate screen: _____

_____

_____

_____

_____

4. Introduction to contact: _____

_____

_____

_____

5. Brief statement describing offer (sequence of 5 and 6 can be reversed): _____

_____

_____

_____

_____

_____

_____

_____

6. Brief statement describing purpose of call: _____

_____

_____

_____

_____

_____

_____

7. Qualify prospect:

- _____

_____

_____

- _____

_____

_____

_____

- _____

_____

_____

_____

- _____

_____

_____

_____

- _____

_____

_____

_____

- _____

_____

_____

8.  If necessary, give more information on product or service: _____

_____

_____

_____

_____

_____

_____

9.  Close: _____

_____

_____

_____

_____

_____

_____

Notes: _____

_____

_____

_____

_____

_____

_____

_____

# Chapter 2

# EFFECTIVE QUALIFYING
# DIALOGUE FOR ANY TYPE
# OF SALES CALL

Top-producing telemarketers and field sales reps continually work on enhancing their probing skills. When key prospect facts and feelings are uncovered by a seller, the cash register is much more likely to ring. Some of the vital areas targeted in probing are:

- How a product or service will be used by a potential buyer.
- What the competitive products being considered by the prospect are.
- How the buying procedure works in the prospect organization.

. . . and other important factors. Good probing should result in a complete and clear picture of the buying company. An adept salesperson will find out exactly where the "hot buttons" are and how to steer around obstacles in order to bring about the desired outcome.

Effective qualifying is the ability to *explore topics that will contribute to closing the sale.* A skillful prober will not stop after asking one question on an important topic, but will work to peel off additional layers of information until the story is complete in every detail.

## PROBING FOR APPLICATIONS

For selling situations in which the *specific* use of a product or service is not perfectly defined, extra qualifying must be done to determine whether there is a fit or not. For example, aluminum siding for a building exterior is a relatively straightforward application. However, the specs of a new printing press will almost certainly depend on a long list of variables.

The first step in good qualifying is to search for and identify a need for your product or service. As soon as that is accomplished, go on to see if your product or service fits the prospect company.

## SCRIPT 2.1a: SEARCHING FOR NEED

By first identifying general applications for a uniform-rental service, a solid foundation is set in place. At this early stage, the telemarketer probes areas like employee morale and appearance.

| | |
|---|---|
| *Telemarketer:* | *If you have a minute, I'd like to briefly describe how employee morale and performance can be improved in your company through our work apparel program.* |
| | *Has your firm ever looked into the advantages of renting uniforms?* |
| *Contact:* | *I recall that we considered it once, but the advantages didn't seem to be very strong.* |
| *Telemarketer:* | *Do you feel that your employees could make a better appearance to your customers—and compare more favorably to competitors' employees who wear standardized garments?* |
| *Contact:* | *We do okay in that respect.* |
| *Telemarketer:* | *Do you have any special safety or sanitary guidelines that are tough to meet with street clothes? For example, certain fabrics may present flammability problems.* |
| *Contact:* | *We'd have to look at that.* |
| *Telemarketer:* | *Another aspect to consider is employee expense. Some of our clients like to help their employees cut down on the wear and tear to their personal wardrobes. So uniforms can be a strong extra benefit.* |
| *Contact:* | *I can see that our warehouse and shop workers might consider that a plus.* |

## SCRIPT 2.1b: IDENTIFYING SPECIFIC USES

Now that the *general* need for this service has been established, the telemarketer moves to pinpoint some *specific* applications in the prospect firm. To do this, it helps when a caller possesses at least a working knowledge of how the business operates.

| | |
|---|---|
| *Telemarketer:* | *Aside from the shop and warehouse, which departments in your company could use standardized work apparel?* |
| *Contact:* | *Probably our counterhelp.* |
| *Telemarketer:* | *Do you have delivery people who might benefit from standardized work apparel?* |

| | |
|---|---|
| *Contact:* | *Could be that our route drivers would be good candidates.* |
| *Telemarketer:* | *What do they wear now?* |
| *Contact:* | *They buy their own overalls.* |
| *Telemarketer:* | *I guess all of them look different, right?* |
| *Contact:* | *Right. There's no standardization.* |
| *Telemarketer:* | *We've seen studies showing that customers feel more comfortable about delivery people in standard uniforms. There's a stronger security factor when a customer recognizes the delivery person. That's especially true with consumers getting deliveries at home.* |
| | *If you haven't seen that research, I can get a copy for you.* |
| *Contact:* | *We deliver to businesses, but I get your point.* |

This telemarketer has kept up with research on how uniforms impact customers. Please notice that information of that nature can have solid, positive impact on the outcome of a sale.

## SCRIPT 2.1c: DEEPER PROBING

To illustrate how an expert prober fully explores an opportunity, we'll go back to the point where the prospect identified the firm's counterhelp as possible uniform users.

| | |
|---|---|
| *Telemarketer:* | *Aside from the shop and warehouse, which departments in your company could use standardized work apparel?* |
| *Contact:* | *Probably our counterhelp.* |
| *Telemarketer:* | *How many people do you have working the sales counters?* |
| *Contact:* | *Eight in this location and six at our southside facility.* |
| *Telemarketer:* | *What do you think they should look like?* |
| *Contact:* | *I've always wanted them in blazers—or in some kind of sharp outfit. One of our competitors has their counter people dressed in blazers, and they really look good. Very professional. We just never got around to it.* |
| *Telemarketer:* | *Do you have a distinctive company logo?* |
| *Contact:* | *Yes.* |
| *Telemarketer:* | *That could be on the front of a custom work garment. Very classy if it's done right. Also, I guess you have your own company colors, right?* |
| *Contact:* | *Well, our stationery is gray with burgundy printing, but I'm not sure we regard those as our company colors.* |

*Telemarketer:*          *I just wanted to let you know that a custom uniform can reflect your image right down to your chosen colors, cut of the garment, pocket location, and any special safety features you want—or are required to have by OSHA.*

## UNCOVERING COMPETITIVE FACTORS

A telemarketer who closes major sales by phone—or qualifies prospects for later follow-up by a field sales rep—has to give special attention to competitors. Although prospects will usually not be quick to reveal the details of their relationships with other vendors, they often *will* give you some generalities about what you are up against.

Questions about rivals are best asked *after* basic qualifying is completed. At that point, the prospect has become more comfortable with the telemarketer and is less apt to be defensive regarding questions about competitors.

The following procedure is successfully used by a proprietary school organization. When their admissions reps understand who the potential competitors are, they can operate much more effectively.

#### SCRIPT 2.2a: LEARNING THE IDENTITY OF OTHER SOURCES

*Telemarketer:*          *Have you discussed training with any other schools?*

*Contact:*          *I'm in the process of gathering information.*

*Telemarketer:*          *I want to be sure you understand the difference between the various courses available around the city. As far as I know, each school does a good job, but they all specialize in different types of education.*

                              *Do you mind telling me who you've spoken to so I can see if you're on the right track?*

If prospect agrees to identify other schools, continue with Script 2.2b. If prospect will *not* identify other schools, stop probing for competitive factors and continue to close for appointment.

Much the same approach can be used in a presentation for a product.

#### SCRIPT 2.2b: DETERMINING THE DEPTH OF COMPETITIVE ENCROACHMENT

When the telemarketer *has* successfully obtained the identity of one or more competitors, the topic can be pursued in order to find out *the level of commitment* between shopper and source.

*Telemarketer:*          *Do you mind telling me who you've spoken to so I can see if you're on the right track?*

| | |
|---|---|
| *Contact:* | *Besides your school, I've talked to Acme Academy.* |
| *Telemarketer:* | *Have you received detailed information about their courses, schedules, and tuition rates?* |
| *Contact:* | *I have their catalogues.* |
| *Telemarketer:* | *Have you reviewed that material yet?* |
| *Contact:* | *Not yet.* |
| *Telemarketer:* | *Did you tour their facility?* |
| *Contact:* | *I have an appointment to see the school on Tuesday morning.* |
| *Telemarketer:* | *It's good that you're looking into different possibilities. We know that many of our most successful graduates are people who paid attention to every step of their training—including selection of the school.* |
| | *Why don't we set aside an hour on Monday to have you visit the school.* |

### SCRIPT 2.2c: GETTING INFORMATION ON THE NATURE OF RIVAL BIDS

When competitive encroachment *is* identified and the prospect indicates that competitive bids *have* been made it is advantageous to get as much information about those bids as possible.

In the following example, the seller opens the questioning by mentioning an *approximate* dollar amount. In some cases, a prospect will respond by correcting that estimate, thus providing a fairly accurate competitive figure.

| | |
|---|---|
| *Telemarketer:* | *Have you received detailed information about their courses, schedules, and tuition rates?* |
| *Contact:* | *I have their tuition sheet.* |
| *Telemarketer:* | *You've figured out exactly what Acme's program will cost and what you'll receive?* |
| *Contact:* | *Yes.* |
| *Telemarketer:* | *My recollection is that Acme's basic fee for that course is $2,200. But that was last year.* |
| *Contact:* | *About $2,400 now.* |
| *Telemarketer:* | *Is that manageable for you?* |
| *Contact:* | *I'd like to get away for less.* |
| *Telemarketer:* | *We might be able to work with you for less money on that program.* |

# PINPOINTING PROBABLE TIME OF PURCHASE

One of the most important pieces of information to be collected in qualifying is *when the purchase will be made. Fast* revenue generation is the primary reason why the telephone must be used by effective sellers in any business. While future sales opportunities are vital to the ongoing success of any firm, the real value of a telemarketing program is the *immediate results* calling is able to uncover.

The question of *when* the purchase will be made is especially important when a telemarketer is finding opportunities for outside salespeople. With the high cost of field selling, a rep's time should be confined to visits that promise *quick results.*

Whether a telemarketer deals with businesses or consumers, questions about purchase timeframe are perfectly reasonable. It is essential for the telemarketer to make note of the intended purchase date so that follow-up can be precisely scheduled.

## SCRIPT 2.3a: ASCERTAINING PROSPECT'S SCHEDULE

Probing for the date of a decision is most effectively done *after* basic qualifying is completed. This sequence is much more comfortable for this reason: It makes no sense at all to ask *"When* do you need this gadget, and *do* you need it?" but it makes complete sense to ask *"Do* you need this gadget and, if so, when would you like to have it?"

| | |
|---|---|
| *Telemarketer:* | *Are you interested in purchasing a remote letter-quality printer within the next several days?* |
| *Contact:* | *I think we'll need a little more time.* |
| *Telemarketer:* | *Within 30 days?* |
| *Contact:* | *Realistically, it might take more like 30 to 60 days from now.* |

## SCRIPT 2.3b: PROBING TO REVEAL LENGTH OF BUYING PROCESS

As soon as the approximate time of purchase is known, the next step is to find out what is involved in the prospect's purchase method. The buying process may also have a bearing on how long it takes to close.

| | |
|---|---|
| *Telemarketer:* | *So I can make sure we'd be able to meet your delivery expectations, I'd like to make sure I understand how the timing works. Will you first start getting approvals in about 30 days, or will the purchase be fully okayed by that time?* |
| *Contact:* | *We'll decide which way we want to go in about three weeks. Then purchase approvals will take another week or so.* |
| *Telemarketer:* | *So it sounds like you'll need all specs and pricing from us by the end of this week. Is that about right?* |
| *Contact:* | *I should have your information by Tuesday at the latest.* |

The preceding example is typical of how a little probing can reveal highly specific information that might make the difference between making or losing a sale. Facts of this sort would usually not come out in normal conversation.

## SCRIPT 2.3c: DETERMINING DESIRED DELIVERY DATE

Having narrowed down the prospect's timeframe, it pays to ask the contact about other factors that might influence a delivery date.

> *Telemarketer:*   *Before I hang up, it would be helpful to know a couple of other things that seem important. Is delivery of the printer coordinated with other system components you are adding?*
>
> *Contact:*   *It'll be part of an overall new system, so the other components will need to be in place.*
>
> *Telemarketer:*   *So you've planned all your system purchases to bring everything together in 30 to 60 days?*
>
> *Contact:*   *We want the whole thing operational by the end of August.*

In point of fact, how many telemarketers probe to that extent to learn about a prospect's time constraints? More often than not, the contact will be favorably impressed with thorough questioning of that kind.

## SCRIPT 2.3d: EXPLORING THE NEED FOR A TRAINING PROGRAM

We'll take the telephone presentation for a printer one step further. This unit requires a special familiarization to system users, as is the case with many devices sold to companies today. This training is very much a part of the package being offered.

> *Telemarketer:*   *Getting an entirely new system up and running will require some personnel training. Do you have that covered?*
>
> *Contact:*   *Our priorities right now are to buy the system components that are best for our needs. But training will be a concern as soon as the pieces are on hand.*
>
> *Telemarketer:*   *If you decide on our printer, we want to make absolutely sure we can devote people to your company so you can meet your target date. How much time do you think will be allocated for training?*
>
> *Contact:*   *A total of two days should do it. We can give a half-day to printer operations.*
>
> *Telemarketer:*   *I'll make a note that you'll receive one morning or afternoon. We'll see that all of your people get handbooks on the printer. So I'll get the exact number of attendees from you later.*
>
> *Contact:*   *That would be a help.*

In this qualifying segment, probing for needed information also serves the purpose of *helping to sell*. By questioning the details of a contemplated purchase, the telemarketer is providing service by assuring that *all* facets of the transaction are being considered and will work smoothly.

## QUALIFYING FOR ABILITY TO BUY

A contact's *desire* to own your product or service may have no connection whatsoever with his or her *ability* to own it. The authority of your contact, budget constraints, and other factors may get in the way of desire or need. Most prospects understand a telemarketer's question about ability to buy and do not take offense. They realize that the potential vendor will incur time and expense in the selling process and reasonable care must be taken.

Another factor to consider is this: Most companies don't want employees who are nonbuyers to get involved in telephone conversations with firms trying to sell. Therefore, when you ask about the authority of the person on the line, that query will be seen by your contact as simply good business practice.

### SCRIPT 2.4a: AFFIRMING AUTHORITY OF YOUR CONTACT

This first step is to establish the credentials of the person on the line. Even when this individual has been named as the right one to talk to, a good telemarketer will verify that beyond any shadow of a doubt.

| | |
|---|---|
| *Telemarketer:* | *Since we've never done business with your company before, I'm not familiar with your purchasing procedure. I understand that you're in charge of placing orders for office items. Is that correct?* |
| *Contact:* | *For certain categories. On small items I send a requisition to our purchasing people and they select a source.* |
| *Telemarketer:* | *So on larger furniture items, you're the person to deal with?* |
| *Contact:* | *Right.* |

### SCRIPT 2.4b: SEARCHING FOR OTHER DECISIONMAKERS

In almost every selling situation, it is wise to find out whether other key people in the firm can influence the decision of your contact. If probing is not done to discover them, these other people who can affect the purchase will usually *not* come to light until it is too late.

| | |
|---|---|
| *Telemarketer:* | *So I'll know how many brochures to mail—and who to send them to—are there any other managers you confer with who would be involved in the selection?* |
| *Contact:* | *It might be a good idea to include Betty Wells, our facilities manager. She likes to make sure about colors and sizes.* |

| | |
|---|---|
| *Telemarketer:* | *I'll make sure she's on the list. Would it be helpful if I contacted her to see if she has any questions?* |
| *Contact:* | *We'll see later.* |

## SCRIPT 2.4c: FINDING THE INFLUENTIAL FAMILY MEMBERS IN SELLING TO CONSUMERS

How many direct-to-consumer sales are lost because a wife, husband, or parent did not attend the initial sales presentation? An overwhelming number of lost sales can easily be avoided if the telemarketer merely asks about influencers, then assures their presence.

To illustrate the process of identifying other people who may be in a position to influence a consumer, we'll continue the private-school example from Script 2.2c, in which a rival school's proposal has been discovered by the telemarketer.

| | |
|---|---|
| *Telemarketer:* | *My recollection is that Acme's basic fee for that course is $2,200. But that was last year.* |
| *Contact:* | *About $2,400 now.* |
| *Telemarketer:* | *Is that manageable for you?* |
| *Contact:* | *I'd like to get away for less.* |
| *Telemarketer:* | *We might be able to work with you for less money on that program. I recommend that we sit down and look at the course, the fees, and what you want for yourself in a career.* |
| | *Do you discuss your plans with any family members or with others who are close to you?* |
| *Contact:* | *I live with my mother and we talk about my school and work.* |
| *Telemarketer:* | *She must be extremely interested in how your future works out.* |
| *Contact:* | *Yes, but I do what I think is right, and it's always okay with her.* |
| *Telemarketer:* | *Well, you're the one who has to make it happen, but it does help to have somebody close to confide in.* |
| | *Is there anyone else you talk to about school and work?* |
| *Contact:* | *No.* |
| *Telemarketer:* | *Since your mother really is so interested in what you do and how things work out for you, it would be a good move to have her join us when we get together. Would that be okay with you?* |

NOTE: While the telemarketer in this example makes the parent's presence sound like an option, many companies wisely insist on having other influencers accompany the prospect.

If the rather soft approach in the example fails to get the prospect's mother involved, a more firm attempt must come next.

| | |
|---|---|
| *Telemarketer:* | *Since your mother really is so interested in what you do and how things work out for you, it would be a good move to have her join us when we get together. Would that be okay with you?* |
| *Contact:* | *I make my own decisions, so I really don't see why she has to join me.* |
| *Telemarketer:* | *I understand you. This is your career and you are the only one who will get into it and make it work. But the school feels that somebody close to the future student can give us information that will help us evaluate your chances. They think of things that neither you or the admissions people would think of. I'll have to ask you to bear with us on this one.* |

## SCRIPT 2.4d: ASSURING AUTONOMY OF A BRANCH OR SUBSIDIARY

It may be that a particular contact has the authority to *recommend* a purchase at a subsidiary level but must defer the ultimate decision to a corporate headquarters or main office at a different location. It is best to find that out *now*.

| | |
|---|---|
| *Telemarketer:* | *Are you an autonomous operation or do you have to get buying clearance from a corporate office?* |
| *Contact:* | *No, all decisions of this kind can be made from this office.* |

## SCRIPT 2.4e: QUESTIONING BUDGET AVAILABILITY

In a corporate environment, availability or lack of a budget is often a basic fact of life. As such, it is usually not an area that employees are overly sensitive about—they talk about budget as they discuss the weather. Therefore, the following question would probably not be seen as aggressive:

| | |
|---|---|
| *Telemarketer:* | *If I may ask, are you budgeted for an office furniture purchase in this quarter?* |
| *Contact:* | *Not this quarter. By the time we make a decision, take delivery, and process the invoice, we would be budgeted. We're looking at the beginning of the third quarter.* |

## SCRIPT 2.4f: PROBING CREDITWORTHINESS

| | |
|---|---|
| *Telemarketer:* | *Sounds good. Since we don't have a file on your firm, can we have you complete an application? That would eliminate a possible delay once you made a decision.* |

| | |
|---|---|
| *Contact:* | *Send one out. I'll see that it's filled out and returned to you in time.* |

# DETERMINING PROSPECT BUYING POTENTIAL

More often than ever before, companies are finding out how much a prospect intends to buy and how often that prospect will reorder. A surprising number of telephone presentations include questions designed to reveal the value of a prospect as a customer.

There are several reasons for getting early clues regarding the potential size of a prospect.

- A vendor may be geared to shipping large quantities and will simply refuse to accept orders under certain minimum amounts.

- A vendor may refer smaller orders to a subsidiary that specializes in lower-volume business.

- A vendor might put all small-scale buyers into a special group of accounts that are serviced exclusively by telephone. The seller's field reps avoid these special accounts due to the high costs involved in visiting them (more about this in Chapter 12, "Cutting the Cost of Dealing With Marginal Accounts").

### SCRIPT 2.5a: PROBING FOR PURCHASE QUANTITY

An office coffee service targets companies that do not presently use such a service. A critical qualifying aspect is the potential account size, as the cost of servicing accounts is exceptionally high in a downtown area.

| | |
|---|---|
| *Telemarketer:* | *Our system provides benefits for everybody in a company—from clerks all the way to top management.* |
| | *For example, we make sure that coffee and other drinks are in abundant supply and individually packaged in quantities large enough to satisfy your people and increase their productivity.* |
| | *How many employees do you have altogether?* |
| *Contact:* | *At last count, a total of 72 people.* |
| *Telemarketer:* | *And how many different work areas do you have? For example, locations in your offices where brewers could be located?* |
| *Contact:* | *Four main work areas.* |
| *Telemarketer:* | *Are there any people who use their own brewers in the office?* |
| *Contact:* | *As far as I know, there are three home coffee machines in various offices and around seven people drink that coffee.* |
| *Telemarketer:* | *Would those people switch from their own brewers to our coffee?* |

| | |
|---|---|
| *Contact:* | *I guess if the quality of your coffee is up to par they would.* |
| *Telemarketer:* | *Do you normally have heavy visitor traffic during a typical week?* |
| *Contact:* | *I imagine about 50 people a week come in, and most of them will have coffee.* |

### SCRIPT 2.5b: REVEALING PURCHASE FREQUENCY

When approximate quantities are known, the next step is to discover purchase frequency. The interval of orders is another major measurement of potential profitability.

| | |
|---|---|
| *Telemarketer:* | *Would you classify the people in your company as light, moderate, or heavy coffee drinkers?* |
| *Contact:* | *That's tough to answer. I'll guess that ten percent are heavy, about 50 percent are light to moderate, and the rest don't drink coffee at all—or not enough to count.* |

### SCRIPT 2.5c: FINDING OUT ABOUT SERVICE EXPECTATIONS

In the estimation of the coffee service, this particular prospect will apparently consume products at a rate that justifies above-average personal attention. Exactly *how much* attention may be needed is now explored by the telemarketer.

| | |
|---|---|
| *Telemarketer:* | *Do you have employees who normally do housekeeping around the offices?* |
| *Contact:* | *We could designate people to do things like sweep the area and keep counters clean, but we'd want the brewers in really good shape and the coffee products kept neat and stocked.* |
| *Telemarketer:* | *We'll thoroughly clean the machines and restock once a week. If that doesn't do it, we can add one visit per week. Does that sound sufficient?* |

## QUALIFYING TO SAVE LOST BUSINESS

Literally millions of dollars in sales are rescued every year by telemarketers who *ask questions* after they learn that the order is no longer on track. A caller who does not bother to find out where a lost sale stands will almost certainly end up at the back of the pack.

When a buyer tells a telemarketer that a project has been shelved or a different supplier has been chosen, it is time to press on and determine the precise status of the purchase. In a remarkable number of these situations, the sale turns out to be salvageable and the telemarketer gains new information about how to get the close.

### SCRIPT 2.6a: DIGGING FOR THE TRUTH ABOUT AN ORDER

In the best approaches for saving sales, the first step is to discover what happened in the prospect's buying process and where the transaction stands at the moment.

| | |
|---|---|
| *Prospect:* | [Decided not to go ahead with a purchase or chose to give the business to a competitive vendor.] |
| *Telemarketer:* | *So we can operate more effectively in the future, we'd value your opinion and insight about how our offer stacked up. Can I ask you a few questions?* |

Most buyers would agree to spend a little time with a source they have just turned down.

| | |
|---|---|
| *Telemarketer:* | *Were our prices in line with your expectations?* |

If no, you have successfully found out why the order went to a different supplier. If yes or too high, continue to next question.

> *In your opinion, are we offering less, about the same, or more than our competitors?*

If less, try to pinpoint where the deficiencies are by asking:

> *Can you tell me exactly where you feel we fall short compared to other suppliers?*
>
> *What areas do you think we should strengthen to become more competitive?*

At this stage, the reason for losing the order should be known. The next step is to explore the possibility of reversing the buyer's decision.

> *If we could eliminate that problem, would it be possible to do business with you on this order?*

If no, keep the door open for next time by saying:

> *Would you consider us as a source for your future needs? We understand a lot more about your requirements now, and I feel we could be an excellent supplier for you.*

### SCRIPT 2.6b: GETTING AN OKAY TO
### TRACK DOWN THE PAPERWORK

In many cases, a buyer is, in the strict sense of the word, a "specifier." He or she will decide on the need for a product or service, then request an acquisition through the purchasing department. In these instances, it is the purchasing agent's job to actually select a vendor.

Quite often, the decision can *still* be influenced when the request is on the purchasing agent's desk. Since it would be poor form to go over the specifier's head and deal directly with the purchasing agent, a telemarketer can get a green light by saying something like this to the specifier:

> *Telemarketer:*        *Since you feel that our product and our prices are competitive with others you've looked at, would you have any objection if I talked directly to your purchasing people? They should be aware of details like our maintenance program and lease arrangements—and I know you're too busy to bother with those issues.*

If yes, get the name and extension number of the correct contact in purchasing. Also ask the specifier if he or she will alert the purchasing agent before you call. If no, fall back to the following position:

> *Telemarketer:*        *Would it be effective if I prepared a letter describing our maintenance program and lease plans? I could either mail it directly to purchasing or send it to your attention.*

### SCRIPT 2.6c: DEALING WITH THE PURCHASING AGENT TO SAVE THE SALE

> *Telemarketer:*        *Mrs. Peterson? My name is Dan York from the Walters Company. Alex Peters in your engineering department told me it would be okay to contact you directly regarding the new lighting system they've requested. I hope you can give me just a moment to describe a couple of features that may be important in your choice of a supplier.*

It's a reasonably safe assumption that a purchasing agent will respond to cost advantages since his or her mandate is to watch expenditures carefully. It makes good sense to add a word about economy:

> *Telemarketer:*        *In addition, there are some ways we can save money for you while keeping the quality of the system at the level needed by engineering.*

## REFINING YOUR QUALIFYING APPROACHES

If you use the telephone to contact other businesses, Form 2.1a provides a menu of qualifying areas. If you call individual consumers, use Form 2.1b.

Once you have a general qualifying routine laid out, use Form 2.2, Qualifying Dialogue Worksheet, to set up the precise language of each main question and any subset questions you think of. This form is also used to arrange a sequence of probing questions that sounds natural to prospects.

Most good presentations include five to eight main qualifying questions, as well as at least two subset questions that uncover additional prospect facts.

As time goes on, you will find that all of these forms can be valuable in modifying a qualifying procedure to better deal with current market conditions.

---

### FORM 2.1a: QUALIFYING CHECKLIST FOR SELLING TO OTHER COMPANIES

While many sellers would like to have almost *all* of these questions answered, it simply is not practical to cover the entire list in a telemarketing program. Select only the *key* questions (a maximum of eight) to be used in the initial telephone call. Then sequence them so they flow logically and smoothly. Use Form 2.2 to work out the precise wording.

Questions that you decide are of secondary importance can be asked during follow-up contacts with a prospect.

1. *Assuring that telemarketer is speaking to the right kind of company and the correct contact.*

   - Is this company a main office or is it a subsidiary or branch?

   - What is the exact nature of prospect's business?

   - Does title of contact appear to be correct?

   - Does contact have authority to buy?

   - Are other decisionmakers or influential people present in the company?

   - Is contact familiar with seller's product or service? (Determine how much product education is needed.)

2. *Questions that reveal company size.*

   - How many years in business?

   - How many employees?

   - Estimated quantity of purchase? (Is quantity an adequate volume for seller?)

   - What are annual sales of prospect company?

3. *Determining ability to buy.*

   - What is firm's credit situation?

   - Is budget available now? (If not, when?)

   - Is distance of prospect within seller's service area?

   - Is required vendor support within seller's ability to perform?

   - What is present stock on hand in prospect company?

   - Would any conflict of interest arise due to seller's existing customers?

4. *Exploring a prospect's uses for a product or service.*

   - Is firm presently using or has firm used this (or similar) product or service in the past?

   - If so, who are or were the suppliers?

- Is or was the prospect satisfied with that supplier's performance?
- What distribution methods are used by the prospect company?
- Are special projects underway—or planned—that would create need?
- Is a project leader designated? (If so, where does that person fit into the decision process?)
- Do the firm's needs appear to be valid?
- Is the firm apparently committed to this acquisition?
- Do any special needs exist in the prospect company?
- Are there any other departments in the firm that might use this product or service?

5. *Getting facts on a prospect's purchasing procedures.*
   - Is the buyer open to visit the seller's facility for a seminar or demonstration?
   - Would the buyer (and other influential people) be available for an appointment at their site?
   - Does the firm attend trade shows?
   - Is a formal proposal required? (If so, is a special format needed?)
   - What are the specific steps in making a purchase?
   - How long does that procedure normally take?
   - Would the firm agree to a trial of the product or service?
   - When would the product or service actually be needed?

---

---

**FORM 2.1b:  QUALIFYING CHECKLIST FOR
SELLING TO INDIVIDUAL CONSUMERS**

1. *Needs of the prospect.*
   - Occupation?
   - Hobbies or leisure-time activities?
   - Educational background?
   - Present or prior use of product or service?
   - Membership in any organized group?
   - Do special needs exist?
   - Level of knowledge about seller's product or service? (Determine amount of education necessary.)
2. *Lifestyle of prospect.*
   - Income?
   - Homeowner or renter?

- Children in household? (If so, ages?)
- Time available?

3. *Ability to buy.*
   - When would product or service be delivered?
   - Does prospect have sufficient disposable income?
   - Acceptable credit rating?
   - Valid credit card?
   - COD delivery okay?
   - Agree to trial purchase?

---

## FORM 2.2: QUALIFYING DIALOGUE WORKSHEET

As soon as the key qualifying questions have been selected, follow this procedure:

- Sequence the questions so they flow just as they would in a normal conversation. On this form, list them in the order they will be asked. There is space on the form for eight qualifying questions, with two subsets for each.

- If appropriate, come up with one or two subset questions to each of the key questions. These are designed to reveal added information about a prospect.

- Work out the exact wording for all key and subset questions.

*FIRST QUALIFYING QUESTION:*

_____

_____

_____

_____

Subset question:

_____

_____

_____

Subset question:

_____

_____

_____

*SECOND QUALIFYING QUESTION:*

_____

_____

_____

_____

Subset question:

_____

_____

_____

_____

Subset question:

_____

_____

_____

_____

*THIRD QUALIFYING QUESTION:*

_____

_____

_____

_____

Subset question:

_____

_____

_____

_____

Subset question:

_____

_____

_____

_____

*FOURTH QUALIFYING QUESTION:*

_____

_____

_____

_____

Subset question:

_____

_____

_____

_____

Subset question:

_____

_____

_____

_____

*FIFTH QUALIFYING QUESTION:*

_____

_____

_____

_____

Subset question:

_____

_____

_____

_____

Subset question:

_____

_____

_____

_____

*SIXTH QUALIFYING QUESTION:*

_____

_____

_____

_____

Subset question:

_____

_____

_____

_____

Subset question:

_____

_____

_____

_____

*SEVENTH QUALIFYING QUESTION:*

_____

_____

_____

_____

Subset question:

_____

_____

_____

_____

Subset question:

_____

_____

_____

_____

*EIGHTH QUALIFYING QUESTION:*

_____

_____

_____

_____

Subset question:

_____

_____

_____

_____

Subset question:

_____

_____

_____

_____

*NOTES:*

_____

_____

_____

_____

_____

_____

_____

_____

_____

_____

# Chapter 3

# CLEAR DESCRIPTIONS OF PRODUCTS AND SERVICES

Most successful telemarketing is powered by the caller's ability to concisely explain what a product does—and what it looks like. Boiling a description down to a few crystal-clear paragraphs does not require any special skills; but it *does* demand the patience to work and rework the words until every sentence is as brief as it can be, yet packed with meaning and color.

When a prospect completely understands the product or service offered by telephone, the chances of rejection are cut down considerably. A number of reliable surveys have shown that unsuccessful telephone sales contacts are largely due to the failure of the caller to adequately convey the offer. A contact's refusal to buy may simply be a way for that person to say, "I'm not really sure what you are trying to sell me, so the safest thing I can do is say no."

Some of the most skillful presentation writers insist that the best descriptions are created to be understood by those at a seventh-grade level of comprehension. That helps assure the following points:

- Long words are eliminated in favor of simpler, shorter words and phrases.
- "Buzzwords," usually understood only by a few industry insiders, are thrown out whenever they can successfully be replaced by more practical language.
- Nothing is taken for granted in terms of a contact's prior understanding. Approach all prospects as if they knew nothing at all about your product or service.
- The description, while brief, must flow logically from start to finish. One major reason for confusion is that callers sometimes deliver statements out of context and a patchwork description comes out that most people won't bother to decipher.

• A firm grasp of a product's facts and figures does help in the process of putting together a good description, although dry specifications should be kept out of product descriptions whenever possible.

In this chapter we'll look at a variety of descriptions for both products and services.

## EFFECTIVELY COMBINING FEATURES AND BENEFITS

In creating an effective description, the most prominent strengths of a product or service are earmarked for use in the presentation. Next, these exceptional strengths will be worded in a way that stresses the *advantages* that will accrue to the buyer—or to the ultimate user.

For example, the fact that a water distillation unit is of all stainless steel construction may, in itself, sound desirable to a potential buyer. But of *more* interest is just how that particular material will enhance performance, reliability, and/or cost-effectiveness.

In the next script, we'll see how the featured aspects of this particular product are linked to benefits in order to create a complete description.

### SCRIPT 3.1a: EXAMPLE OF A FEATURE/BENEFIT STATEMENT

*Telemarketer:*   *Let me take an extra minute to give you a rundown of what our midsized distiller can offer you.*

*Most important is that our 240C model is rated 97 percent effective in removing impurities from ordinary tap water.*

*It's a countertop unit—about the size of a toaster oven—so you can keep it in a convenient spot. You'll want it out because it's extremely attractive—all stainless steel.*

*That stainless construction means the distiller will provide years of reliable performance with very little maintenance. There are no glass parts to break and no plastic or metals that might give the water a bad taste.*

*This unit is really safe and easy to use. It takes about two minutes to start a distilling cycle, and you can go about your business while the machine does its work. It shuts off automatically when two gallons of crystal clear water are ready. That takes about four hours.*

In this description, the important points touched are

• Effective
• Convenient size
• Attractive

- Good construction, rugged
- Low maintenance
- Free of parts that may impair water taste
- Safe
- Easy to use
- Automatic

In planning a sales approach for the distilling unit, the product distributor came up with this list of attributes as being of primary importance to the average household buyer who was interested in home water distilling.

Each major point is made in a remarkably brief description. There is no need for the telemarketer to go into lengthy detail. If necessary, the caller could provide more information on any given aspect of the product—including technical data—but only if the prospect specifically requested additional facts. The following example shows caller dialogue used when a prospect asks for more information about portability of the distiller.

### SCRIPT 3.1b: SUPPLEMENTAL BENEFIT STATEMENT

*Contact:*            *You mentioned that the unit is a countertop model, but we're looking for one that can be easily transported to our summer home when we spend time there.*

*Telemarketer:*       *That's exactly what sets the midsized distiller apart from our big units. It's completely portable.*

*At only twelve pounds, you can pick it up and move it to any location where there's a water faucet and an electrical outlet. You'd have nothing else to move or hook up.*

*Also, the extremely rugged construction of the 240C model means it can absorb bumps with no problem.*

The preceding dialogue illustrates the tremendous advantages you can achieve by preparing statements in advance and having those prepared statements at the caller's fingertips. The telemarketer is immediately ready with a perfectly crafted response that deals accurately with almost *any* question that may be posed by the prospect.

In the next dialogue, *features* are stressed a bit more heavily but are still closely tied to corresponding benefits.

### SCRIPT 3.1c: ISOLATING FEATURE/BENEFIT SETS
### FOR MAXIMUM SELLING IMPACT

An interesting method sometimes used for describing product strengths is to *isolate one feature along with its matching benefit* when preparing the description. This technique departs from the standard dialogue designed to sound like spontaneous speech, and the description produced more closely resembles a simple "shopping list" of product attributes, as you will see.

One distinct advantage of this approach is its simplicity. It is easy for a prospect to understand because the product's leading points are not mixed into other dialogue from the telemarketer. Another plus is this: The preparation of simple feature/benefit sets is very easy for a presentation writer to produce. It successfully avoids the problem of trying to make written speech sound natural.

*Telemarketer:*      *I feel it would be helpful to you if I run through a few of the main strengths of the midsized distiller.*

*Number one, it has a timer dial. You turn it to the exact quantity of water you want to produce during the day then walk away and forget it.*

*Two, this model has an overheat switch. It'll shut down completely if the heating element gets too hot. So there is no danger of fire.*

*Three, we provide a "quick-tap" that instantly hooks up to any water faucet. There's no need to tamper with house plumbing.*

*Four, you get a specially designed bottle that fits into the machine and holds the distilled water. When a cycle is complete, you just pick up that container and put it in the refrigerator.*

The feature is stated, then the corresponding benefit is explained in the same paragraph. Each set is very brief and punchy. In the preceding example, the sets have been numbered by the telemarketer. This helps the listener keep one point separate from the other.

When a telemarketer has difficulty in making speech sound natural—or tends to muddle language by running thoughts together—simple feature/benefit sets could be the ideal solution.

Closely related to providing a matching benefit for each feature is how to relate *specifications* to a telephone contact.

## SCRIPT 3.2: MAKING COLD, HARD SPECS MORE INTERESTING

In some high-tech telephone selling, engineering facts and figures will almost certainly enter into the conversation. Generally speaking, the more technical the prospect, the more likely it is that specs will be discussed.

Most managers in telephone selling operations make an effort to steer clear of specs. When the subject comes up, the caller is instructed to refer the call to somebody in the firm who is more technically qualified to handle it. But the reality is this: Basic performance numbers and other measurements will often be needed, and it simply isn't possible to avoid all of the occasions when numbers come up. The answer then is to handle specs in a way that helps to make the sale.

To illustrate how ordinarily dull numbers can be animated to build increased listener interest, we'll remain with the water distiller presentation. The following dialogue is the caller's *response* to a prospect's question. In this particular telemarketing program, facts and figures on unit capacity and size are not given until the data is requested by the potential buyer.

| | |
|---|---|
| *Contact:* | *Can you give me more specific information about water output and unit size?* |
| *Telemarketer:* | *Sure, I'd be happy to do that. Let's start with the size of the 240C model.* |
| | *It's 20 inches wide, 14 inches deep, and 13 inches high. That's roughly the same as a large toaster oven. What is interesting about the size is the fact that the water storage container is designed to hang over the edge of your countertop. So it's out of the way and doesn't take up additional working space.* |
| | *Exact dry weight is 12 pounds, or about the same as a small portable TV set.* |
| | *Now I'll fill you in on output. As I mentioned earlier, the 240C puts out two gallons per day. That quantity is based on using the quick-tap where you hook up to any water faucet. If you decide to tap into a cold-water line in the house plumbing, you can get about two gallons per cycle — but the machine wouldn't be as portable.* |
| *Contact:* | *How about water quality as compared to other treatment methods?* |
| *Telemarketer:* | *Okay. Distilling is the only process that boils water. The other methods use filters that clog up and hold contaminants until the filters are cleaned or replaced. Boiling kills viruses, bacteria, and other organisms. In addition, distilling removes most solid contaminants.* |
| | *I'll give you a sampling of an analysis we had done by an independent testing lab:* |
| | *Our 240C model removed 97 percent of the chloride and magnesium as well as a long list of other solids commonly found in a typical water supply.* |
| | *If you've ever seen the objects that catch in the filter of your water faucet, you can imagine how many smaller particles get through into what you drink and cook with. Distilling removes virtually all of it.* |

Here again, the program works best when the telemarketer's responses are *prepared in advance*. Even when the caller changes the dialogue to fit his or her individual style, the essence of the response comes across intact, clear and logically sequenced.

When providing specs, the key to making them more interesting is this: With every set of numbers, include a comparison that can easily be related to a known quantity. This simple approach enables the prospect to mentally picture the product, which greatly enhances telephone selling punch. To repeat two examples in Script 3.2: "That's roughly the same as a large toaster oven" or "Exact dry weight is 12 pounds, or about the same as a small portable TV set."

Then, in the description of how distilling removes solid contaminants, tremendous impact is added through the graphic example of how particles get through the filters in ordinary faucets.

### LETTER 3.1: REINFORCING THE TELEPHONE DESCRIPTION

When a close does not materialize by telephone, or when a later field appointment is used to get the sale, a follow-up letter to the prospect is good strategy. Stating the product features and benefits in straightforward "bullet" form is one effective way to design the follow-up letter. Also, don't forget to end the piece by setting up the next contact.

Dear Mr. Harmon:

We are delighted that you are considering the purchase of our 240C model water distiller. For the needs you described, it appears that this unit is an excellent choice.

For your convenience, I have noted some of the important points we covered during our recent telephone conversation:

- Daily output of the unit is two gallons. Operation is completely automatic . . . . and *safe.*
- Compact, lightweight design allows countertop operation. You can easily move the distiller to other locations.
- Distillation is the most effective process for purifying water. Tests prove that the 240C model provides 97 percent effectiveness.
- Construction is stainless steel for easy care and years of reliability.

When you meet with our representative, Liz Blair, next Monday, she will explain other capabilities of the distiller that we have not discussed. In addition, any questions that come up can be covered.

We look forward to being of service to you.

Sincerely,

James D. Katz

Of course the feature/benefit sets in the letter can be tailored to conform with the interests and concerns expressed by the prospect.

## BRINGING SERVICE DESCRIPTIONS TO LIFE

One of the most vexing problems to a telemarketer is how to convey a coherent description of an *intangible.* A product can be seen and felt. It is a definite color and shape and performs a more or less definable task. But a service can be as nebulous as the morning fog.

Many salespeople see intangible services in the following way:

- *Insurance* is merely a document that explains what is covered in the policy and what is not. The sole measurable aspect of insurance seems to be real only when a loss might be suffered by the insured individual.

- *Consulting* can never really be explained in terms of what the project outcome will be; too many variables can alter the results. The *process* of a consulting task can be described, but that story is often slow to unfold and may bore a prospect.
- *Training* can be difficult to describe because, again, so many variables can obscure the final picture. Benefits are affected by how the student and instructor interact and, to some degree, by general conditions prevailing when a job is sought.

Therefore, a somewhat different approach is necessary when describing a service by telephone. The feature/benefit sets used for a product might miss the mark because the benefits of an intangible are not quite as clear as they are for most products.

To bring a service to life in a telephone call, a much more intensive hunt for prospect motivation is needed. In other words, the specific hot buttons must be identified by the caller. Then, those hot buttons are targeted in a very specific way.

While hot buttons are most helpful when selling products, they are *essential* for selling intangibles. A telemarketer identifies hot buttons by opening the description with a brief overview of each major advantage of the service being sold. Next, the prospect is probed to find out *which* advantage is most important. When that becomes clear, the telemarketer can stress the point or points that have the best chance of making the sale.

Here are scripts that show how it is done.

### SCRIPT 3.3a: AN OVERVIEW THAT HELPS TO CUT THROUGH PROSPECT CONFUSION

A management consulting firm uses telemarketing to locate prospects that warrant follow-up by one of the company's nine consultants. The consulting firm's telemarketer tested a number of approaches and found that the one shown here consistently produces solid results when the prospect president or chief financial officer is contacted.

*Telemarketer:*     *Mrs. McElroy, my name is Steve Eng of Management Services, Inc. We're management consultants and we've established a reputation for helping companies like yours improve their profit performance.*

*I'll mail you a brochure, but first I'd like to briefly describe some of the things we do.*

If the contact does not protest, the telemarketer continues with an overview of the leading benefits that would likely result from a successful consulting program.

*Telemarketer:*     *Our initial focus is squarely on the financial aspects of a client's operation. By doing an in-depth analysis, we can work with a company to reach a variety of important goals. Some of those goals are improvement of net profits; increasing cash flow and reducing debt; setting up short- and long-range financial plans—or complete business plans and strategies; helping organize management succession; and working out plans for merger or acquisition.*

> *Plus scores of other areas that tie into the main categories I just described.*
>
> *Which of those objectives have you been considering?*

When a prospect identifies one or more of the consulting advantages, the telemarketer is ready with a short statement that further enhances the potential value of that particular area.

### SCRIPT 3.3b: PUTTING EMPHASIS ON A PROSPECT "HOT BUTTON"

The prospect will reveal an interest in one of the main advantages highlighted in the overview. Now the telemarketer will lock into that apparent hot button in order to reinforce its importance in the prospect's mind.

| | |
|---|---|
| *Telemarketer:* | *Which of those objectives have you been considering?* |
| *Contact:* | *We've been thinking about succession. We have senior people who are owners, and most of them will be retiring over the next few years. So we'd like to keep some of the younger middle managers in the organization.* |
| *Telemarketer:* | *As part of succession, a program can deal with compensation designed to keep key people. Also, some firms consider employee stock ownership plans—if you don't already have one.* |
| | *Does that generally fit your situation?* |
| *Contact:* | *Yes, I feel that both of those items can be part of what we eventually do.* |

Once the value of the main benefits has been established, this consulting firm has found it enormously convincing to make three additional points.

- The amount of the prospect's time that can be saved *must be* stressed. The fact is, most firms *can* successfully undertake a financial planning project using their present people, but they don't have time. Companies freely admit that they utilize consultants primarily because staff people can't be allocated due to ongoing work.
- *Convenience* definitely justifies mention at this crucial stage of the telephone presentation. This is simply assurance that the presence of a consultant will not disrupt normal operations in the prospect company.
- *Reliability* of the consulting company is underlined by the telemarketer. The best way to do this is by mentioning the client base and how confidentiality is strictly maintained.

Each of these major presentation points are presented now.

## SCRIPT 3.3c: POINTING OUT THE TIME SAVINGS

Time problems in a busy company are usually severe and represent a very strong selling point when offering intangible services by telephone. It is an area that *must* be covered by a telemarketer if a solid appointment is to be set. We'll go back to the end of Script 3.3b to see how the telemarketer makes a transition into the issue of time savings.

| | |
|---|---|
| *Telemarketer:* | *As part of succession, a program can deal with compensation designed to keep key people. Also, some firms consider employee stock ownership plans—if you don't already have one.* |
| | *Does that generally fit your situation?* |
| *Contact:* | *Yes, I feel that both of those items can be part of what we eventually do.* |
| *Telemarketer:* | *If your company is anything at all like so many others we talk to, you must have a real challenge in taking the time to build a program like this.* |
| *Contact:* | *Only a few people here can do it, and we do have a few other responsibilities to take care of.* |
| *Telemarketer:* | *Our best clients—and our most successful projects—are with companies that* have *the internal capabilities to do the job themselves but just can't devote the time to get it done. Part of our role is to solve the time problem for you.* |

It is appropriate for the telemarketer to add the convenience statement at this time because it reassures the prospect that the company will not be overrun by an army of intrusive people who disrupt ongoing business activities.

## SCRIPT 3.3d: HIGHLIGHTING CONVENIENCE

A surprisingly large number of businesspeople feel that consultants often create unrest among employees, who may suspect that their jobs are in jeopardy. The lower the profile maintained by the consultant, the better. That point must be made when selling a service.

| | |
|---|---|
| *Telemarketer:* | *I'd like to add something that might **be important** to you and other managers in your company.* |
| | *We're extremely sensitive about the possible impact our people may have on a client's employees. We know employees tend to worry when strangers visit the office and talk to their bosses.* |
| | *Our preference is to stay out of the way as much as we can and to occupy as little management time as we can.* |
| | *Most of the work we do on financial programs is handled in our offices, so clients really don't see us much, and that is far more convenient for you.* |

Reliability is closely linked to convenience. The financial firm realized that prospects envisioned complete strangers looking at their most confidential facts and figures. That has no doubt prevented a number of prospects from going ahead with consulting programs, so it *must* be covered by the telemarketer.

## SCRIPT 3.3e: STRESSING RELIABILITY

When your company is unknown to a prospect, it is usually rather hollow for the telemarketer to talk about how reliable and trustworthy it is. More than a few well-meaning words will be needed to establish trust.

The financial consulting company overcomes the trust hurdle by offering references that can vouch for the firm's integrity. A reference from an impartial third party will certify the consultant's ethics, which generally solves the credibility problem.

> *Telemarketer:*    *Since this company was founded 16 years ago, we have been fanatical about protecting client data. If you decide to go ahead with us, we'll provide a list of clients you can call directly to verify our integrity.*

NOTE: Most companies that offer references will provide a client list *only* when a project appears to be near approval. When client lists are given to new prospects, valued customers will be bothered much more than necessary and may decide at some point to stop taking calls from prospects. In a situation like that of the financial company, only the field consultant is authorized to provide references to a prospect. That decision is usually made after the initial face-to-face meeting is concluded.

When it appears that some time will elapse between the telephone call and the field appointment, the telemarketer sends a letter to the prospect. This letter recaps the major points made during the telephone conversation.

## LETTER 3.2: RECAPPING SPECIFIC ADVANTAGES OF THE SERVICE

This letter is used when the telemarketer has succeeded in identifying a specific prospect hot button. It recaps the telephone conversation and helps reinforce the qualifications of the consultant who will call to set an appointment.

Fast, efficient generation of follow-up letters is done by word processing in the financial firm. Thus, a letter like the following one looks highly customized, but in reality is composed mainly of stock paragraphs residing in the memory of a small computer.

Dear Mrs. McElroy:

Your plans for a management succession program are exciting, and we would like very much to work with you on setting one up. A number of our clients have instituted similar plans, and they report an increased sense of continuity among managers along with dramatically reduced turnover in those key positions.

We fully understand the time constraints faced by you and other executives and feel that our assistance will enable you to create and implement a succession program with minimum demands on your schedule and facilities.

Also, please be assured that confidentiality of company data is carefully observed. As I mentioned when we spoke, references can be provided so that you can verify the high ethical standards we have built over a period of many years.

Our consultant in the area of management succession programs is Don Graber. He has been deeply involved in this specialty for the past eight years. Don has an MBA in finance, and we are certain that you will find him helpful, knowledgeable, and sensitive to your needs.

Don will be in touch with you before the weekend to set a convenient meeting time. Please call me if I can be of any further assistance.

Sincerely,

Steve Eng

## USING APPLICATION STUDIES TO GET YOUR MESSAGE ACROSS

In selling to either organizations or consumers, one of the most powerful strategies available to a telemarketer is a *user report* developed from an application study.

Almost *any* potential buyer is interested in a user's experience with the product or service being considered for purchase. To most prospects, a user's opinion has far more weight than *any* brochure or spec sheet prepared by the manufacturer or distributor since these are often regarded by hard-headed buyers as self-serving propaganda.

A user report has special impact under the following conditions:

- When the user applies the product or service in ways that are similar to how the prospect will apply it.
- When the user appears to be frank about the pros and cons.
- When the prospect can directly contact some of the users in order to verify the pros and cons, and fill in missing details.

In some notably successful telemarketing programs, user reports completely replace traditional product descriptions. When the caller tells a prospect how a certain industrial sewing machine is working for another apparel manufacturer, the contact can instantly and accurately *visualize* the operating environment. That is vastly more effective than trying to make sense of a general description of the machine.

Effective user reports are developed from carefully formulated application studies. An application study is a simple questionnaire completed by one or more customers who currently use the product or service. A telemarketer can easily create excellent telephone selling dialogue from a completed study. The process of creating that dialogue is demonstrated in this section.

You will first see, in Form 3.1, a blank questionnaire used to document a customer's experiences. This particular one is used by a temporary-help agency that specializes in financial personnel. Next, the same questionnaire is shown after it has been completed by a client of the placement agency.

Following the application study, Script 3.4 shows the telephone dialogue that was developed from the study by the agency's telemarketer.

The section closes with a follow-up letter that ties into this very effective program.

### FORM 3.1:  DOCUMENTING CUSTOMER APPLICATIONS:
### THE APPLICATION STUDY

A form used to document the experiences of a user can easily be customized to work for almost any product or service. Companies that utilize user reports as part of their selling strategy follow a procedure like this:

- Close postsale contact is maintained with the customer.

- After 60 to 90 days of use, the manager responsible for the product or service in the client company is asked "Would you agree to give us your opinions about how the product is working in your organization?"

  Some will agree to provide an evaluation; others will not. Select several who will give you the time to complete a questionnaire.

- For best results, a representative of the *selling company* should ask the questions and record the customer responses. When the customer is asked to fill out the form, less than satisfactory results often occur.

- Sometimes it may be helpful to interview other employees in order to obtain complete and definitive opinions. Ask the manager whether it is appropriate and feasible to speak to others, such as the people who actually operate your machine or work directly with your service, whatever it may be.

On occasion, a customer may consent to give you opinions, but only under the condition that the company identity is not publicized or mentioned by the selling firm. These "anonymous" user reports are valuable only if they are accompanied by reports from companies that *are* identified by name.

*APPLICATION STUDY*

Date: _____

Company name: _____

Address: _____

City: _____ State: _____ Zip: _____

Telephone: (_____) _____ Extension: _____

Contact names:                              Titles:

_____        _____

_____        _____

_____        _____

_____        _____

Type of business: _____

Service to be evaluated: _____

_____

Date placement order was received: _____

Personnel requested: _____

_____

_____

_____

_____

Details of order: _____

_____

_____

_____

_____

Date order was filled: _____

PERFORMANCE EVALUATION

Job description of Position 1: _____

_____

Strengths: _____

_____

_____

_____

_____

_____

Weaknesses: _____

_____

_____

_____

_____

_____

Job description of Position 2: _____

_____

Strengths: _____

_____

_____

_____

_____

_____

Weaknesses: _____

_____

_____

_____

_____

Job description of Position 3: _____

_____

Strengths: _____

_____

_____

_____

_____

Weaknesses: _____

_____

_____

_____

_____

Job description of Position 4: _____

_____

Strengths: _____

_____

_____

_____

_____

Weaknesses: _____

_____

_____

_____

_____

_____

Job description of Position 5: _____

_____

Strengths: _____

_____

_____

_____

_____

_____

Weaknesses: _____

_____

_____

_____

_____

_____

Overall advantages to client: _____

_____

_____

_____

_____

_____

Notes: _____

_____

_____

_____

_____

_____

*APPLICATION STUDY*

Date: _____

Company name: _____

Address: _____

City: _____ State: _____ Zip: _____

Telephone: (_____) _____ Extension: _____

Contact names:                          Titles:

_____    _____

_____    _____

_____    _____

_____    _____

Type of business: _____

Service to be evaluated: _____

_____

Date placement order was received: _____

Personnel requested: _____

_____

_____

_____

_____

Details of order: _____

_____

_____

_____

_____

Date order was filled: _____

PERFORMANCE EVALUATION

Job description of Position 1: _____

_____

Strengths: _____

_____

_____

_____

_____

_____

Weaknesses: _____

_____

_____

_____

_____

_____

Job description of Position 2: _____

_____

Strengths: _____

_____

_____

_____

_____

_____

Weaknesses: _____

_____

_____

_____

_____

Job description of Position 3: _____

_____

Strengths: _____

_____

_____

_____

_____

Weaknesses: _____

_____

_____

_____

_____

_____

Job description of Position 4: _____

_____

Strengths: _____

_____

_____

_____

_____

_____

Weaknesses: _____

_____

_____

_____

_____

_____

Job description of Position 5: _____

_____

Strengths: _____

_____

_____

_____

_____

_____

Weaknesses: _____

_____

_____

_____

_____

Overall advantages to client: _____

_____

_____

_____

_____

_____

Notes: _____

_____

_____

_____

_____

_____

_____

### SCRIPT 3.4: USING CUSTOMER FEEDBACK
### TO CREATE A SELLING SCRIPT

When the client has reported on the various merits of a product or service, an extremely credible description can be constructed, then used in the telephone sales presentation. More often than not, the resulting description has extra impact since it is actually a replay of a customer's first-hand experience.

A little over one hour was needed for the personnel agency's telemarketer to build the following description from the completed application study just discussed.

*Telemarketer:*        *I can give you an example of how we typically serve our clients.*

*A local film distribution company called us recently and asked whether we could provide a temporary accounting clerk and tax consultant by the end of the following week.*

*Both people had to be experienced. For example, the tax person needed specific background in royalty accounts and in depreciation work.*

*We keep at least 150 experienced financial specialists in our temporary workforce at all times, so we're pretty sure we can meet difficult requests like that on short notice.*

*Five people were identified and prescreened. Then the two front-runners were sent over to the company for interviews. They were just about perfect. The accounting clerk proved to be extremely reliable. And during the time he was at the film company, the tax specialist came up with some changes that will save the client lots of money over the years.*

*All it took was one phone call for this company to get past a major workload crisis. We immediately understood what they needed, and we came very close to perfect choices.*

*If you'd like more details on how our people performed for that company, I can put you directly in touch with their personnel manager.*

Examples can pertain to almost *any* job in the prospect firm. The point is, there is *nothing* more convincing than how similar clients fared when they used your product or service successfully.

In cases calling for a follow-up letter to a prospect, this version is used by the agency:

### LETTER 3.3: A FOLLOW-UP LETTER DEVELOPED FROM APPLICATION STUDIES

Several positive customer reports were used to create this excellent piece for prospects. It is designed to be mailed immediately after the initial telephone contact.

Please note the fact that specific client experiences are not included in this letter. The personnel agency feels that the letter must be devoted to explaining *how the best temporary employees are selected* because this area is not covered sufficiently in the phone call, which emphasizes how people fit into jobs.

One other feature that sets this letter apart from many other follow-up pieces is its length. The agency is certain that worthwhile prospects *will* spend the extra few moments to discover more about how the firm operates.

Dear Ms. Bachman:

Your interest in our temporary financial personnel is appreciated. Since 1973, one basic rule has guided Baily & Harkins in serving the hundreds of companies that rely on us for financial personnel. It is simply this:

*We are every bit as diligent in selecting people for client organizations as we are in choosing people for our own staff.*

Screening and skill-to-job matching go only part of the way toward the goal of creating good fits between people and companies. We believe that an agency must also be willing to put its reputation on the line *every time* it recommends a temporary employee to a client. Baily & Harkins *is* willing to do that because we go a few steps farther to properly fulfill your needs. For example:

- When we judge that an individual's skills match your specific requirements, we have looked carefully at professional knowledge, prior experience in successfully practicing that knowledge, and background in businesses similar to yours.
- Years of experience observing people in various environments has revealed some things to us about matching personalities as well as skills. Baily & Harkins makes as certain as possible that your financial team will work as well together after the new person is aboard. We do that by visiting your facility to see how the chemistry works.

- Reference checking is done thoroughly and without compromise by our staff. It takes a good deal more than an imposing resume and a crisp interview to sell us. We demand a bonafide, verifiable track record.
- Actual skill testing will not do much more than confirm or modify our impressions about an individual's effectiveness, so test results in themselves are just a part of the complete picture we present to you. But it's a part we never miss.

The results of our meticulous approach to finding exceptionally qualified financial specialists is this: Leading companies express unprecedented loyalty to Baily & Harkins. Equally important, these unusually skillful men and women consider us their connection to the financial world.

Let's get you together.

Sincerely,

Derek K. Knutson

## DESCRIBING SERVICE AND SUPPORT

Surveys strongly indicate that a majority of people who buy from telemarketers attach tremendous importance to whatever kind of service and support is offered as part of the deal. A large number of the individuals who receive calls are not familiar with the telemarketer's company, so the *reassurance of a guarantee* becomes essential in gaining that buyer's confidence. Amazingly, very few telemarketing programs include dialogue about how the buyer is protected.

While it may not seem to be very exciting in terms of dramatic impact, information about service and support could very well have more impact on a prospect than *any* other single item in the description.

Service, support, and guarantees of customer satisfaction are especially critical when a telemarketing program is designed to close a sale during the initial call. In this case, buyer confidence must be established *immediately*. There is no rep visit to do the job.

In a calling program that sets appointments for outside salespeople, mention of service and support can be played down somewhat since the field rep will have an opportunity to properly explain that area to the prospect. It still must be covered, however, in order to help make sure the appointment itself holds up.

Here are three separate dialogue segments used by the telemarketing department of a highly successful computer software company. All three are used immediately after the system is described.

### SCRIPT 3.5a: SPELLING OUT GUARANTEES

This firm sells a complex system for large computers and markets the product *exclusively* by telephone and direct mail. Therefore, the buyer is expected to commit major dollars to the purchase, then take the responsibility of installing the system and making it work. If there was ever a product that needed strong assurance from the telemarketer, this is it.

*Telemarketer:*          *We've sold over 700 systems to mainframe sites all over the world. More than 90 percent of those customers installed the system and got it running without a hitch.*

*We're sure you will also find it easy to get the package into operation, but if you do encounter any kind of problem at any stage of installation or implementation, you can return the system, no questions asked and no obligation.*

*In other words, your satisfaction is unconditionally guaranteed. That guarantee covers installation and ongoing performance of the system.*

The terms of this satisfaction guarantee are repeated in a document that accompanies the system package, so the company provides written backup of the money-back guarantee.

*Note:* As you may know, any sale that is consummated by telephone or direct mail is, by law, returnable by the buyer for a refund. An astute seller will turn that into an advantage by making the legal requirement appear to be an act of extreme generosity.

## SCRIPT 3.5b: OUTLINING SUPPORT

Mechanical devices such as machines and vehicles demand continuing assistance from the seller. This is also true of some services. In the software example of Script 3.5a, the data processing manager who purchased the package might require advice from the manufacturer later on if changes to the computer system suddenly caused the need for adjustments.

If manufacturer support were *not* available, the software could be rendered useless. For that reason, sophisticated buyers try to look into the future in order to judge the reliability of the seller's support, and a decision often hinges on the verdict.

Support for the software is described by the firm's telemarketer this way:

*Telemarketer:*     *Part of the reason why our customers are so successful in operating the system is our continuing service. There are two main parts to that program:*

- *First, our telephone technical advisory service is available to assist you with solutions to any problems you may encounter. You can call during all normal working hours, and there's no charge—no matter how long it may take to get finished.*

- *Second, you'll receive regular bulletins with information about what other users are doing. There are excellent ideas in every mailing you receive.*

*So we work very hard to make sure you always have the best backup available at all times.*

## SCRIPT 3.5c: EXPLAINING FUTURE UPDATES

From support in Script 3.5b, it is easy to move directly to a short statement about the software firm's update policy.

*Telemarketer:*        *In case you weren't already aware of our update service, I'll go through it briefly.*

*Whenever we introduce the newest version of Utility 900, you get a copy of the program automatically—at no additional charge.*

*Along with the software, we provide new documentation, and everything else you need to support the enhanced system.*

With a service-intensive approach like the one illustrated above, this software company has captured a hefty market share and unusually high customer loyalty.

## REFINING YOUR DESCRIPTIONS

Copy the following forms and use them to help build your telemarketing descriptions.

Form 3.2, Description-Building Checklist, will help assure that all of the most important components are present in your description.

Use the Description-Building Worksheet, Form 3.3, to actually write your descriptive dialogue. Two distinct advantages in using this form is that it compels you to keep the dialogue brief and helps keep the *flow* of the description smooth and logically sequenced.

### FORM 3.2:  DESCRIPTION-BUILDING CHECKLIST

Select *one* product or service that is well suited to telephone selling. Consult the following list in order to make the best selection. Product or service:

- is used by a large market.
- is easily identified by that market.
- can be priced competitively.

For the product or service you selected, list the five most prominent features, along with matching benefits. List in order of importance (1 is most important, 5 is least important).

*FEATURE 1:* _____

_____

_____

BENEFIT 1: _____

_____

_____

_____

*FEATURE 2:* _____

_____

_____

BENEFIT 2: _____

_____

_____

_____

*FEATURE 3:* _____

_____

_____

BENEFIT 3: _____

_____

_____

_____

*FEATURE 4:* _____

_____

_____

BENEFIT 4: _____

_____

_____

_____

*FEATURE 5:* _____

_____

_____

BENEFIT 5: _____

_____

_____

_____

NOTE: If you are able to list more than five feature/benefit sets, take a harder look at each of them and retain *only* the best five for your description.
  In the above feature/benefit sets, have you covered . . . ?

- Convenience
- Time savings
- Economic advantages

- Reliability
- Guarantees
- Support
- Future updates

Will specs, or any other facts and figures, be included in the telephone description?

\_\_\_\_ Yes     \_\_\_\_ No

If so, which ones? _____

_____

_____

_____

_____

If the successful sale of your product or service depends on equipment or systems already possessed by a prospect, will that information be covered in the telemarketing description?

\_\_\_\_ Yes     \_\_\_\_ No

Do you have customer experiences documented well enough to use in the telemarketing description of your chosen product or service?

\_\_\_\_ Yes     \_\_\_\_ No

If so, which features/benefits do the customer experiences cover?

- _____
- _____
- _____
- _____

Will price be included in your description?

\_\_\_\_ Yes     \_\_\_\_ No

If price is to be included, will various models or versions of your product or service be quoted?

\_\_\_\_ Yes     \_\_\_\_ No

If price will *not* be included in the description, how will the telemarketer respond if a prospect requests price information?

_____

_____

_____

_____

Notes: _____

_____

_____

_____

_____

_____

_____

_____

## FORM 3.3: DESCRIPTION-BUILDING WORKSHEET

*Opening Statement of Description*

This brief statement leads your prospect to the description itself. It could sound something like this: "If you have just a few moments, why don't I briefly cover a few of the leading points about the _____."

_____

_____

_____

*Point One*

State the *most important* feature/benefit set. *Or,* use a customer experience to get each point across.

_____

_____

_____

_____

_____

_____

*Point Two*

Now relate the second most important point. Continue until you have covered up to five leading points.

*IMPORTANT:* After *each* point, ask your contact if the description you gave was completely clear.

_____

_____

_____

_____

_____

_____

*Point Three*

_____

_____

_____

_____

_____

*Point Four*

_____

_____

_____

_____

_____

*Point Five*

_____

_____

_____

_____

_____

*Explain Vital Specs*

If absolutely necessary, provide vital statistics such as capacity, size, etc. Remember to make this rather dry information as interesting as you can! (See Script 3.2.)

_____

_____

_____

_____

_____

_____

### Give Price Information

If your policy is to provide prices, insert this statement here. If you quote *only* on customer request, keep the price statement ready to use as needed.

_____

_____

_____

_____

_____

_____

### Sum It Up

After all feature/benefit sets have been related by the telemarketer, this statement points out exactly *how* the product or service would fit the prospect's situation. For example, "So it appears that the Criteria 7B model would work nicely in the environment you described earlier (when the telemarketer qualified the prospect). In addition, it would appear to serve the needs that seem most important to you."

_____

_____

_____

_____

_____

Try to keep the overall length of the description down to about 90 seconds, based on the normal speech rate of the telemarketer who will be using it. Do this by (1) keeping the text within the allotted space on the form and (2) editing several times to keep the language as crisp and brief as it can possibly be.

_____

# Chapter 4

# SETTING UP FIELD SALES APPOINTMENTS BY TELEPHONE

With the cost of one field sales visit well over $100 in most industries, outside appointments *must be* reserved for only the very strongest prospects. A strong prospect has the following attributes:

- Is in the market for your product or service right now.
- Is financially able to make the purchase.
- Will buy enough to make the sales effort worthwhile.
- Expresses at least mild enthusiasm for your offer.
- Qualifies in every other respect, according to the criteria that you set up in your telemarketing program (review Form 2.1a Qualifying Checklist in Chapter 2).

When qualifying has been done and the prospect warrants priority follow-up, a telemarketer's next move is either to (1) set up a specific appointment for a field salesperson or (2) pave the way for a follow-up call from a field salesperson who will select the time for a visit.

In either situation, the telemarketer must have the ability to sell the concept of an appointment. The prospect must be left with a clear impression that valuable and interesting information will be provided by the representative, that questions will be answered frankly and expertly, and that honest advice regarding the wisdom of buying will be imparted by the rep.

In reality, a great number of telemarketers do *not* succeed in creating these expectations in the prospect. For example, immediately after qualifying, too many callers will say something like this: "Mr. Jones can come out and see you on Tuesday." That pathetically weak language almost always results in feeble appointments that end up wasting a field rep's valuable time.

This chapter provides a rich selection of reasons for an appointment that consumers or business buyers respond to. When these reasons are hooked up to thorough qualifying questions, the result is a happy marriage between skillful telephone work and outside sales.

# DESCRIBING THE ROLES OF CALLER AND FIELD REP

In the eyes of many buyers, a telemarketer who calls on behalf of a field salesperson essentially builds trust, then vanishes forever—no sooner does the caller establish rapport with the prospect, then he or she steps out of the picture. Replacing the friendly voice of the caller is the shadowy presence of a "heavyweight" who will show up at the prospect's office or home, obviously to do some fancy selling.

Because of that break in the continuity of a transaction, the field seller is often faced with the task of overcoming prospect defenses. The potential buyer frequently doesn't even know the name of the person who will visit, much less what will happen during the meeting!

A skillful telemarketer will not only eliminate that clumsy switch from caller to "closer," but will successfully *build up* the importance of the field rep and underline the benefits of the coming sales visit. When this is done correctly, a telemarketer can drastically slash appointment cancellations and no-shows. On top of that, the field seller more often walks into situations in which prospects are far more relaxed and receptive.

Properly paving the way for an outside rep normally takes just a few seconds of the caller's time. One or two paragraphs prior to closing for the appointment is usually all it takes to assure a prospect's comfort with the so far unknown second person.

This section shows how some leading telemarketers go that extra inch to assure stronger field appointments.

### SCRIPT 4.1a: STRESSING THE FIELD REP'S
### PROBLEM-SOLVING CAPABILITIES

Whenever possible, the telemarketer stresses the rep strengths that match the needs of a particular prospect. In the following example, caller qualifying revealed the existence of certain problems that needed solutions. This prospect was looking for guidance on developing an in-house microfilming capability.

| | |
|---|---|
| *Telemarketer:* | *Our field representative is Hank Foreman. His background is in records storage, so I feel that he'd be able to give you some extremely valuable advice on microfilming and storing your legal files. He has designed a number of systems like the one you apparently need.* |
| | *Hank is one of our most experienced people. He keeps up to date on the newest ways to deal with records problems, so I'm sure your questions will be answered clearly and expertly when you talk to him.* |

## SCRIPT 4.1b: EMPHASIZING THE REP'S CREDENTIALS

When specific prospect hot buttons do not emerge during qualifying, the telemarketer is always on safe ground by focusing on the field rep's general qualifications. This can effectively take the shape of a mini-resume.

> *Telemarketer:*        *Hank Foreman is our representative in your area. Let me take just a few seconds to fill you in on his background in records storage.*
>
>        *Hank has a master's degree from Columbia University. From there, he worked at Farleigh Corporation where he spent seven years developing microfiche systems—a number of them for legal firms. In fact, he has written numerous articles on this topic for national publications. Hank has been with us for five years, advising customers on the best ways to set up microfilming capabilities.*

## SCRIPT 4.1c: THE SERVICE TEAM

After establishing the field rep's credentials, the telemarketer can clarify his or her continuing role with respect to the prospect or customer. This conveys to the contact a team picture, which strengthens the seller's service image.

> *Telemarketer:*        *So Hank's primary responsibility is to work with a customer to build an efficient in-house microfiche capability.*
>
>        *My job is to work with the customer to keep the total project organized and on track. Any time you call with any kind of request, I'm here to see that it gets taken care of. I'm your contact and Hank is the system designer.*

## SCRIPT 4.1d: TRANSFERRING THE PROSPECT'S TRUST TO THE SALESPERSON

Some prospects develop a surprisingly high level of rapport with a telemarketer during the initial telephone contact. One very successful outside salesman said this about the relationships built between caller and buyer:

> Our telemarketer only talks to prospects one time, and that conversation rarely lasts more than ten minutes or so. When I finally meet these prospects face to face, however, many of them talk about Anne as if they knew her for years. The trust is incredible. She builds a strong bond with total strangers in a very short period of time.
>
> I actually had problems establishing *my* identity at first. Prospects said "Anne said this and Anne said that." Then we developed a simple way for her to transfer much of the prospect's trust to *me.*

> *Telemarketer:*        *We really hit it off! I hope we get to work with you on this project. When you meet Eva and the other people on our*

*staff, you'll find that all of us care a lot about what we do. We feel that every project has to get the best we can give it—and every job turns out to be fun.*

*I'm looking forward to getting the two of you together.*

Please realize that the above words fit the unique personality of this particular telemarketer. The fact is, a majority of prospects find Anne's style spontaneous, honest, and refreshing. It cuts through the standard and sometimes stilted face of business that is considered "safe" by many people at all levels of business. She puts the transaction on a very human basis.

While Anne's dialogue would not necessarily be appropriate for use by other business people, a *version* of her script—modified to fit an individual caller's personal taste—might come across as effectively as the above text does for her.

Next, the basic follow-up letter Anne uses to pave the way for a field rep.

### LETTER 4.1:   REINFORCING THE NEXT CONTACT

In a busy organization, it may be realistic to suffer delays between a telemarketer's successful first contact and the follow-up call from the field salesperson designated to call for the appointment. While sales strategists urge *immediate* action, it is sometimes out of the question when schedules are filled with other important events.

When Anne sees a follow-up lag of three days or more (which occurs about 30 percent of the time), she sends this letter to those prospects who have expressed interest in talking to a sales rep. Its purpose is twofold:

- It adds to the prospect's perception of the rep's ability.
- It reminds the prospect that the rep will call for an appointment.

Dear Mr. Gomberg:

As promised, I have enclosed a packet of information about the microfiche system we discussed on Tuesday.

After our conversation, I briefed our sales representative, Hank Foreman, on some of the key items that came up. In the next several days, Hank will research these areas so he can put together the latest facts and therefore guide you more effectively when you meet with him.

Hank will also describe for you some of the microfiche installations we've handled that accomplish tasks similar to the ones you are dealing with. This should prove to be particularly interesting to you.

Please list any questions that come up as you review the enclosed material.

Please expect Hank to call you on Monday to schedule an appointment that is convenient for both of you, as well as others in your company who you may want to participate.

I look forward to talking to you again soon.

Sincerely,

Anne Thomas

# ESTABLISHING STRONG REASONS
# FOR THE FIELD APPOINTMENT

As mentioned earlier, the most common downfall of telemarketers is the fact that they fail to convince prospects that an appointment would be beneficial. Unfortunately, a large number of calls come across as if the telemarketer were saying "Sounds to me like you may be interested enough to buy what we're selling. So I'll send someone over to try to close the deal."

If the prospect's need for a product or service is strong enough, he or she will look past that kind of hopelessly weak plea for an appointment and agree to sit down with a sales rep—sometimes a sale is made *despite* the inadequacies of the telemarketer. But a prospect that is not quite as motivated will find a way to escape a wishy-washy telemarketer.

When a call is handled professionally, the telemarketer will provide one or more very solid reasons why the prospect should get together with a field sales representative. A few of the prominent reasons are

- To keep up with the latest developments in a field that touches his or her industry in some way.
- To get ideas on how to solve specific operating problems.
- To achieve the means to reduce expenses, increase income, or both.
- To discover systems or methods that may provide a leg up on competitors.

After the telemarketer has used these or other reasons to make the idea of an appointment attractive, it becomes the responsibility of the field rep to actually *deliver* the kind of guidance pledged by the telemarketer. Therefore, the caller's mandate is to build in the prospect the highest possible expectations for the appointment. When the time of the meeting arrives, it's strictly up to the outside salesperson to come through with a presentation that will get the close.

The scripts that follow are used by a contract furniture company to build a prospect's expectations for the appointment.

## SCRIPT 4.2a: LAYING A FOUNDATION FOR
## SELLING SALES APPOINTMENTS

A southwestern U.S. company that sells high-quality office furnishings finds 70 percent of its customers through telemarketing. This firm's search for the right telephone approach was a struggle that went on for almost two years, during which time the program was almost aborted on several occasions due to management frustration.

This company found that fancy office furniture, no matter how distinctive, could *not* be sold by telephone. They also learned that those who made decisions about corporate refurnishing needed compelling reasons before they would consent to an appointment with one of the firm's field consultants.

Armed with those two facts, the furniture company constructed a telephone presentation that actually avoided most mention of sofas, chairs, and desks. In place of trying to describe items of decor, the caller explained that the field consultant would sit down with the buyer and point out an array of advantages that would likely accrue to a client that updated its furnishings.

The front end of this presentation follows:

> *Telemarketer:* *Our specialty is the creation of custom interiors for corporate and professional office suites. We've handled design projects small and large, from ones for start-up law firms all the way to ones for very large clients such as Stevens & Ashmore. That was six full floors in the building.*
>
> *You'd be interested in how we approach the problem of furnishing offices so they are more conducive to productivity and at the same time capture the personality and style of the people who use the space.*

At this stage, the telemarketer will check the interest level of the contact and attempt to draw the individual into the discussion by asking "Did you *know* that productivity can be increased through interior design?"

As often as not, this question evokes an attempt at humor from the contact, such as a comment to the effect that there is no design that could increase productivity in the firm. This, of course, serves to lighten the moment and build rapport between the caller and prospect.

Another question can now be asked by the telemarketer: "Do you feel that your present office furnishings convey your company's personality—or the image you desire?"

Most frequently, the contact response is either that no serious thought had ever been given to image, or another thrust at humor regarding personality is made. After sharing the joke, the caller continues.

## SCRIPT 4.2b: BUILDING IMAGE AND PERSONALITY

Most intelligent contacts at a corporate decision-making level do recognize the value of image, so it has proved to be a worthwhile topic to review with the furniture company. A review will often bring the question of image into sharper focus and may succeed in magnifying its importance.

> *Telemarketer:* *When we get acquainted with a client, one of our first goals is to come up with the kind of look their offices should have. The look I'm referring to goes from the carpet on the floor to the smallest accessories. It encompasses not only executive offices and reception areas, but all work areas as well.*
>
> *When done right, offices should not only be impressive to your clients but also completely comfortable for your employees. The end result definitely does have a personality that perfectly fits a company's role in the business world.*
>
> *I should add the fact that most of our clients have employees who insist on having some of their own pieces in*

*the office—like pictures, desktop items, and even furniture*
*pieces. When that's the case, we can integrate a design*
*around those items.*

To make certain that the description appeals to the more hard-headed buyers who
look for some kind of payback, the telemarketer takes the following direction:

### SCRIPT 4.2c: KEEPING PACE WITH COMPETITORS

*Telemarketer:*          *Most clients tell us that their new offices are not only more*
*beautiful and comfortable than ever, but that they look a*
*lot better than the competition—and that helps them win*
*new customers.*

*An important part of our job is to help make sure that our*
*client is a leader in how they appear to the public.*

At this point, a subtle "plug" for the field consultant:

*Before we suggest anything at all for a client, a senior con-*
*sultant spends time with you and gets to understand the*
*nature of your organization and your industry.*

Next, more substance about payback.

### SCRIPT 4.2d: SOLVING LOGISTIC PROBLEMS

There are few busy offices that do not contend with glaring inefficiencies in the following areas:

- Traffic patterns in offices: How people and data get from one site to another
- Storage of equipment and records
- Optimum working conditions
- Potential for expansion

It is very likely that the preceding points will have more impact than any others
on some companies. Years of unplanned growth can result in logistic chaos.

*Telemarketer:*          *I'd like to cover an area in which we might be able to provide*
*a significant amount of help. A well-planned refurnishing*
*program can give your company an immediate boost in pro-*
*ductivity.*

*When people and information can move more quickly and*
*efficiently from one spot to another, things happen faster*
*and more gets done.*

*Another big change we almost always make is to achieve*
*effective storage. When a firm grows, it acquires equipment*

> *that can't be absorbed properly, so the equipment sits in the wrong places and gets in the way. These things are designed into the new office. They're integrated the way they should* be.
>
> *Some clients say that suddenly they find they can add needed personnel without renting new space. The footage can be utilized so much more efficiently, it's amazing.*

Another plug for the field consultant:

> *Our consultant would be able to tell pretty quickly how much productivity of your company might increase.*

Now the telemarketer summarizes the advantages—with emphasis on the economic gains that stand to be obtained.

### SCRIPT 4.2e: CAPSULIZING THE ADVANTAGES

Presenting the bottom line brings out the desirability of sitting down with the furniture company's field consultant. This no-obligation visit will give the prospect a picture of the cost of refurnishing and the gains that can be achieved through a redesign project.

*Telemarketer:*   *In a 90-minute meeting with you, we can get enough background to prepare a proposal consisting of these main points: Sketches of how your offices should look, based on your preferences, desired image, and budget; the cost of refurnishing and how long the project would take; the estimated increases in productivity, and what the dollar gains could be; and the space we might be able to pick up for expansion.*

*And there is absolutely no obligation to you.*

This telemarketer successfully provides a series of good reasons why an appointment would be beneficial. When the valuable time of an outside salesperson has to be maximized, there is no better way to handle the initial telephone contact.

Some companies require their telemarketers to set the appointment for the field rep. Others prefer to have the rep make a call to set a day and time (*after* the prospect is qualified by the telemarketer). We'll look at both methods now.

## WHEN THE TELEMARKETER SETS UP
## AN APPOINTMENT FOR THE FIELD REP

Busy outside salespeople usually elect to keep control of their own appointment activity. These high achievers work on developing new sales opportunities as part of their daily routine. For example, they seek referrals, sometimes cold-call in the field when it is convenient and economical to do so, make their own telephone contacts between scheduled outside appointments, and do other things that create extra business.

As a result of these personal efforts, an aggressive field rep really can't accommodate the appointments set by a telemarketer. Frequent time conflicts and rescheduling would occur, and because appointments probably would not be properly grouped, difficulties might arise due to excessive travel time from one appointment to the next.

A few firms have tried to perfect systems in which the rep would reserve blocks of time for the telemarketer. In such a case, the outside seller continues to develop personal opportunities but does not schedule meetings during the reserved time. There are two potential problems with this approach:

- If the telemarketer sometimes fails to set appointments to occupy the reserved times, those hours are essentially wasted and can never be recovered.
- There are still a good number of outside sellers who are reluctant to venture out on an appointment until they themselves have had a chance to prequalify the prospect. In these instances, a high level of trust has not yet been established between caller and rep.

Because of these very real complexities, a majority of productive telemarketing programs are based on a system in which the caller sets up a second telephone contact. In that second contact, the rep talks to the targeted buyer to get acquainted and do a little more qualifying.

Most companies that use the two-call method find it advantageous to organize their telemarketing programs so that certain qualifying questions are asked during each call. The telemarketer proceeds to a preestablished point, then, when the rep follows up, he or she completes the questioning routine.

A midwestern art-supply retailer uses telemarketing to sign major corporate accounts. The caller lines up the most promising buyers for follow-up by one of the company's outside salespeople. Management devised the system shown next under Splitting Up the Qualifying Questions to accomplish the following objectives:

- To assure that qualifying would be complete when both the telemarketer and the outside rep had concluded their respective calls to a prospect.
- To help avoid duplication of questions when the rep followed up. It might be irritating to a prospect if the same ground were inadvertently covered.

## SPLITTING UP THE QUALIFYING QUESTIONS

This is simply a list of qualifying questions used by the art-supply firm. It shows *who* asks the questions, the telemarketer or the rep. Please notice that the rep's questions are generally more specific—and somewhat more sensitive—than those asked by the caller.

*Qualifying Questions to Be Asked by Telemarketer.*

- Identify buyer of art/drafting equipment.
- Find out how many departments in the company use these supplies.

- Determine applications for art/drafting supplies.
- List product groups most commonly purchased.
- Identify immediate needs.
- Note best days and times to reach the buyer.

*Qualifying Questions to Be Asked by Sales Representative.*

- Find out annual dollars spent on art/drafting supplies.
- Determine present sources of supply.
- Ask about current budget.
- Determine decision process for major art/drafting purchases.

Between the two calls, one from the telemarketer and the other from the rep, the story about any given prospect becomes reasonably clear, and the rep would certainly be prepared to sit down with the buyer and work toward a sale.

We'll look now at how the telemarketer for the art-supply firm sets up the rep's contact.

### SCRIPT 4.3a: PREPARING THE PROSPECT FOR A SECOND ROUND OF QUALIFYING

In the case of the art-supply company, both of the firm's outside salespeople stated a strong preference for doing their own qualifying before committing to going on a field visit. This attitude was partly due to the relative inexperience of the caller and to some fear that a large percentage of the appointments would not be as solid as the telemarketer represented them to be.

While the reps had no problem with the caller finding solid leads, they still wanted to verify the quality of those leads, then set their own appointments if warranted after qualifying. A telephone presentation was designed with these circumstances in mind. The following script includes *only* the qualifying questions just listed and prepares the prospect by emphasizing the call that will come from the field rep.

| | |
|---|---|
| *Telemarketer:* | *Do you have any art-supply or drafting-supply needs that are pressing?* |
| *Contact:* | *As far as I know, we don't have any emergencies, but we'll be getting a routine order ready in about a month.* |

If the telemarketer *had* uncovered an immediate need, the situation would be ideal for having the field rep personally deliver the urgent order—the same day if at all possible.

| | |
|---|---|
| *Telemarketer:* | *Can you usually be reached on Wednesday mornings?* |
| *Contact:* | *Usually. Why do you ask?* |

|               |               |
|---------------|---------------|
| *Telemarketer:* | *Tim Brock, our rep in your area, can call you and explain some of the advantages of using us as a source. For example, we have a volume discount program that might save you considerable money and help assure that you never run out of important supplies.* |
|               | *Mainly, I think it would be valuable for you to talk with Tim because he's extremely knowledgeable about what you're doing and the products you use. He might have some suggestions that will make your ordering task easier and more economical.* |
|               | *If you spend just a few minutes on the phone with him, I'm sure you'll be able to tell whether he can help you, so it's worth looking into, don't you agree?* |

Since there is virtually no threat to the prospect in spending a little more time on the phone—and there *is* a chance that some money and/or time could be saved—most prospects *would* agree to taking the rep's follow-up call.

When agreement is expressed, an effective telemarketer will go an extra step toward nailing down a *precise* follow-up time.

### SCRIPT 4.3b: PINPOINTING A TIME FOR THE REP'S CALL

When special emphasis is *not* placed by the telemarketer on the exact time of follow-up, the entire idea of later rep contact loses importance in the eyes of the prospect. It becomes just so much loose conversation, and most contacts promptly forget about the promised call-back *and* the essence of the art firm's offer.

Setting a precise follow-up time should be something of a formal ritual. The importance of the coming call from the rep is built up to maximum extent.

|               |               |
|---------------|---------------|
| *Telemarketer:* | *Let's reserve 15 minutes next Wednesday morning at 10:00 A.M. Is that the best time for you?* |

As soon as agreement on time is reached, ask the contact to *write down* the information about the call-back date.

> *Would you please jot this information down?*

When the contact is ready to write, the specific information is given.

> *That's Wednesday, April 8, at 10:00 A.M. Our rep's name is Tim Brock. That's spelled B–R–O–C–K.*
>
> *If there is any change in your schedule, call me at 871-9490, extension 24. Again, my name is Judy Price, P–R–I–C–E.*
>
> *I'll talk to Tim later today. If that time isn't perfect for him, I'll call you tomorrow morning.*

*I'll brief Tim on our conversation so when he calls he'll have more information on the areas of interest to you.*

This meticulous approach for setting the date and time for the rep's call leaves every prospect with the distinct impression that the call-back event is held in high regard. In addition, the formalized approach helps assure that the contact will remember the date, the time, and the *purpose* of the rep's call.

Finally, the telemarketer has to make absolutely certain that the rep *does* make the call precisely at the established time. To slip on time will essentially undo all the good accomplished by a hard-working telemarketer.

When at least four days will elapse between the telemarketer's call and the rep's follow-up, a brief confirming letter will help reinforce the agreed upon arrangements.

### LETTER 4.2: CONFIRMING CALL FROM REP

Dear Mrs. Stein:

Just a note to confirm the arrangements we made during our conversation on Thursday.

Our western regional field representative, Tim Brock, will call you on Wednesday, April 8, at 10:00 A.M.

Tim will have additional information on the various items you use in your art and drafting tasks. This will include facts on volume discounts that you apparently qualify for.

We look forward to exploring a business relationship with your fine organization.

Sincerely,

Judy Price

If the two-call appointment system is to work as well as it should, a company must have a way for the telemarketer to transmit data to the rep who will follow up.

---

### FORM 4.1: TRANSMITTING FOLLOW-UP DATA TO THE REP

Any number of forms are used to relay prospect data to the field salesperson who will make the second call and set up the initial outside visit. One version is shown here.

### CONTACT FORM

Company _____ Date _____

Address _____ Source of Inquiry _____

City _____ State _____ Zip _____

Telephone ( ) _____

Contact by Priority

1 _____ 2 _____

3 _____ 4 _____

Comments _____

_____

_____

_____

_____

_____

Qualifications _____

_____

_____

_____

_____

Rating _____

_____

Regardless of how your form is designed, certain key components should be included. They are now described.

Aside from basic address information, the telemarketer lists the contacts in a prospect company in order of their buying authority. It can be helpful to include the title and extension number of each individual, if appropriate.

Contact by Priority

1 _____ 2 _____
3 _____ 4 _____

The comments section should include any information that will help the field rep understand the prospect company and the primary contact.

Qualifications give the rep a quick look at how the company stacks up in terms of its ability to buy. Most telemarketing departments preprint each qualification question that will be asked by both the caller *and* the outside salesperson. Blank space is provided next to the printed question so a yes, no, or maybe can be entered as qualifications proceed. The box for a rating is described later.

Comments _____

_____

_____

_____

_____

Qualifications _____

_____

_____

_____

_____

Rating _____

Follow-Up Action Record is where the telemarketer notes exactly what kind of action has taken place and what actions should follow—and *when.*

When the outside salesperson takes charge of the form then makes a follow-up call and goes on the appointment, those events are also recorded. In this way, a complete history of activity is maintained, in addition to information about future steps that will be needed to obtain the sale.

**Follow-Up Action Record**

| Date | Talked To | Comments | Send | Appointment | Call Again | Other |
|------|-----------|----------|------|-------------|------------|-------|
|      |           |          |      |             |            |       |
|      |           |          |      |             |            |       |
|      |           |          |      |             |            |       |
|      |           |          |      |             |            |       |
|      |           |          |      |             |            |       |
|      |           |          |      |             |            |       |

## RATING THE QUALITY OF PROSPECTS

A rating can be extremely helpful to the field rep. The rating is simply a grade that sums up the perceived quality of the company as a buying candidate. Here's a sample of how one firm's telemarketing department rates each prospect they talk to.

*TYPE A*   Prospect is qualified, interested, and has an immediate need. Arrange personal visit as soon as possible.

*TYPE B*   Qualified and interested, but certain factors put time of appointment about 30 days away. Call back within 30 days.

*TYPE C*   Qualified and interested, but can't take action until one to six months from present date.

*TYPE D*   Neither qualified or interested. Call back in about six months.

Some companies use as many as seven letter designations to describe prospect readiness; and the definitions can vary widely from one firm to another.

As a given prospect goes through a series of sales contacts, it is likely that the letter rating will change, thus demanding higher or lower follow-up priority. For example, a B-rated prospect when called back in 30 days may very well become A-rated.

In some companies, the telemarketer has the green light to book the appointment for an outside sales representative. We'll now look at some of the presentations used for that purpose.

## WHEN THE TELEMARKETER CLOSES
## THE APPOINTMENT FOR THE FIELD REP

A system called *closed-loop selling* is an ideal environment for having the telemarketer set the appointment. Closed-loop selling involves a tightly knit team composed of *one* telemarketer and *one* field sales rep. The two work so closely together and understand each other so well that communication is usually flawless. Therefore, the caller in such a team is generally in charge of the field appointment.

One other situation in which the caller sets the visit date is, of course, when the salesperson makes his or her own telephone calls. This is common in most small businesses and in some firms that don't believe in the concept of dedicated telemarketers prospecting for the benefit of outside sellers.

When the telemarketer does bear the responsibility of setting appointments, there is usually *no* second call from a rep that can be used for additional qualifying. Thus, the *initial call* has to be strong enough to make sure there is definite commitment from the prospect. Much more pressure is placed on the telemarketer, since a bad appointment is blamed on nobody else but the caller.

Field reps who depend on telemarketers to set their appointments consider the following areas to be of chief importance:

- The caller has to take extra steps to obtain agreement from the prospect. The appointment must be rock solid.
- A prospect has to understand exactly what the rep will cover at the time of the appointment.
- Prospects can't feel at all threatened by the impending visit.
- All decision makers should be present at appointment time, and the telemarketer is the one who must assure their presence.

Scripts in this section cover these points.

### SCRIPT 4.4a: SETTING AN EXTRA-SOLID DATE FOR
### THE FIELD SALES APPOINTMENT

There is nothing as aggravating to an outside salesperson as traveling to an appointment, then finding that the contact either doesn't expect the rep, or is out of town. A few repeats of this situation will almost surely wreck the sometimes fragile relationship between telemarketer and field seller. A good outside salesperson can overcome a variety of adversities, but walking into an appointment when unexpected or unwanted is an exceptionally tough one to beat.

Telemarketers who want to take extra measures to avoid failed appointments must take special precautions to nail down a prospect's commitment for the meeting. The following dialogue is used by the telemarketer *after* a prospect has agreed in principal to meet with a sales rep.

Please keep in mind that the following approach is optional. It goes a big step farther to emphasize the appointment date. Some callers and telemarketing managers prefer to set a date and time, then leave it at that—hoping the appointment holds up.

| | |
|---|---|
| *Telemarketer:* | *Our representative in your area is Cynthia Herbert. She has an hour open on Friday, May 11, at 2:00 P.M. Can you check your schedule to see if that time is open?* |

*Note:* Many telemarketers prefer to offer two alternative times.

| | |
|---|---|
| *Contact:* | [Affirms availability of spot or suggests an acceptable alternative.] |
| *Telemarketer:* | *I know this may be impossible to answer, but how much chance do you think there is that something else will come up in that time slot? Cynthia will be out on calls Friday, and we won't be able to reach her if there's a cancellation.* |

A telemarketer doesn't really expect a legitimate answer to the above question. It is asked mostly for effect—to underline the selected date and time, and to help sanctify the appointment.

| | |
|---|---|
| *Contact:* | *As far as I can tell right now, that time should be okay. But nobody ever knows about sudden interruptions.* |
| *Telemarketer:* | *Sounds good. Will you jot down my number in case something does come up?* |

The telemarketer now gives contact complete information to write down. This includes name, telephone number, appointment date, and rep's name. It is also a very good idea to get directions from the contact on how to find the company and where to park.

The second phase of this approach is to recap what will take place during the appointment.

## SCRIPT 4.4b: DESCRIBING WHAT WILL HAPPEN AT THE MEETING

Even if the purpose of the rep's visit has been discussed earlier in the call, it is now *repeated* by cautious callers who set appointment dates for reps.

Assuming that the prospect has just written down the appointment date, there is no better moment for the telemarketer to provide a short list of items that will be covered during the appointment.

| | |
|---|---|
| *Telemarketer:* | *Let me briefly review for you exactly what Cynthia will cover when you meet with her on Friday.* |
| | *First, she'll ask you some questions about what you use copies for and how heavy the traffic is on each of the machines you have now. That will provide clues about what kind of unit might fit best.* |
| | *Then she'll describe some solutions and estimate what the costs would be to upgrade.* |
| | *An important part of the meeting can be for answering your questions. Cynthia really knows the copier market, and she'll give you very frank answers.* |
| | *After about 45 minutes, we'll have enough information to come back and prepare a formal proposal for you.* |

That final paragraph in the above dialogue would, of course, be eliminated when the close is attempted at the time of the field visit.

When a close *is* part of the appointment strategy, the telemarketer often finds it helpful to use the next dialogue.

### SCRIPT 4.4c: REMOVING THE THREAT FROM THE APPOINTMENT

Most seasoned decision makers are under no illusions regarding the reason for an appointment. Very simply, the vendor wants to *sell* something, and the sooner the better.

Therefore, when a prospect agrees to sit down with a rep, the buyer fully expects to be "pitched." Some prospects see that as unpleasant and may avoid appointments for that reason. In order to try to neutralize such a reaction from a prospect, the telemarketer can add the dialogue in the next script.

We'll begin with the end of Script 4.4b, when the final paragraph is *not* used.

| | |
|---|---|
| *Telemarketer:* | *An important part of the meeting can be for answering your questions. Cynthia really knows the copier market and she'll give you very frank answers.* |
| | *We are definitely against high-pressure selling. We like to sell copiers—but not until our customer is absolutely certain that the best solution has been worked out.* |
| | *If that decision can be made rapidly, that's fine. But if it takes more work and additional time, we will completely understand.* |

If used, this dialogue should be carefully formulated and approved by the outside rep who ultimately has to live with the consequences.

A very important final step in setting solid appointments for reps is trying to assure that *all* decision makers will be in attendance.

## SCRIPT 4.4d: MAKING AS SURE AS POSSIBLE THAT THE ENTIRE BUYING COMMITTEE WILL BE PRESENT AT THE APPOINTMENT

In a very new business relationship, a telemarketer should take care when talking about other buyers or influential people. The established contact may be insulted or irritated if the caller pushes too hard on getting others involved in the appointment. At this stage, a passing mention of other decision makers is sufficient.

> *Telemarketer:*      *I almost forgot to ask you whether the time we decided on will be convenient for others whom you ask to sit in on the meeting with Cynthia.*

When it is imperative that the telemarketer find out how many others will attend the meeting, the following strategy works nicely.

## SCRIPT 4.4e: GETTING A DEFINITE COUNT ON WHO WILL ATTEND

Every outside rep has walked into an appointment where every chair in a big conference room was occupied by a manager waiting to hear the presentation and pass judgment on it. When the rep was expecting just one or two people, that can be quite a shock. A telemarketer can neatly prevent a situation like that through this simple tactic.

> *Telemarketer:*      *Cynthia will prepare special literature packages for each person you want to include in the meeting. Can you give me a count and the names of people who'll be there?*

Aggressive outside salespeople can get outstanding results by utilizing their "in-between" time to the maximum extent. Here's how a telemarketer can help in that respect.

## SCRIPT 4.5: INFORMAL APPOINTMENTS: GETTING A FOOT IN THE DOOR

When a rep has a little extra time between appointments, and travel to the next visit is under control, a telemarketer can set up *informal* field visits for the rep. Since the rep is out in the field anyway, the high cost of personal visits does not become a factor.

A program of "fill-in" visits can be highly successful because this kind of contact is completely nonthreatening to most prospects, and their resistance is kept at a comparatively low level.

Essentially, the caller is getting a foot in the door and does not go into detail. After the introduction, this dialogue is used by the caller:

> *Telemarketer:*      *Our rep in your area is Cynthia Herbert. She has an appointment in your neighborhood next Friday at 2:00 P.M. She'll have five minutes just to introduce herself to you and give you some literature on our line of copiers and fax machines.*
>
> *Can you break away for a few minutes at about ten minutes to two?*

If the contact can't or won't break away, the rep can at least drop off a literature package with the prospect's receptionist.

When a fill-in visit *is* successful, the rep uses the brief exposure to set up a full-scale appointment later.

### LETTER 4.3:   CONFIRMING THE APPOINTMENT FOR THE FIELD REP

When the field appointment is four days or more from the time of the telemarketer's call, a confirming letter helps reinforce the visit and reminds the contact about what will happen during the appointment.

Dear Mr. Nielsen:

Since you are so busy, I thought it would help to recap the arrangements we made when we spoke this morning.

Our north city representative, Cynthia Herbert, will be at your Clement Street offices on Friday at 2:00 P.M. to present Westland's line of copiers.

Normally, about forty minutes will be needed to cover the following important items:

- Your present applications, and how many copies are usually made on each machine during the course of a typical month.
- Other desired capabilities you would like to have in new copiers.
- Any questions that come up.

Our objective is to help you find the best possible solution.

If there are any changes in your schedule prior to Friday, please contact me at 247-3470, extension 12.

We look forward to serving you.

Sincerely,

Dave Tyner

There are numerous occasions when the prospect is again called before the rep's visit. Some of these are covered now.

## CALLS THAT CONFIRM THE FIELD APPOINTMENT

Any active field rep can tell stories about apparently good appointments that don't materialize. The telemarketer does a round of qualifying as carefully and thoroughly as possible, and the contact agrees to a meeting time. But at some point, for unknown reasons, the arrangements fall apart. This occurs frequently enough to prompt a large number of sales organizations to insist on confirming appointments.

Another widely held point of view takes the opposite stand: If the telemarketer or field rep calls to confirm an established appointment, there is a high risk that the prospect will cancel or postpone the appointment due to some form of "buyer's remorse."

Those who advocate the confirmation of appointments say that they do experience a few cancellations, but they feel that these particular prospects are marginal in any event and not really worth a trip through traffic.

In the end, each seller has to make an individual decision about whether to confirm or not. If a firm opts to confirm, the following scripts are used successfully.

## SCRIPT 4.6a: CONFIRMING THE APPOINTMENT

A commonly used confirming call is a brief, straightforward contact between the telemarketer and the targeted buyer. Telemarketing managers say that the buyer's secretary or assistant can also be a completely reliable person to speak with when confirming an appointment. Confirming is often simple and usually does not involve hassles with screens since communications have already been established.

Immediately after a standard reintroduction, the caller says this:

| | |
|---|---|
| ***Telemarketer:*** | *I'm calling to confirm the appointment between Mr. Nielsen and Cynthia Herbert on Friday at 2:00 P.M.* |
| | *Can you tell me if that day and time are still okay?* |

Contact or assistant will verify or change, as the case may be.

> *Great. I appreciate your checking on that for me. We look forward to Friday (or to the modified date).*

Confirming calls can be made as late as an hour or two before the actual appointment time. If an outside salesperson is facing a trek through heavy traffic of at least an hour, he or she may be strongly inclined to confirm that meeting before hitting the road.

Another version of a confirming call follows.

## SCRIPT 4.6b: CHECKING ON RECEIPT OF LITERATURE PACKAGE

Many telemarketers set an appointment during their initial call to a prospect and at the same time promise to mail an information package to the prospect.

If a sales rep is scheduled to visit the prospect in a matter of days, a brochure or information sheet seems superfluous and perhaps may even be detrimental to the cause. Still, this practice is not unusual. Telemarketers who *do* send out literature use that mailing as a pretext for confirming the appointment. For example:

| | |
|---|---|
| ***Telemarketer:*** | *[After reintroduction.] When we set the appointment between you and Mrs. Faber, I promised to mail information on the telephone system. Did you receive that package okay?* |

If yes:

> *Good! While I've got you on the line, I'd like to confirm that appointment. That's next Monday at 9:00 A.M. Is that still clear?*

If yes:

> *We'll see you then. Thank you very much.*

One leading objection to this confirmation method is that to duck the appointment, a prospect merely claims that the mailing must have been delayed in transit or was misplaced internally. The inevitable next step is a request for you to mail a new package, then call in a week or so to set a new appointment.

A significant number of telemarketing managers will never permit the mailing of an information package to a prospect if an appointment has been booked. These managers maintain that the rep is the one who now controls the flow of data to the prospect. When information mailings are not sent to booked prospects, the telemarketer can give this response to a request for brochures:

### SCRIPT 4.6c: POLITELY REFUSING TO MAIL BROCHURES

A prospect who has agreed to sit down with a sales rep is a valuable property indeed, and the telemarketer would never risk this budding relationship by turning down the contact's simple request for a brochure, spec sheets, or any other kind of data. But if company policy insists that mailings are *not* to be sent to booked prospects, such requests from prospects have to be declined. The turndown must be as polite, and as logical, as it can possibly be. Here's one possibility:

| | |
|---|---|
| *Contact:* | *Will you mail all available product information to me this afternoon? I'll look it over before the appointment on Tuesday.* |
| *Telemarketer:* | *We have so many packages going out every day, I doubt if we can get the package to you before the appointment. Those mailings are done by a separate department and my request goes into channels with everyone else's. You know how that works. But, if you don't mind, I'll make sure that Bob brings all available product information when you meet.* |

Next, forms to help you create appointment-setting dialogue for your telemarketing program.

## REFINING YOUR APPOINTMENT-SETTING APPROACHES

Form 4.2 provides a checklist that can be used for both the call that sets up a later contact from the field rep and the call that makes the appointment for the rep. This checklist will help assure that all points are covered when you create this part of your presentation.

A worksheet for writing appointment-setting dialogue is supplied in Form 4.3. Make as many copies as you need.

## FORM 4.2: APPOINTMENT-SETTING CHECKLIST

When setting up a call, or actually *making* the appointment, for the field salesperson, be sure to cover the following points:

— Emphasize credentials of the outside sales rep.

— Describe the role of both the telemarketer and the field rep as they pertain to the relationship with the prospect.

— Establish definite reasons for the field appointment. Identify the best reasons from the following list or note others that are important for your product or service:

  • To help solve problems for the prospect.

  • To improve logistics in the prospect company.

  • To build image and personality for the prospect.

  • To improve prospect's profits and/or reduce expenses.

  • To help prospect keep up with or remain ahead of competitors.

— If call is to set up a telephone contact from the field rep, stress *exact time* of next contact.

— If call is to set an appointment for the rep, strongly emphasize the date and time of the meeting.

— Describe to the prospect exactly what will take place during the appointment.

— Remove all elements of threat from the telephone dialogue.

— Try to ensure that all buyers and other influential people will be present at the meeting.

— If necessary, create a form for documenting prospect data.

— Make certain that key data about the prospect are transmitted to, and understood by, the field rep.

Other points important to your product or service: _____

_____

_____

_____

_____

_____

_____

## FORM 4.3:   APPOINTMENT DIALOGUE WORKSHEET

Use this form to write telephone dialogue that *immediately follows* the product/service description. Try to keep the total time of this dialogue segment at two minutes or less.

In order to obtain smooth, logical flow to the appointment-setting dialogue, think of this segment in terms of three distinct parts:

1. Stress the qualifications of the field rep. The prospect has to feel that a meeting with the outside seller will be beneficial.

2. Provide at least two reasons why an appointment will be well worth the prospect's time.

3. Get a definite time commitment for either a call from the rep or for the appointment itself.

Again, review the checklist (Form 4.2) to make sure that all desired points are included in the dialogue.

1. Create dialogue that describes the rep's qualifications: _____

_____

_____

_____

_____

_____

_____

_____

_____

_____

_____

_____

_____

_____

_____

_____

_____

_____

_____

_____

2. Provide at least two reasons why an appointment would be worthwhile:

- _____

_____

_____

_____

_____

- _____

_____

_____

_____

_____

_____

- _____

_____

_____

_____

_____

3. Get a definite time commitment from the prospect: _____

_____

_____

_____

_____

_____

_____

_____

_____

_____

_____

_____

_____

_____

_____

Notes: _____

_____

_____

_____

_____

_____

_____

_____

# Chapter 5

# CLOSING A SALE ON
# THE FIRST TELEPHONE CONTACT

A rapidly increasing number of companies are working on ways to sell without outside salespeople. In almost every instance, management recognizes these realities:

- The cost of a field sales visit can cut deeply into profits for many companies. That problem is compounded when multiple visits are needed to sell, then support, a customer.

- Firms that seek wider distribution frequently can't afford to finance an expanded rep organization, so they look at alternatives such as selling exclusively by direct mail and telephone.

- Many companies that sell through independent rep organizations or distributors find they do not receive enough exposure to potential buyers. Their lines are often lost among scores of others, all fighting for attention.

When faced with these disadvantages, it is understandable that many firms would look with interest at the creation of a "rep-less" selling capability.

Another major group of firms that must close their sales by telephone are those marketing low-ticket items. For example, a $50 sale simply cannot be profitably closed in the field unless the transaction is consummated in a retail store.

This chapter provides telephone presentations and supporting letters designed to do the job of closing without personal salespeople. Of special interest is a presentation successfully used to sell custom products by telephone. The customer never sees the finished product until it is completed and delivered. There are two striking features about this particular program. First is the remarkable fact that it costs about $28 to obtain a close when the sale is made by telephone compared to $240 when the company got the close through field visits in earlier days! Second, customer complaints are not a factor. Problems are at the same low level today that they were when field reps were on the job.

Closing by telephone is vitally important to almost any small business. An entrepreneur cannot spend intensive time out in a territory selling if he or she must also do the work to keep clients happy. The telephone seems to create more time in each day for small companies.

## COMPLETE SCRIPTS FOR
## GETTING THE ORDER IMMEDIATELY

When the telemarketer's goal is to close the sale on the initial telephone contact, there are a few differences in how the call is conducted. For example:

- Since there will not be a follow-up call from an outside sales rep, complete qualifying must be done during the first contact, and a quick, accurate judgment must be made by the caller regarding the quality of a prospect.

- Prospect objections have to be handled firmly, decisively, and immediately. A caller who closes sales has no choice but to be well informed about how the product or service works and how it benefits the buyer in every respect.

- Knowledge of the caller should extend to the background of the selling company and its intimate workings. Prospects will rarely buy unless they understand who they are dealing with. Credibility is magnified in importance when closing by telephone.

- Perhaps most important, the telemarketer must *expect* to close the telephone sale. This assumptive attitude helps to sweep a prospect toward a positive decision. If the caller personally doubts that one telephone call can obtain an order, the prospect will almost certainly pick up on those doubts.

Since there are differences between this call and the calls we have covered in the prior chapters, we'll look at several complete closing presentations. By reviewing the start-to-finish dialogue, the differences will be easier to identify.

### SCRIPT 5.1a: CLOSING ON AN OUTBOUND COLD CALL

Script examples in this section are used by independent business form/computer supply distributors. These companies sell to other businesses, and many of them depend rather heavily on telemarketing to find prospects and sell to them in this highly competitive industry.

Our first script is used to close an order on the first call. This particular forms distributor targets two kinds of prospects in its cold-calling program:

- Companies in need of certain standard business forms such as invoices or employment applications. Almost every business goes through a supply of these forms periodically, but often not in large quantities.

- Companies in need of computer supplies.

This distributor's business philosophy maintains that a telephone sale can be closed if the dollar volume is low enough to eliminate any feeling of risk on the part of the buyer. As the business relationship is solidified, larger and more profitable sales will follow.

| | |
|---|---|
| *Receptionist:* | *Good morning, Whiteside Company. Can I help you?* |
| *Telemarketer:* | *Good morning, my name is Tim Hughes. Can you connect me with the person who takes care of your business forms?* |
| *Receptionist:* | *That's probably Bob Fillmore, our office manager. May I tell him why you are calling?* |
| *Telemarketer:* | *Sure. I mailed some literature about a special on business forms and computer supplies to your company recently, and I'm calling to find out if it got to Mr. Fillmore.* |
| *Receptionist:* | *Hold on, I'll see if he's available.* |
| *Contact:* | *This is Bob Fillmore. What can I do for you?* |
| *Telemarketer:* | *I'm Tim Hughes with Morgan Business Supply. We supply a number of customers in town with standard business forms and computer supplies. In fact, we've been working with your neighbor Ekman & Tabor Company for several years.* |
| | *We sent out a bulletin announcing a special. Do you remember seeing it?* |

Mention of a nearby customer helps establish the identity of Tim's company. Also, mentioning the bulletin serves to hold the interest of Bob Fillmore.

| | |
|---|---|
| *Contact:* | *No, I don't remember a bulletin.* |
| *Telemarketer:* | *You're in charge of buying business forms, is that right?* |
| *Contact:* | *Right.* |
| *Telemarketer:* | *We have a new service that might be an extremely effective money-saver for you. I can describe it in a few seconds.* |
| *Contact:* | *Okay—but please make it fast.* |
| *Telemarketer:* | *We can supply as few as 100 standard business forms with your company imprint. That saves you cash and storage space since most suppliers insist on selling a minimum of 500 forms—especially when imprinting is required. And we sell the smaller quantity at the same per-unit price you pay for larger orders.* |
| | *What kind of standard forms do you use?* |
| *Contact:* | *Bookkeeping forms and packing lists come to mind.* |
| *Telemarketer:* | *Does the concept of buying smaller quantities make sense to you?* |
| *Contact:* | *It might in some cases.* |

At this point, the telemarketer explores the types of accounting forms used and obtains information such as how many parts the company needs in its forms. As soon as precise needs are known, the caller closes:

> *Telemarketer:*         *As a trial of our service, why don't we send you* [a rundown of the forms previously identified, and the quantities and prices].

Whether or not the close succeeds, the telemarketer proceeds with dialogue that introduces other key aspects of the distributor's business:

> *Telemarketer:*         *What kind of computer do you use in your company?*
>
> *Contact:*         *We have a _____ in our accounting department.*
>
> *Telemarketer:*         *We may be able to help you with printer ribbons, diskettes, and stock tab. Again, no matter what quantities you need, we can send the items along with your order and still give you large-volume pricing.*
>
>         *Can I put a box of printer ribbons in your shipment?*

After this area is settled one way or another, the caller concludes with one final point:

> *Telemarketer:*         *While we specialize in small quantities, we're also geared to handle your biggest requirements for standard or custom forms.*
>
>         *Do you use custom forms in your firm?*

At the very least, the telemarketer wants to plant the seed that will lead to major form business in the future. Just a mention of this other capability will suffice at this point. The telephone presentation for custom form orders is covered in Script 5.3a.

For this distributor, an average order obtained by telephone comes to $87. This sale in itself is marginally profitable, but is only the very beginning of a continuing business relationship for these reasons:

- Virtually *all* sales subsequently made to a typical customer are handled by telephone, so costs are very nominal and profits much better than they would be if the sale was made by visiting the account.

- Later sales tend to grow in dollar volume since the building of trust leads to a larger share of the customer's needs. Therefore, the initial transaction can be less profitable if it gets the door open.

- Reorders are obtained about every five weeks. This frequency helps assure that the customer will remain loyal; competitors don't have much of a chance to gain a foothold.

- Eventually, large form orders will be won by the distributor, and these will more than compensate for the early lean pickings.

Telephone inquiries generated by ads, trade shows, and other types of publicity are all too often neglected by busy companies. Here's how one firm makes money on leads that many other companies stuff into a box and forget.

### SCRIPT 5.1b: CLOSING ON THE FIRST CALL TO AN EXISTING LEAD

Recent studies show that about 70 percent of the people who inquire about a certain product or service will eventually purchase it. These lookers may buy from a source different than the one originally queried, but the purchase will be made by most of them sooner or later.

In view of that fact, it is extraordinary that so many firms spend big money to generate inquiries but take little or no action to follow those leads up.

Perhaps the sheer number of responses is a problem to some advertisers. For example, exhibiting at a trade show can easily produce hundreds of names and telephone numbers. These shoppers range in quality from students or tinkerers who gather data for research (definitely nonbuyers) to prospects who are on the verge of placing an order.

Even with the mixed bag of interest in any group of leads and the effort that must be given to checking each one out, astute firms consider their leads valuable. They know it's a "numbers game"—a certain quantity of calls *will* uncover the ones that are ready to buy.

A majority of the companies that do follow up their leads take a highly assumptive approach. They view a lead this way: *You,* the prospect, took action by expressing interest in our offer. That action identifies you as a likely buyer. Therefore, we'll presume that you are ready to buy unless you tell us something different.

Here's the follow-up call used by a maker of automotive test equipment.

| | |
|---|---|
| *Receptionist:* | *Lubin Company. May I help you?* |
| *Telemarketer:* | *Hello, I'm Tim Meineke of Farber Instrument Company. Ray Ghorley, please.* |
| *Receptionist:* | *Is he expecting your call?* |
| *Telemarketer:* | *Mr. Ghorley requested information about our test instruments, and I'm calling in response to that request.* |
| *Receptionist:* | *Please hold a moment.* |

Screens should *not* present a serious problem when a caller is following up a lead. Name and title of the contact are usually known, and an adept telemarketer should be able to make the call sound like a response that has been initiated by the inquirer, which indeed it *is.*

| | |
|---|---|
| *Contact:* | *This is Ray Ghorley.* |
| *Telemarketer:* | *Ray, I'm Tim Meineke of Farber Instruments. We received the card you sent requesting information on our 3200 analyzer. I felt it was important enough to warrant getting in touch with you personally.* |
| | *What kind of work do you see the 3200 doing for you?* |

| Contact: | We modify truck engines, so we're reviewing some ways to improve our methods. I thought you'd send out literature on your instruments. |
|---|---|
| Telemarketer: | We do. In fact, information will be in the mail this afternoon. But sometimes the customer's need is urgent, so we try to make things happen a little faster than usual. |
| | What is your timeframe for obtaining a new analyzer? |
| Contact: | There isn't any. We're just exploring right now. |

Regardless of timeframe, the telemarketer remains on the following track.

| Telemarketer: | Are you in charge of testing? |
|---|---|
| Contact: | In the area where we might use an analyzer like yours, I'm in charge. |

At this stage, the telemarketer probes for available budget and establishes both the purchase price and the alternative lease arrangements for the instrument.

Next, basic specifications of the machine are reviewed for the prospect. Again, this is not an intensive discussion about specs, but merely a confirmation of what the analyzer can and can't do for the prospect. Immediately following that review of capabilities, a highly assumptive close is attempted.

| Telemarketer: | I can't imagine a more ideal application for the 3200 than what you have in mind. I have a suggestion I think you'll like. |
|---|---|
| | We can send a new unit out to you for a field trial. If it doesn't give you everything you're looking for, there's no obligation of any kind. Just ship the unit back to us freight collect. That's the only way to really find out how the 3200 may fit your needs. |
| | Can you give me a P.O. number now, or should I call back? |

Since this caller had contacted the prospect while the acquisition of an analyzer was still a hot issue, a strong close was the only way to go. A timid approach might have lead to weeks of procrastination and an eventual loss of interest—or loss of the prospect to a more aggressive competitor.

Companies that manage to maximize telephone sales from inquiry calls make the following key assumption: Since the prospect has taken the first action, there is no better moment to close. Interest is at an absolute peak *immediately*.

A major trade association builds seminar attendance with the next presentation.

## SCRIPT 5.2: SELLING SEMINAR SEATS BY TELEPHONE

In past years, a national trade association had depended primarily on direct mail to fill seminars and workshops for member firms. Mailings, supported by publicity in a private newsletter, were the only methods used to sell seats. Typically, sessions were only 62 percent full and the break-even point was barely reached.

Since seminars are given on a regional basis, about 550 prospects could be identified in each region. This number could be telephoned by association staff members over a six-day period. Therefore, it was decided that telemarketing would be used to support the print promotions.

Please keep in mind the fact that all prospects in this example are acquainted with the "seller," just as the association knows who the prospect is. This familiarity eliminates the need to qualify and establish credibility.

> *Telemarketer:* [After introduction to the person who answers the call, ask] *Can you please connect me to (name of owner/operator of company)?*

If screen asks what the nature of the call is, say:

> *The association would like to invite Mrs. Jansen to a special conference.*

When owner/operator comes on line, start by introducing yourself, then ask:

> *Do you know about RBTA's financial workshop in Atlanta on May third and fourth?*

If yes, ask:

> *Do you plan to attend?*

If yes, find out whether registration has been mailed. Whether yes or no, go directly to *Quick Close* (next step). If no, say:

> *It's a complete how-to program specific to (our industry), given by Mr. Anthony Peters, who's a nationally recognized authority in this field.*
>
> *Most of the content deals with how other association members are doing their accounting and financial planning to make more money, cut expenses, and save on taxes.*
>
> Quick Close
>
> *Let's make absolutely certain there's a spot reserved for you. Can you take another moment to give me registration information, or should I get it from your membership records?*

If yes, ask:

> • *How many will attend?*
>
> • [Names and titles.]
>
> • [Other arrangements such as local accommodations needed.]

If no, say:

>*Let me take another few moments to highlight the leading benefits of this program.*
>
>Detailed Program Description
>
>*This is a hands-on, two-day session for management-level people. Each participant will actually build a complete and functional financial strategy that fits his or her own business in every way.*
>
>*All content emphasizes financial issues that are proven in this industry. For example:*
>
>*A review of systems that are especially effective in our industry. They've been field-tested and are definitely superior to the methods recommended by many accountants who don't know our business.*
>
>*Complete coverage of how to get tax advantages that are perfectly legal but are not used by a majority of firms in our industry. This advice alone can make the difference at year end.*
>
>*How to use commercially available computer software to cut way down on accounting time. And even if you are on computer now and use one of the popular software packages, you'll find out how to use the system more efficiently.*
>
>*Unlike the content of many seminars, the discussion here is not of theories. Instead, tactics being used today by other industry firms will be covered. You can start using most of these ideas—and making them pay—immediately.*
>
>*Do you feel knowledge like that would help you and make your business work better?*

Whether yes or no, ask:

>*Would any other people in your company benefit by attending?*

Uncover objections and overcome.

>*We'd really like to have you with us in Atlanta. Can I put your name down?*

If yes, make arrangements as necessary. If no, say:

>*Would you mind if I call you again in about a week to see if anything has changed?*

If no, politely terminate call.

This association discovered that a remarkable number of members were only vaguely aware of the scheduled seminar and its specific purpose. That minimal awareness was due to the extensive mailing effort and other print exposure. A majority had glanced at the materials, but very few gave it the attention required in forming a yes or no decision.

The telephone call served to effectively drive the benefits home. This resulted in clear decisions. From the time calling became part of the selling effort, seminar attendance rose to 95 percent of capacity.

A large segment of business operators maintain that sales of custom merchandise or services can't be negotiated by telephone. These people believe that outside salespeople *must* handle the task of matching the finished item to a buyer's needs. While this is true in some cases, countless firms are highly successful in closing custom orders by phone. How they do it is covered next.

## SCRIPT 5.3a: SELLING CUSTOM ORDERS BY TELEPHONE

In the strict sense of the word, custom orders are usually not totally consummated during the initial call. The sale can be *closed* at the time of the first conversation, but further discussions are generally needed to work out important details. Still, the results of this method of selling are especially dramatic when compared to those acquired through expensive field selling.

Some custom products and services just do not lend themselves to handling *exclusively* by telephone; for example, in cases requiring complex and/or extensive modifications; when no earlier versions can be used as a model; and when personal contact is absolutely needed. In those cases the phone can support the transaction but will not successfully carry the entire burden.

Exclusive use of the phone to close a custom order *will* work in many of the following situations:

- When samples or drawings of earlier versions can be sent to and reviewed by the prospect, then desired changes communicated to the supplier.
- When the purchase price does not represent a major amount. The risk has to be acceptable to the seller, who stands to forgo payment and redo the order if the buyer is not satisfied.
- When the seller can make a reasonable case for the advantages in ordering by telephone. If the vendor is merely offering to duplicate the buyer's present source in all particulars, it probably will not make sense for either party to proceed with a transaction.

An office-supply chain sells office partitions by telephone and has made this niche a hot area for volume and profits. Generally speaking, there is *no* personal contact between seller and buyer until the installers arrive with the partitions.

The firm's telephone approach looks like this:

*Step 1: Locate Contact.* Introduce yourself to the person who answers your call, then ask for your contact by name if possible. If a specific name is not available, find out who is in charge of facilities or office furniture and ask to be connected.

*Step 2: Key-Point Statement.* When the individual you are seeking comes to the phone, start by introducing yourself. Verify that this person has authority to buy office partitions, then say:

> *Telemarketer:*      *We're a major office-supply and furniture dealer in town. We specialize in designing and installing portable partitions that precisely meet a company's office space needs. I'm calling to acquaint you with our capabilities. Do you have a moment?*

If yes, proceed to Basic Qualifications (step 3). If no, ask:

> *Would it be better if I called about 1:00 P.M., or would noon Tuesday be more convenient?*

Then end call and file for appropriate follow-up.

*Step 3: Basic Qualifications.* Begin the qualifying phase of your presentation with this statement:

> *We have a number of customers in your industry, so we're at least partly familiar with your working area requirements . . . Do you have any space needs we can help you with now?*

If yes, go into further qualifying:

> *Are those needs similar to partitions you have used before in some other area?*

*Note:* If a similar configuration *has* been used by the prospect in the past, a simple sketch of that space, or the original partition order, can be used to formulate the new specs.

Answers to the next two qualifiers provide more information on what kind of extra refinements might be included in the design.

> - *Which departments will use the new office areas?*
> - *Specific purpose? (If not answered in the prior question.)*
> - *How many new offices do you need?*
> - *When will they be needed?*

Include any other information that will contribute to accuracy in the design and quotation. If no, probe future need and set up later follow-up.

*Step 4: Brief Description of Capabilities.*

> *We can handle the complete design and installation by telephone. Our customers like the service we provide because*

> *we're fast, accurate, and economical. You'll save a tremen-dous amount of time because you won't have to sit down and go through the details with a salesperson.*
>
> *For example, it sounds like the office partitions you just described can be done by us through a couple of quick tele-phone conversations. There is no need to take a lot of valu-able time. The results will be perfect—and you'll find the price right.*
>
> *Does that make sense to you?*

If yes, go to next step. If no, try to deal with objections.
  *Step 5: Close (Request Sketch).*

> *Can you do a quick sketch of the desired office, showing dimensions of the office space? I'll send you a special grid that makes it easy for you. We'll use your rough sketch as well as facts from our discussion today to prepare a de-tailed drawing for your approval.*

If yes, go to step 6. If no, say the following:

> *Let me suggest this: I'll research the requirements you out-lined and find plans we've done that come close to what you need. I'll mail several out to you this afternoon.*
>
> *Then we can talk again after you've received them. Would that work out for you?*

If yes, set up follow-up call. If no, file for future contact.
  *Step 6: Make Follow-up Arrangements.* For best results, arrange a definite date and time for the next call. That next contact will serve to finalize design of the office space. By providing a specific time for this next contact, your prospect is much more likely to either mail sketches or review the sketches you provided.
  If the prospect has agreed to send sketches, say:

> *I'll make sure the grids go out to you today. I look forward to receiving your sketches no later than Wednesday. We'll review them before Friday noon so I can get back to you at about 3:00 P.M. Friday. Do you expect to be in then?*

As you can see, the most critical step in obtaining a custom order by telephone is the prospect's response by providing sketches and other needed data to the vendor. Therefore, the grids must be sent to the buyer *immediately*, and they should be accom-panied by a letter that reminds the prospect about what's expected next and when future contacts will take place.
  Here's the cover letter used when a prospect is unable to provide sketches due to time problems or other reasons.

*LETTER 5.1:   COVER LETTER TO SUPPORT THE CUSTOM ORDER*

Dear Ms. Davies:

My appreciation for the time you were able to give me when I called on Thursday.

Based on your description of the office spaces you need, I have researched our files and came up with three variations that appear to fit your situation. I realize that modifications will be required, but these can be made quickly and to your complete satisfaction.

As I explained when we spoke, we'll be able to prepare a precise sketch of the area you desire if you indicate exactly where changes have to be made. I have enclosed a stamped and addressed envelope for your convenience in returning the corrections to me.

If I receive your corrections in the mail by Wednesday, I can have a quote ready for you by the following Friday morning. At that time we can go over the details just to make sure the partitions fulfill your office-space needs in every way.

We look forward to working with you on this important project.

Sincerely,

Manuel Reyes


In reality, getting a response from some prospects may require several calls. This is often due to the fact that the prospect is simply preoccupied. But persistence does pay.

When your contact has provided information on desired changes, it is time for the first follow-up call, which serves to clarify the details of this custom order.

## SCRIPT 5.3b: FIRST FOLLOW-UP CALL TO THE CUSTOM ORDER PROSPECT

Again, this call is made after the prospect's sketches have been received, or after you are certain that your sketches are in the prospect's hands.

*Step 1: Locate Contact.* Talk to the individual you spoke to initially. If not available, get the time he or she will be in and call again. It is usually not as effective to begin with a new decision maker at this point unless absolutely necessary.

As soon as former contact is on the line, proceed to step 2.

*Step 2: Establish Accuracy of Sketch.* If sketch was sent by prospect:

- Clarify any areas of uncertainty regarding layout, dimensions, and other specs.
- Confirm number of office spaces needed.
- Determine special furniture items and/or accessories needed.
- Confirm when delivery and installation are desired.
- Include any other data needed for quoting.

If vendor's sketches have been received by prospect:

- Decide which sketch is closest to desired office.
- Discuss necessary changes. (Ask prospect to mark up sketch with corrections.)
- Confirm number of offices needed.

- Determine special furniture items and/or accessories needed.
- Confirm when delivery, installation are desired.
- Include any other data needed to establish a quote.

*Step 3: Close.* Many custom orders are closed on this contact. A little gentle probing will reveal the prospect's readiness to okay the order. If both you and your contact are in complete agreement on what the office space should look like—and price has been established—the following approach can be effective:

> *Telemarketer:*     *If you are completely comfortable that these partitions are exactly what you want, we can start working on it today. Can we go ahead?*

If there is hesitation, go to step 4.
*Step 4: Set Up Call to Close Order.*

> *So we're both completely sure that the new partitions are perfect in every detail, we'll prepare a final sketch and get it in the mail to you. You'll receive it on or before Friday. I'll call you again on Monday and we can finalize the order.*

As mentioned, the above contact will succeed in getting a full commitment, but a number of very good prospects will insist on maximum caution and hold out for completely approved drawings before they agree to part with a P.O. number. The next call is used in such cases.

### SCRIPT 5.3c: FOLLOW-UP TO CLOSE THE CUSTOM ORDER

*Step 1: Locate Prior Contact.*
*Step 2: Review Any Additional Modifications.*
*Step 3: Close Order.*

- If you have not provided an exact quote during previous contacts, do so now.
- Give delivery information.
- Explain any other details that may have a bearing on price or delivery.

Then say:

> *I've alerted our design and production people, and they're ready to start on your order. If you give me an okay, we'll begin right away.*

In highly competitive markets, an extra push is often needed to move a buyer toward the close. The next pages cover how this is done in productive telemarketing programs.

# SPECIAL INDUCEMENTS TO ORDER IMMEDIATELY

A retail store can *merchandise* in order to attract buyers. This includes window and counter displays, in-store product demonstrations, strategically placed sale signs, and other tactics. To some extent, even an outside sales rep can do some merchandising to boost the appeal of products and services.

Because many companies don't take sufficient time to build effective telemarketing strategies, their callers function without the various benefits brought by merchandising. Firms that give some thought to their telephone sales programs *do* provide their callers an array of special inducements that often produce surprisingly good results.

Inducements are particularly valuable when the telemarketing program is designed to close on the initial call. Every advantage a company can give the caller is needed.

Firms that are especially sensitive to their image must proceed carefully when offering inducements to buy. The following ground rules are generally observed:

- An inducement has to be *real*. For example, if the caller offers a special discount, the *regular* price should actually be the amount usually charged. When the regular price is artificially inflated so that a special looks better, the more sophisticated buyers will catch on and see the offer as a scam.

- Overstocks or factory slowdowns can sometimes be verified by dubious buyers. Again, the situation should be factual.

- To stay strictly within legal limits, an inducement should be offered to *every* prospect. If presented only in difficult sales situations, its use is considered discriminatory, and the company may be opened up to possible legal action.

- Any special that runs constantly is not special at all. A store that screams "sale" for months or years on end illustrates that point. Alert customers quickly learn to ignore such phony announcements.

This section provides an opening to a special, as well as a series of closes that have extra selling punch.

## SCRIPT 5.4a: SETTING UP A SPECIAL OFFER

Any of these scripts can be used to introduce the special inducements in Scripts 5.4b through 5.4d.

| | |
|---|---|
| *Telemarketer:* | [Immediately following a product or service description, the caller says] *I'd like to describe a situation that may make a purchase extremely attractive to you* [or] *We're in the position to present a special offer to you if you make a decision today* [or] *Let me explain a set of circumstances that can save you substantial money if you order now.* |

Immediately following that statement, one of the inducements is delivered.

## SCRIPT 5.4b: LIMITED-TIME PRICE BREAK

Credibility is often shaky when a price break is offered by a seller. When it's a bolt out of the blue, offered for no apparent reason, almost every prospect will consider the deal a desperate attempt to get the sale and will question whether the offer is real or not. Therefore, a solid reason has to accompany the offer. A reason will help dispel the questions Why the reduction? and Won't it also be available in six weeks—or six months?

To do it right, a telemarketer describes both a reason for the price break and the effective period of that break.

This dialogue is linked to one of the introductory scripts in Script 5.4a.

> *Telemarketer:*      *We're in a position to present a special offer to you if you make a decision today.*
>
> *Twice a year—now and in August—we reduce prices on our complete line of drill presses to make room for new models on order.*
>
> *You can order now and save 18 percent, or wait about six months. The problem with waiting is this: Due to inflation, increasing material costs, and other factors, prices go up an average of 12 percent a year. So waiting probably means that a big chunk of your savings would be eaten up by a price increase.*
>
> *The special is good through Friday, but the machines are moving fast, and I can reserve the model you want right now if you give me an okay.*

In some selling environments, a rep will say something such as:

> *If I pledge to give you a substantial discount, can I count on you to give me the order?*

This represents the most obnoxious kind of high-pressure selling, and it is not recommended if the building of long-term business relationships is desired by the supplier.

In the preceding dialogue, it *is* plausible that prices might increase in six months. It *is* likely that the special prices are creating more demand which would reduce selection. The offer *is* believable.

A bloated and sluggish inventory is also an excellent pretext for offering specials.

## SCRIPT 5.4c: OVERSTOCKED CONDITION

*Overstocked* is a word that has been overused by aggressive merchants at every level of marketing. As a result, the shopping public is somewhat skeptical about this appeal unless the seller can relate a believable story to back up the claim and give it a semblance of legitimacy.

Attaching a limited-time proviso to the overstocked plea has a phony ring for this reason: If a retailer or manufacturer *is* heavy on certain items, the firm would want to keep the special open until the excess stock is reduced.

The following dialogue, from factory rep to retailer, tells the story in a way that reinforces plausibility. It follows one of the openings in Script 5.4a.

> *Telemarketer:*
>
> *I'd like to describe a situation that may make a purchase extremely attractive to you.*
>
> *As of this morning we had 340 units over our normal inventory of model H4 drill presses. Our costs for warehouse space are much too high, so we have to sell off the excess stock regardless of profit margins.*
>
> *We can give you 28 percent off five or more, or 18 percent off one to four units.*
>
> *You know that's a steep break, and so do our other dealers, since they've been ordering heavily. We'll keep the special open until we're down to normal stock levels, but that may only take another few days.*
>
> *How many can we ship to you on this special?*

While the retailer is not being seriously pressured to order right now, he or she should be astute enough to realize that fast action will save money and that other dealers *will* act on this good deal. However, the impact of the dialogue would of course be minimal if this factory was regularly overstocked.

That seasonal industries suffer slowdowns during certain periods is well documented. The next approach fits that situation.

## SCRIPT 5.4d: FACTORY SLOW PERIOD

Most firms in seasonal industries can plot with fair accuracy the months during which sales dip, and they can plan to have inventory at low levels in those comparatively lean times. But to keep the cash flowing, extra selling effort is made during the doldrums.

When prospects are *not* aware of a certain vendor's seasonal slowdown, the seller explains the predicament this way:

> *Telemarketer:*
>
> *Let me explain a set of circumstances that can save you substantial money if you order now.*
>
> *We have a seasonal business slowdown during January of every year. For exactly five weeks, we take orders at one third off all prices. It's absolutely the only time of the year we discount our drill presses.*
>
> *Since this special break attracts extra orders from our dealers, I'd suggest that you tell me how many units you want shipped.*

A telephone selling strategy that enjoys enormous success in many industries is covered next.

# NO-OBLIGATION FREE TRIALS

When a purchase is consummated by telephone or by mail, a seller is required by law to refund the purchase price if the buyer desires, within a reasonable length of time from the date of purchase. Since the decision to buy is made without the benefit of inspecting a product, the buyer must be entirely satisfied before the sale is legally considered final.

A number of companies doing heavy business by telephone and mail use that regulation to their advantage. Knowing full well that their customer can return a recently delivered product without the need to explain why, many marketers base their offer on the following proposition: "Try it out for 14 days. If you are not *totally* satisfied, just send it back—no obligation, no strings of any kind."

That, of course, is what the vendor would have to do in any case.

There are several key components that are needed to make this selling method a success:

- The prospect *must* be exceptionally well qualified. Any firm that ships products on trial to poorly qualified prospects will eventually fail due to the losses that are bound to result.

- A product delivered on trial must be of sufficient dollar value to warrant the effort that will go into arranging the trial. As you will soon see, this includes at least three telephone calls and a minimum of one mailing. Another expense is delivery to, and possibly from, the prospect.

- It helps tremendously when a trial product possesses advantages that can be clearly demonstrated in actual use.

- A trial product probably should not be open to customization.

- Customer installation is a must. If assembly and/or operation are exceedingly complex, a trial will flop. Remember, there is no field rep to help the prospect.

- Products on trial can't be subject to disposal when returned to the seller. This would apply to undergarments, food products, certain medical devices, and anything else used on a highly personal basis. The fact is, most returned items are refurbished by the supplier, repackaged, then used for new trials.

Kitchen devices, tools, electronic products, books, art objects, and many services fit well into a trial program. There are many other possibilities. The product in our telephone selling scripts is a home speaker system.

## SCRIPT 5.5a: DESCRIBING THE OFFER

Immediately after describing the speaker system, the telemarketer closes on a 30-day free-trial period. Trial periods can range from 10 days to 45 days or more. Prospect qualifications, including creditworthiness, have been deemed to be solid prior to making the trial offer.

*Telemarketer:*         *With a product like this, I think you'll agree that the only way to make a decision is to put the speakers through a test with the music you prefer. You really can't make a fair judgment by reviewing this system in strange surroundings, reproducing sounds you aren't familiar with.*

*We'd like very much to have you try these speakers in your home, with your other components, for 30 days. There is no charge and no obligation. We'll deliver a set at no cost. If you decide to keep them, just pay the invoice. If not, we'll pick them up at our cost.*

*I'm so sure you'll like them, there's no question in my mind that you will never want to part with this system.*

*Let me verify your address and other information.*

In carefully monitored tests, several leading marketing firms discovered that the conversion of free trials to sales improve dramatically when extra effort is made by the seller to obtain a pledge of responsibility from the prospect.

After verifying delivery information, the telemarketer makes that important extra effort.

### SCRIPT 5.5b: GETTING PROSPECT'S COMMITMENT TO SUPPORT THE TRIAL

*Telemarketer:*         *Let me take just a few more seconds to explain how this trial works.*

*Your opinion on system performance is extremely valuable to us since you are obviously a discerning listener. In view of that fact, I'd appreciate your assurance that you will personally conduct a fair test of the system and frankly let me know what you think.* [Get verbal assent.]

*I'll be in touch with you in about three weeks to get your comments.*

This dialogue subtly informs the prospect that the trial is his or her responsibility. It also suggests that the seller's property should be protected to the extent practical.

Some marketers go a step further and find out whether the prospect's home contains any unusual hazards (housepets, small children, or other factors) that could damage merchandise or present risk to the potential buyer.

Right after shipment of the trial products, which should occur within a day or two of the phone call, the following letter is sent. It recaps the initial transaction.

### LETTER 5.2: REINFORCING THE TERMS OF THE FREE TRIAL

Dear Mr. Albelli:

It was a pleasure talking to you yesterday. We are most excited about getting your reaction to the X15 speakers. Two units were shipped to you this morning via Midwest Trucking Company.

Installation instructions should be clear, and proper set-up takes only a few minutes. If you encounter any problems at all, please contact Jack Lawrence in our service department.

As we discussed, you have agreed to review the speaker system with your present stereo components. This review will proceed over a period of thirty days from the date of delivery. There is no obligation whatsoever on your part to make any purchases.

To get your initial comments, I will call you at about 7:00 P.M. on April 18. I expect to find you as enthusiastic as we are!

If any questions come up before that time, please call me at 772-2400 during normal office hours.

Sincerely,

Pat Josephson

### SCRIPT 5.5c: POSTINSTALLATION FOLLOW-UP CALL

Without a doubt, the most crucial phase of a free trial is the first follow-up call. This vital contact is made after the prospect has received delivery of the trial product. The call works best when timed to reach the prospect one week to ten days after product delivery. This provides enough time for the individual to use the product, yet, not so much that the prospect's initial excitement can fade appreciably.

A version of the first follow-up call is next.

> *Telemarketer:* [After reestablishing rapport with contact, say] *By now I guess you've had an opportunity to play some of your favorite selections on the new system. Which ones sound best?*

This opening dialogue *assumes* that the system has been tested. It does not encourage the prospect to procrastinate by saying, "You'll have to call me back. I haven't had a chance to hook 'em up yet." Also, the opening goes directly to one of the prospect's favored topics: his or her preferred music.

After listening to prospect comments, objections are handled as necessary. Telemarketer then asks:

> *Do you have any questions about the system?*

If yes, provide thorough answers, then attempt to close the sale. If no, attempt to close the sale.

> *It sounds like you're really excited about the way you can hear your music now. I knew you'd love those speakers.*
>
> *Do you feel you'll want to pay cash, or can we set up financing for you?*

In a certain number of trials, the telemarketer will follow up by telephone only to find that the product is still in a shipping carton. In those instances, patience must be the chief virtue of the caller. After some reselling, a time is set for a new follow-up call. In other instances, the prospect will need more time to evaluate. Here again, another follow-up is arranged after some reselling.

Next, we'll look at *assurance*, an extremely valuable way to close by telephone.

## ASSURANCES THAT HELP GET THE CLOSE

When prospects can be convinced that there are few risks in buying, a telemarketer's close ratio will improve drastically. Buyer surveys, conducted at both the business and consumer levels, prove that *believable guarantees* do more to get the sale than any other aspect of the presentation. Evidence shows that prospects need the assurances that:

- The product or service they are committing to can be cancelled if not satisfactory. Furthermore, cancelling has to be hassle-free and accepted graciously by the seller.

- Actual quality and performance come up to the levels represented by the vendor. Some purchasers, unfortunately, are reconciled to settling for less than they expected.

- Vendor service and support will be on a par with that given by leading suppliers. A good many buyers fully expect a smaller company to provide inferior service and post-sale support.

- They will not be forgotten as soon as they pay the invoice. In general, most prospects express this concern.

While some firms don't utter a word about assurances, others go to an opposite extreme, but often fail to state anything specific about guarantees and support. This particular telemarketer tells a prospect "We're the greatest company and our product is superior to anything on the market" or "We'll always be there to help when you need it."

These meaningless generalities are probably detrimental to the outcome of a sale. Any sophisticated buyer will instantly recognize them as devoid of substance. Specifics *must be present* to make assurances plausible. The dialogue you review now accomplishes that.

### SCRIPT 5.6a: GUARANTEED SATISFACTION

To some extent, a free-product trial period replaces the need to assure a prospect. Therefore, the following scripts are used in a standard telephone close where *no* free trial is involved.

Following the description of a product or service, assurance is provided. This script gives a prospect the right to return a product or cancel the order (as they have to under the law in any event).

> *Telemarketer:*
>
> *We realize that you'll be making a commitment without the benefit of trying or seeing the product.*
>
> *I want you to know that we unconditionally guarantee your complete satisfaction. That means you can return the air purifier to us within 30 days if it doesn't do everything we claim it will do. Our policy is no obligation, no questions asked if you change your mind within the first month.*
>
> *There is absolutely no risk to you in any way.*

A mention of the guarantee terms will effectively underscore the satisfaction guarantee dialogue just covered.

## SCRIPT 5.6b: EXPLAINING SPECIFIC TERMS OF A WARRANTY OR GUARANTEE

In order to demonstrate the context of the complete assurance statement, we'll begin this dialogue with the final sentence of Script 5.6a.

> *Telemarketer:*
>
> *There is absolutely no risk to you in any way. In fact, we essentially remove the risk from ownership on a long-term basis as well. If there are any failures of mechanical parts during the first year of use, we'll cover the cost of all parts and labor, no matter what caused the problem.*
>
> *From the second through the fifth year there is no charge for parts. The owner pays only labor costs.*
>
> *That's probably the most comprehensive warranty in the industry. It reflects our confidence in the quality of this product.*
>
> *You'll get that in writing when the unit is delivered to you. You'll see that there are no restrictions or special requirements. It's a straightforward, armor-plated assurance of trouble-free use for at least five years.*

That kind of assurance sells with enormous power. Even when you are selling a product backed by a comparatively weak warranty, telemarketing language can still be developed that provides a high degree of prospect confidence.

Finally, service/support dialogue can be nicely linked to the statement about guarantee terms.

## SCRIPT 5.6c: ONGOING SERVICE AND SUPPORT

A prospect's fear of being forgotten after the sale is made has to be laid to rest by any telemarketer who is responsible for closing. In the imagination of the prospect, the caller could just as well be operating out of a car trunk and using public telephones.

There is simply no way for the buyer to be sure about the later availability of the seller until reassured to the contrary.

Dialogue that establishes ongoing support is now shown. To maintain logical flow, it is preceded by the final paragraph of the warranty statement in Script 5.6b.

> *Telemarketer:*
>
> *You'll get that in writing when the unit is delivered to you. You'll see that there are no restrictions or special requirements. It's a straightforward, armor-plated assurance of trouble-free use for at least five years.*
>
> *To make certain that you realize the full potential of your air purifier, we have an 800 advisory line to our plant. During working hours, you can get answers to operating questions and expert help in solving any problems that come up. There is no charge for this service, and you're entitled to use it as often as you need it—as long as you own the unit.*
>
> *Also, after one year you get an on-site inspection and cleaning of the unit by one of our factory service reps. There's only about ten minutes of down time—and you pay nothing for this check.*

In sales environments for which guarantees, service, and support are magnified in importance, for example, when selling costly high-tech equipment, a follow-up letter can effectively recap the key points of the telephone dialogue.

## LETTER 5.3: BLANKET ASSURANCE STATEMENT

This letter is targeted to prospects who were not closed on the initial telephone call, but who are strong possibilities for eventual purchases.

Dear Mr. Snyder:

Your interest in our line of lathes is appreciated. We look forward to having you as a customer in the near future.

Since the founding of our company in 1961, our point of greatest pride has been the outstanding quality of our 4400 and its performance track record in some of the most demanding production environments.

By virtue of that tradition of value and dependability, we are able to offer you the strongest warranty in our industry (specifics are described here).

As a leader in your industry, we are certain you will see our warranty and our service/support policies as the only program worthy of your own high standards.

Please don't hesitate to contact me if I can answer any questions.

Sincerely,

Fran Warneke
V.P. Manufacturing

## REFINING YOUR TELEPHONE CLOSE APPROACH

Use the following form to help build the strongest possible telephone close. It provides the most important points that can go into high-impact telephone closes.

### FORM 5.1: CLOSING CHECKLIST

Check the components you feel would be most valuable to your telephone close.

1. Are prospect qualifications thorough enough to permit a close with no further scrutiny of the buyer?

   ____ Yes   ____ No

2. Are qualification questions designed to identify prospect uses for your product or service?

   ____ Yes   ____ No

3. Have you focused on *one* product or service on which to close? (This is *essential* to avoid confusing the prospect.)

   ____ Yes   ____ No

4. Is your *description* of the product or service clear enough to assure prospect's understanding?

   ____ Yes   ____ No

5. Make sure the following points are settled:

   • Will you require a purchase-order number to complete an order?

   ____ Yes   ____ No

   • If a credit card number will be needed to make a purchase, are you set up to handle that kind of transaction?

   ____ Yes   ____ No

   • Will a written order be required from the buyer before you deliver?

   ____ Yes   ____ No

   • Are prices and payment terms described adequately in the close or description?

   ____ Yes   ____ No

6. For custom orders, is a system worked out for communicating changes between buyer and seller?

   ____ Yes   ____ No

7. Does the dialogue in the telephone close firmly request a decision from the prospect?

   ____ Yes   ____ No

8. Have you identified appropriate inducements to order now?

___ Yes     ___ No

9. Are those inducements credible?

___ Yes     ___ No

10. If a free trial is to be offered, is the follow-up system strong enough to convert trials to sales in an organized way?

___ Yes     ___ No

11. If a free trial, is installation easy enough to assure customer use?

___ Yes     ___ No

12. Does your closing dialogue go far enough to let the buyer know that he or she must take responsibility for the trial?

___ Yes     ___ No

13. Is the product or service of high enough value to warrant a free trial?

___ Yes     ___ No

14. Can customer-caused wear and tear during trials create unacceptable losses to you?

___ Yes     ___ No

15. Does your close include enough information about guarantees, warranties, and vendor support?

___ Yes     ___ No

16. If a telephone close fails, is your follow-up system designed to get the sale later?

___ Yes     ___ No

17. When a telephone close is successful, does your follow-up system assure that contact will be maintained with the customer?

___ Yes     ___ No

Notes: _____

_____

_____

_____

_____

# Chapter 6

# SCRIPTS THAT INCREASE THE IMPACT OF FIELD SALES REPS

As telemarketing became a force to be reckoned with in the marketing of products and services, many of the more aggressive sales managers started to see the telephone as a formidable tool for their outside salespeople. A called dedicated to the task of finding prospects may have been the primary direction of most programs, but telemarketing also included the following facets for sharp managers:

- Better utilization of "in-between" time—those inevitable time gaps between field appointments could be effectively used to contact prospects and customers.

- Routine follow-up calls to prospects in the decision process. These are contacts that often should not be handled by anyone but the person who conducted the presentation.

- In some special cases, the field rep is in a position to confirm appointments or change scheduled times due to unforeseen events that regularly come up.

In short, the best outside sellers today are adept telemarketers. Although they usually prefer to operate on a face-to-face basis, they are not in the least apprehensive about using the telephone when it is expedient and profitable to do so.

This chapter provides an array of scripts that cover virtually every situation that might be encountered by a field sales representative.

## TURNING FIELD "IN-BETWEEN" TIME INTO PROFITS

Cellular phones have, to a significant extent, revolutionized field selling approaches. A rep no longer has to search for miserably uncomfortable public telephones when trying to make the most of the time before the next appointment. Even sitting in traffic can be fruitful. Now, scores of valuable contacts can be made daily from the comfort and relative quiet of an automobile.

To calibrate the precise impact of spending in-between time on the phone, a test was recently conducted in three companies selling an industrial service. In each firm, half of the field reps used cellular phones during each time gap between appointments. After six weeks, the cellular-equipped reps averaged 4.8 *more* appointments per week and increased their closes by some 18 percent.

Public phones *do* serve the purpose if cellular phones are out of the question. The point is, slack time between sales visits is far too precious to waste. Here are the most common in-between calls.

### SCRIPT 6.1a: USING URGENCY TO CONTACT HARD-TO-REACH PROSPECTS

Some of the very best leads to take along on a trip to the field are those that appear to be strong but have proven to be exceedingly difficult to reach. If a telemarketer has tried to make contact and failed, the inquiry generally goes to the bottom of the stack and a new attempt may not be made for another three weeks or more—far too long if the prospect looks like a buyer. These elusive targets are favored by field sellers who like to do some calling themselves.

When a field rep is harried and calls a hard-to-reach contact, a natural sense of urgency is conveyed to a receptionist or screen. That urgency in itself often helps to get the buyer on the phone. When this rushed mood is reinforced by the correct words, the dialogue might sound like this:

*Field Rep:*                [Usual but rather hurried introduction to receptionist or screen. Then] *I hope you can help me. I have to hang up in about two minutes, and it's really important that I get in touch with Mr. Campbell.*

An optional addition to that dialogue is

*There's no way I can call again today, so I'm counting on you.*

A key here is the apparent race against the clock. Some screens will feel that they can't qualify according to their normal standards when the caller only has seconds to spend on the phone. Others, of course, will disregard the near panic.

When that high-urgency approach fails to get through to the contact, a field rep can go to the following alternative.

### SCRIPT 6.1b: SETTING UP A DROP-OFF

An office-equipment manufacturer sells many hundreds of big ticket machines every year through literature drop-offs. Whenever possible, these drop-offs are *prearranged* by field reps who set them up by calling nearby firms during in-between time.

| | |
|---|---|
| *Field Rep:* | [Standard but hurried introduction to receptionist or screen. Rep attempts to get through to contact but is rejected. Rep follows with] *I have to get some important information to Mr. Campbell today. I'm within a few minutes of your office right now.* |
| | *I'll swing by in a moment with a big white envelope. If at all possible, I'd like to hand it to Mr. Campbell personally. I'm on the way . . . thank you.* |

In some cases, the contact *is* available to accept the literature package. If not, the receptionist or screen often makes sure the contact gets it because of the urgency conveyed by the rep.

Whether or not drop-offs are delivered directly to the contact, follow-up is the essence in making a program like this successful.

Another firm in the same industry takes an extremely aggressive approach by setting up demos during in-between time.

## SCRIPT 6.1c: USING SPARE MOMENTS
## TO ARRANGE PRODUCT DEMOS

Similar to setting up drop-offs is the arranging of product demos, again utilizing for telephone work the short stretches of time between some field appointments.

Office equipment lends itself to demos particularly well, and one company in the southwest does big business through this method: Every morning, reps load a small number of machines into their cars. The assortment includes large calculators, desktop copiers, and one or two memory typewriters. The target of the rep is to demonstrate a machine, then leave it in an office—in the custody of a responsible individual—for one week of use.

In a majority of instances, if there is even a glimmer of need, the company will decide to keep the machine at the conclusion of the week.

Demos are set up by outside sales reps when field time permits. Here's the telephone approach they like to use:

| | |
|---|---|
| *Field Rep:* | [Usually tries to contact the office manager. After standard introduction, rep says] *We're reviewing the performance of three new office products, and we'd love to have you put one of them through a week of actual use in one of your busier departments.* |
| | *I can give you a choice of a multifunction recording calculator, a memory typewriter, or a desktop copier. Which one can you get the most use of for a week?* |

If objections arise, they will generally come up here. At this point, the rep may have to reassure the prospect that there is no obligation to buy, no charge for the week of use, and no responsibility to the prospect if damage is done to the machine. If one of the units is selected, the rep says:

> *I can drop in briefly at about 3:00 P.M. It'll take about ten
> minutes to set the copier up and show you how to operate it.
> Is that time okay?*

If so, the rep sets up the future sale:

> *As I told you, there is no obligation of any kind. We need
> your frank opinion about how the unit performs. If you find
> it a major help in your office operation, of course we can sell
> it to you. But right now, I'm especially concerned about
> getting your opinion.*

About 80 percent of the products on demo are reused. In other words, they have been out on other demos and returned to the manufacturer. That fact is not hidden from prospects, so discounts are given freely when items are not perfect. Because there is some loss to the manufacturer due to prospect neglect and normal wear and tear, that extra cost component must be taken into consideration when operating a program like this one.

If after one week of use the prospect requests pick-up of the machine, reps offer a different kind of device for a similar one-week demo. About one third of these attempts are successful.

In this type of sale, extensive qualifying as to specific application is *not* done. The prospect's choice of a certain machine is, in itself, the very best qualifier.

A call frequently made by field sellers is the one intended to make sure of, or strengthen, *existing* outside appointments. We'll look at those calls now.

## CONFIRMING AND STRENGTHENING
## FIELD APPOINTMENTS

Investing in a two-minute telephone call can be a good move if it assures a solid field appointment later in the day. This is particularly true when a block of expensive selling time is on the line.

Some outside salespeople insist on personally confirming every appointment set earlier by a telemarketer. Invariably it turns out that a certain percentage of those scheduled appointments are flawed in some way, *regardless* of the experience and skill of the caller. Problems can include:

- Appointment time was misunderstood or forgotten by the prospect.
- Qualifications were not reviewed with care by the telemarketer, so an appointment is set with a prospect who can't make a purchase.
- For some reason, the prospect is no longer interested in the seller's offer.

When around two hours have been set aside for an appointment and travel time and the appointment then fails to materialize, it's a serious blow to a rep who is hustling to produce business. Still, there are many field sellers who maintain that the strategy of calling to confirm an appointment carries a certain element of risk. They cite these situations:

- As the time of the appointment draws near, prospect apprehension may be at a peak. Then, when the rep calls to confirm, cancelling becomes a much more convenient option for the uncertain prospect. However, when the rep does *not* call to confirm, and shows up as expected, the buyer's fear can be overcome and the sale made.

- A routine confirming call sometimes invites a change in the appointment day, time, or both. This can play havoc with a packed appointment schedule.

These arguments are countered by proconfirmation salespeople who say this in rebuttal: It's far better to *know* of those prospect changes in advance instead of walking into them. When changes are known, new appointments can be scheduled in the suddenly vacant time slots.

For those who *do* confirm, the following scripts may offer some ideas.

### SCRIPT 6.2a: REVIEWING QUALIFICATIONS

Almost *every* mature telemarketing program has gone through a phase in which new callers are entrusted to pass judgment on the merits of prospects. Experienced field salespeople then discover that too many of those appointments should not have been set. After suffering a number of unqualified prospects, the reps decide to personally verify prospect qualifications before committing time to the appointment.

This dialogue is used by a building contractor. The call is made between two and six hours before the scheduled appointment.

*Field Rep:*   [Gets the correct individual on the phone and proceeds in this direction] *Mr. Myer? I'm Steve of De Rosa Builders. My associate, Peggy Jones, spoke to you last Tuesday and arranged for us to meet this evening at 6:30 P.M. Do I have that time right?*

When time is verified, seller moves into a review of qualifications.

*If you have just a few moments now, it would be a big help if I could check some facts so I'll be better prepared when we get together.*

When prospect consents to additional time on the phone, seller asks:

*My understanding is that you are interested in adding a garage. Do I have that right?*

After confirming the specific nature of the project, the caller reviews two or three of the requirements that were stated by the prospect at the time of the first contact. Finally, the caller asks:

> *You told Peggy that you were looking at an early September completion date. Is that still your objective?*

This contact normally occupies no more than two or three minutes, unless other conversation is generated. It serves to verify the meeting time and verifies some of the key facts of the project.

A highly successful stockbroker uses the following tactic to make sure of appointments he feels are shaky.

### SCRIPT 6.2b: CHANGING TIMES TO ASSURE THE APPOINTMENT

Every time an appointment seems weak to one east coast securities salesman, he calls the prospect and changes the meeting time. He claims this tactic provides the following advantages:

- It offers one more opportunity to check the validity of the appointment.
- It allows one more conversation with the prospect—however brief—which builds a little more needed rapport.
- By changing the meeting time, even by a mere 30 minutes, the message is conveyed that the broker is busy and therefore in demand by other investors.

Typically, the broker's call sounds like this:

> *Broker:*     [Gets targeted prospect on the line. After reintroduction, he says] *Bob, I hope we can work out a different time for our meeting. A client has to see me before he returns to London. Can we reset our time to either 2:00 P.M. or 4:00 P.M.?*

When a new time is agreed to, caller concludes with:

> *I know how busy you are, and I deeply appreciate your understanding.*

This broker also uses the following tactic to strengthen scheduled appointments.

### SCRIPT 6.2c: MAKING REQUESTS THAT COMMIT THE PROSPECT

Last-minute requests for information can be extremely effective in building prospect commitment. The broker handles it this way:

> *Broker:* [Gets targeted contact on the phone. After reintroduction, he says] *Bob, I've been thinking about the telephone conversation we had the other day. First of all, I want to tell you how challenging your situation is and how much I'm looking forward to meeting with you at 3:00 P.M. so we can look for some constructive solutions.*

If that appointment time is no longer good, the prospect will say so now. When time is confirmed, caller continues:

> *I'm calling to ask if you can bring along some information that might help us get a better picture of your current market position and your objectives.*

The broker now identifies the documents he would like the prospect to bring to the meeting. If those papers are not readily available, the appointment is reset so the papers can be produced.

Quite often, the added prospect involvement achieved by the broker is far more important than the information he requested.

An alternative to asking for documents is to call and simply ask for certain figures. This call resembles the one in Script 6.2a, but its purpose is to go over pertinent numbers, not prospect qualifications.

## SCRIPT 6.2d: GETTING ADDITIONAL SPECS

This is a believable pretext for calling to confirm and strengthen a scheduled appointment. The broker asks for certain figures that he claims will help in the coming meeting.

> *Broker:* [Gets targeted contact on the line. After reintroduction, he says] *Bob, before our 1:00 P.M. meeting, I want to spend some time analyzing your present investment portfolio. I'm sure that would save us some valuable time when we sit down to talk about finances.*

Here again, if rescheduling or cancellation is to occur, it will come up now.

> *When we spoke originally, we covered your holdings in a general way. If you don't mind, I'd like to get a few quick specifics now.*

Now the broker asks two or three fast questions. He is careful to request figures that would not be considered confidential, since a high degree of trust has not yet been formed.

While there is often debate among reps about the wisdom of confirming future appointments, there is virtually unanimous agreement about the advantages of calling a prospect after the meeting. We'll discuss that now.

# POSTAPPOINTMENT CALLS FOR REPS

Some of the highest-earning outside salespeople in America believe that a personal call, placed within one day of the appointment, is an essential part of a successful transaction. This postappointment call is outside of any preset follow-up routine that goes into action.

A personal contact of this kind is almost always made by the field sales rep. It is rarely delegated back to the telemarketer who may have initially uncovered the opportunity.

The importance of a postappointment contact is magnified in this era of relationship building. The fact is, a majority of outside sellers just do not bother to spend a moment to call a recent appointment. Therefore, the reps who *do* call stand a much better chance of getting the order.

In this section we'll cover *postappointment* calls. The section after this one deals with *postsale* calls.

## SCRIPT 6.3a: CLARIFYING INFORMATION

By far the most intelligent and functional postappointment call is the one aimed at eliminating prospect confusion that may exist about the product or service offered. The information conveyed by a salesperson during a face-to-face meeting may be the only knowledge a buyer has. Quite often, that simply isn't enough education for even a bright buyer. There is usually a lot of lingering fog after the rep departs.

When the postappointment call is made, the field rep goes over the key points and generally makes sure that prospect comprehension is sufficient for decision making.

An exercise machine distributor, selling to sports stores and health clubs, urges its reps to make the following personal call to *all* prospects within 24 hours after the field appointment.

| | |
|---|---|
| *Field Rep:* | [After getting the targeted buyer on the line and reintroduction.] *After our meeting, I sat down and made some notes about the things we discussed. It occurred to me that I may not have been clear on certain important details.*<br><br>*If you have just a few minutes, I can cover those critical areas for you again.* |

After the time is cleared, rep continues:

> *Before I begin, may I ask if you have any specific questions?*

On occasion, prospect questions will open some of the topics that the rep wants to clarify.

Before this call is made, the rep must spend some time recalling the field meeting and how the dialogue shaped up. This review, if done soon after the presentation, should reveal several areas that could stand further illumination. With this particular product, common areas of clarification deal with engineering details, user safety, and overall effectiveness.

Here's another strong reason for a postappointment call.

### SCRIPT 6.3b: LATE NEWS ABOUT THE PRODUCT OR SERVICE

A call to the prospect soon after the field appointment can include news about delivery time, recent price changes, quality enhancements, or any number of other developments that were not mentioned or were glossed over during the presentation.

More than one rep in the exercise equipment company purposely withholds a key bit of information so that it can be delivered in the postappointment call. They claim that the morsel of data can be described more dramatically during the postappointment call. The contact sounds something like this:

> *Field Rep:* [After getting the targeted buyer on the phone and reintroduction.] *When we met yesterday, I'm afraid I skipped some information that's extremely important. It's about recent construction changes on our number 102C machine. Can you take a moment so I can bring you up to date?*

When time is cleared, rep continues:

> *Can you get the spec sheets I left with you?*

This rep stresses the importance of having the buyer retrieve the printed piece. It serves to get the seller's products out of a file and out in the open again.

When the spec sheet is available, the rep says:

> *We've added two tubular steel reinforcements that run all the way from front to rear on the bottom of the chassis. They add tremendous rigidity. In addition, soft rubber handgrips have been added on the bottom handlebars. Do you see the points I'm referring to?*
>
> *That model is now a much more expensive unit, but we're holding the line on prices for the immediate future. It's an outstanding value, and I can't believe I almost forgot to tell you about those upgrades.*

There is no question that this particular machine will occupy a prominent position in the minds of most prospects who receive such a call.

One more excellent subject for the postappointment call follows.

### SCRIPT 6.3c: FURTHER COMMENTS ABOUT PROSPECT OBSERVATIONS

This is a very popular postappointment call among seasoned sales representatives. The rep calls the buyer to request further comment on something the buyer said during the meeting. It is especially effective for this reason: Without a doubt, the most important thing to the prospect is his or her own opinion. Therefore, when the rep calls later and wants to further discuss the buyer's remark, it commands attention.

To make this tactic work, a rep has to listen to and remember certain words spoken by the buyer during the presentation. When a statement by the buyer can be recalled by the rep in its original word-for-word form, better yet.

> *Field Rep:*                [After getting the targeted buyer on the line and reintroduction.] *Something you said during our meeting really hit me after I left. Can you take just a moment and tell me more about it?*

After time is cleared, rep says:

> *As I recall, you said you weren't sure that buying the best quality products was the answer in your firm due to the rapid obsolescence that occurs in your industry. That's really interesting. Can you explain a little more about how you see that working?*

A vast majority of prospects will jump at the opportunity to expound on one of their own theories. It rarely fails to increase the rep's stature in the eyes of a buyer.

When proposals are submitted to prospects after a sales visit, reps have a perfect reason to place a postappointment call.

### SCRIPT 6.3d: VERIFYING RECEIPT OF A PROPOSAL

Sales reps who conduct a strong presentation, mail a proposal to the prospect, then neglect to call immediately after the proposal is received, are missing golden opportunities to land more and bigger accounts.

If there is *ever* a reason to make a postappointment call, following up on a proposal is it! Here are the reasons why:

- Several days have passed since the meeting, and the prospect's recollections, and perhaps impressions, have dimmed.
- Even when the best proposals may have sections that need further definition. An example of that follows shortly.
- A review by telephone prepares the buyer to do a better internal selling job on the proposed product or service.
- Most important, on some occasions, review of a proposal by phone leads to preparation of a *revised* proposal. The prospect simply asks the bidder to make a few critical changes before presenting the proposal to a decision-making committee or individual.

On occasion, this particular postappointment call, the proposal-verification call, is set up at the end of the field visit. A time is established between buyer and seller to review the proposal item by item.

This is the proposal-verification call used by a leading training consultant. In this instance, the call is not prearranged.

*Note:* An excerpt from the consultant's proposal follows. Please notice that while the language is fairly concise, the core message definitely can use clarification. The call dialogue in Script 6.3e attempts to do that.

SCRIPT 6.3e

---

*EXCERPT OF PROPOSAL*

*SECTION II, PART 3, PARAGRAPH 2*

*Therefore, the program is designed around a preestablished progress cycle of approximately six months. For example, each contact between a Regional Manager and a broker should cover specific ground and advance the relationship to a prescribed point. By the end of each period in the progress cycle, there should be reasonable movement of the broker toward complete acceptance of fresh product—or definite reasons why not. The causes that impede progress with a broker should be diagnosable, with distinct remedies available to Regional Managers.*

---

| | |
|---|---|
| *Field Rep:* | [After contacting targeted buyer and reintroduction.] *Paul, did you receive our proposal for the training program we discussed last week?* |
| *Contact:* | *It arrived Monday.* |
| *Field Rep:* | *Have you had an opportunity to go through it?* |
| *Contact:* | *Just a glance really. I'll review it, along with some others, on Friday.* |
| *Field Rep:* | *Okay. There's one section I'd like to take you through verbally so you're sure of how it works. In looking at it again, one paragraph seemed a little vague, and I thought it needed further definition.* |
| | *Can you spend another minute or two now?* |

When time is cleared, rep asks the buyer to get the proposal.

*Do you have the proposal in front of you?*

As soon as the buyer has located the proposal, the specific part is referenced by the rep.

*Please go to section two, part three, the second paragraph. That's on page four . . . got it?*

*Paul, please give that paragraph a quick read. That's the one starting with "therefore" and ending with "managers."*

After buyer completes reading rep says:

> *In plain English, we're saying that we measure the progress of a broker every six months. At those six-month points, we have the ability to find out why objectives were made or not made, and we'll know the reasons one way or the other.*
>
> *Also, regional managers will have a clear program to work with so that every contact they have with a broker will get that broker one step closer to the next six-month goal.*
>
> *Does that make sense to you?*

In most cases, such a verbal simplification *does* make sense. One might legitimately argue that proposals should be written clearly in the first place. But that still wouldn't eliminate the advantages of the above postappointment call.

In the next section, we'll look at calls used after a field *close*.

## POSTSALE CALLS FOR REPS

Any person who has even the most remote connection to selling *or* buying should understand this: In probably 70 percent of all sales, communication between the seller and buyer stops at the close. Delivery is made, the invoice is paid, and perhaps an occasional mailer is sent to the customer. Far more often than not, there is no *personal* dialogue of any consequence—until the seller wants another order or a service problem prompts the customer to initiate contact.

When asked about this phenomenon, a surprisingly large number of field salespeople make the excuse that the relevant topics were all exhausted during the appointment, and, furthermore, a postsale call might open the door to cancellation due to "buyer's remorse," which, some say, exists to some degree in all new purchases.

While some reps apparently believe that neglect is a viable strategy, others start building an armor-plated relationship with their customers as soon as they can. The reason they give is that with today's intense competition in most industries, there is really no way to protect a hard-won account from rivals except by lavishing it with service and attention. Low prices can always be shaved to steal a customer. Selection may be a little wider from another source. Terms might be slightly more liberal elsewhere, and so forth. But *staying in close touch* is the one thing sharpshooters have trouble dealing with. A customer who is getting attention from a supplier will definitely *not* be vulnerable to deal makers who, generally speaking, don't understand service.

A move as ridiculously simple as a two-minute call to a recent buyer will build rapport faster than almost anything else a vendor can do for a few cents of expense.

For sellers who insist that all topics are spent during the appointment, here are a number of postsale calls used by successful outside sales reps in various industries.

### SCRIPT 6.4a: GENERAL CALL TO A RECENT BUYER

This call is widely used by reps who *do* advocate post-sale contacts. It is simply an expression of appreciation, and there is really no other message except "thanks for your business." It *is* popular among the pros for this reason:

Because there *is* no ulterior motive, the customer is almost always amazed. For many buyers, this is *the first time* any seller ever bothered calling just to express appreciation for the order.

Typically, the call sounds like this:

> *Field Rep:*  [After recontacting the decision maker.] *Frank, I won't keep you because I know how busy you are.*
>
> *I just wanted to let you know how much we appreciate your business and what a pleasure it was to help you solve those problems.*
>
> *We're going to work very hard to make this installation operate exactly the way you want it to. Based on the way our meeting went, I'm confident we'll make it happen by working together.*
>
> *I'll be in touch again as soon as we're ready to deliver. In the meantime, please call me if any questions come up.*

It is true that similar sentiments may have come out at the time of the appointment, but there is certainly nothing but good to be gained by repeating those sentiments a day or two later.

Our next postsale call supports the buyer's choice.

## SCRIPT 6.4b:  AFFIRMING WISDOM OF DECISION

This postsale call is sometimes used in cases where the rep senses some doubt in the buyer about the sale. When the transaction is at all shaky, there can never be too much reassurance.

A number of top outside reps agree that the best reassurance is to review the reasons why the purchase was made. These items were probably emphasized during the appointment, but going over the points again can strengthen the deal considerably.

Please note that this approach can begin with dialogue very similar to the paragraphs in Script 6.4a.

> *Field Rep:*  [After recontacting the decision maker.] *Frank, I won't keep you because I know how busy you are.*
>
> *I just wanted to let you know that we really appreciate your business, and we're looking forward to helping you in the future.*
>
> *When I got back to the plant after our visit, I sat down with our head programmer and we went over each sample report you gave me.*
>
> *After checking every one of your requirements against our standard formats, we verified that the match-up is incredible. Just about as perfect as you could want.*

> *Your selection of this system looks like a very good move. I*
> *think you'll see that for yourself as soon as we get it up and*
> *running on your machine.*

This particular postsale call works well *only* if the rep can cite specific reasons why the prospect's choice appears to be astute. In the case just illustrated, the buyer's reports would be compatible with the purchased software.

Here's an effective postsale script that's closely related to the one we just looked at.

## SCRIPT 6.4c: REPORTING NEW DISCOVERIES

An information "bonus" can help solidify a sale that isn't considered strong. This morsel of data can be a new application, the throwing in of an accessory that enhances the value of a product or service, or any other news that would be positive to the buyer.

Some reps draw on existing product information. They keep one wild card in reserve to be used at the optimum moment. Others don't hold anything back at the time of the appointment but prefer to go back over the facts, then develop new ideas that will be valuable to the buyer.

This example demonstrates a newly uncovered benefit. As before, the script is opened with dialogue similar to that in Script 6.4a.

*Field Rep:*         [After recontacting the decision maker.] *Frank, if you*
*have just a second, I wanted to tell you how much we appre-*
*ciate your decision to go with P. Newton Company. Also, I*
*have some news that I think you'll find exciting.*

*After our meeting, I went over the schematics you gave me*
*with our chief engineer. He discovered that you'll be able to*
*use your new system not only for all the machines in your*
*main plant, but also for your Stanford facility. You won't*
*have to purchase an extra package for remote installations.*

It is important to note the kind of impact such a call can have on a buyer of marginal strength. The news itself is not necessarily where the real value is. The *real* power comes into play when the decision maker sees that the seller is giving extra effort to the transaction. Any normal buyer will reason this way: "I'm impressed because I have *already* made a commitment to buy from these people. Yet this rep is doing more than necessary for me, and *that's* the kind of supplier I want to deal with."

When new discoveries are not available, a number of field reps base a postsale call on reviewing some key bit of operating information. Here it is:

## SCRIPT 6.4d: CLARIFYING INFORMATION

A rep for a moving and storage company is regarded by his residential and business customers as exceptionally meticulous and deeply involved in a customer's welfare. He has achieved this reputation by never failing to place a postsale call. The purpose of his call is to once again cover certain key aspects of a move sold just a day earlier.

*Field Rep:* [After recontacting the decision maker.] *If you can give me just a couple of minutes, I'd like to go over some of the most important aspects of your move.*

*First of all, we're delighted to be working with you. I want you to know that we won't spare any effort to make this move go smoothly for you.*

*There are three points we should go over again because they're extremely important in making everything run right. We did talk about them the other day, but I want to be sure that every detail is completely clear to you.*

The rep simply summarizes the selected areas. This call rarely takes more than four minutes. While there is no dramatic exchange of information, the reps who use this approach generate *double* the number of referrals obtained by reps who do not. Here's how they handle referrals:

## SCRIPT 6.4e: ASKING FOR REFERRALS

When good service and abundant attention are given a customer, the stage is set for getting referrals. A buyer who is well taken care of is usually happy to assist an effective rep. More important, a pampered customer wants his or her relatives, friends, and associates to enter relationships that are proven to be beneficial.

Immediately after the moving company rep delivers Script 6.4c or 6.4d, this dialogue is used:

*Field Rep:* *Most of our customers come to us on word of mouth. Other satisfied people or companies tell them about the quality work we do.*

*So if you know anybody who is planning a move—even a year from now—I can get information to them. Can you recommend anyone?*

If a referral does not result immediately, it often does later.

One of the most obvious postsale calls, and one that should be made by *every* outside sales rep without exception, is the next one.

## SCRIPT 6.4f: CHECKING ON OPERATION OR SERVICE

This postsale call is designed to check up on the customer's success with a newly purchased product or service.

Amazingly, a huge number of vendors don't bother to ask their customers how the purchase is working out. Perhaps they operate on the theory that no news is good news. Other firms give the follow-up chore to a telemarketer or customer-service representative. Only a handful of outside sales reps undertake that crucial task.

There is no better example of this particular postsale call than the version used by a highly successful automobile body shop in a southeastern U.S. city. This call is made within 48 hours of job completion.

*Manager:*                    [After introduction to customer.] *If you have a moment,
                              I'd like to get your opinion of how we did on your car. Was
                              our work satisfactory?*

If any complaints come forth, the customer is invited in so the manager can see the
problem and rectify it. Additional questions asked are

- Was everybody in the shop courteous and cooperative?

- Was the work completed by the promised date?

- Is there anything the shop can do to help with the insurance claim?

Finally, the manager goes for the referral:

                              *If you know anyone who needs quality bodywork, we'd ap-
                              preciate a recommendation. Please tell them to ask for Jim,
                              and be sure they mention your name. I'll personally make
                              sure everything possible is done for them.*

This task involves an average of five calls per day. Total time is less than 30 minutes. By virtue of this small investment, the shop outproduces all competitors in the city.

## REFINING FIELD SALES TELEPHONE SCRIPTS

Use the following checklists to make sure you consider all available strategies when
planning postappointment and postsale calls. Checklists are followed by worksheets
for creating telephone dialogue.

### FORM 6.1:   CHECKLIST FOR THE POSTAPPOINTMENT CALL

1. Would a postappointment call coordinate with your established follow-up
   system?

   ____ Yes    ____ No

2. To avoid duplication of effort, should other people in your company be informed
   about postappointment calls?

   ____ Yes    ____ No

3. If there *is* a danger of duplication, what modifications should be made to the
   follow-up program?

   _____

   _____

   _____

_____

_____

_____

_____

4. Aside from building a relationship with the prospect, are there any other objectives you want to attain through a postappointment call?

_____

_____

_____

_____

_____

_____

_____

5. How long after the appointment should this call be made?

_____ hour to _____ hours later

6. If proposal is to be provided to the prospect, will a postappointment call be made prior to submitting that proposal?

_____ Yes _____ No

7. In the kind of selling you do, what are the strongest reasons for the postappointment call (expressing appreciation, clarifying information, etc.)?

- _____
- _____
- _____
- _____

Notes: _____

_____

_____

_____

_____

_____

_____

_____

_____

## FORM 6.2: POSTAPPOINTMENT CALL DIALOGUE WORKSHEET

Reintroduction
to buyer: _____

_____

_____

_____

_____

Clear time: _____

_____

_____

Express appreciation
for appointment: _____

_____

_____

_____

_____

Reason for call: _____

_____

_____

_____

_____

_____

_____

## FORM 6.3: CHECKLIST FOR THE POSTSALE CALL

1. Is your product or service delivered a few days from the time of the appointment?

   ____ Yes    ____ No

2. If delivered quickly, should your postsale call be deferred until customer has used the product or service for a certain length of time?

   ____ Yes    ____ No

3. Describe timing strategy: _____

_____

_____

_____

_____

4. Will your postsale call conflict in any way with follow-up contacts from others in your company?

_____ Yes     _____ No

5. If so, describe how call can be coordinated with other efforts to avoid duplication: _____

_____

_____

_____

_____

6. If sale seems weak, how can the postsale call bolster the buyer's commitment?

_____

_____

_____

_____

_____

7. In the kind of selling you do, what are the strongest topics you can use for your postsale calls?

● _____

● _____

● _____

● _____

Notes: _____

_____

_____

_____

_____

_____

_____

---

## FORM 6.4: POSTSALE CALL DIALOGUE WORKSHEET

Reintroduction
to buyer: _____

_____

_____

_____

_____

Clear time: _____

_____

_____

Express appreciation
for sale: _____

_____

_____

_____

_____

Reason for call: _____

_____

_____

_____

_____

_____

_____

_____

_____

_____

# Chapter 7

# SCRIPTS FOR BUILDING RETAIL SALES AND PROFITS

In any retail operation that carries medium to big ticket items or services, it is a tragic waste when salespeople passively wait around in the showroom for customers. For example, in almost every auto dealership, furniture store, or appliance store, employees can be seen watching the door waiting for buyers to wander in. There are scores of other types of stores that suffer the same malaise. It affects hundreds of businesses.

Taking an auto dealership as a prime example, such a business is typically sitting on the following gold mine of sales potential:

- Previous buyers of new and used cars and trucks
- Service customers
- "Walk-ins" who stop by to pick up brochures or enter the showroom to see a certain vehicle
- "Call-ins" to get prices and other information

This rich arsenal of top-quality leads is essentially identical in nature to the resources possessed by other kinds of stores, so the problem is not limited to the car business by any means.

With all of these excellent prospects on hand, only a few retail dealers make an effort to turn names into quick, low-cost sales. As a case in point, have *you* ever had a call from a store where you recently made a major purchase?

Stores that *do* make an ongoing effort to convert their enormous stores of leads into new business are among the most successful. Their salespeople don't sit around *waiting* for customers, they *create* new sales by using the approaches in this chapter.

# CALLS TO CURRENT ACCOUNTS

Without question, the best prospect a store could possibly hope for is a current customer. Anyone who has recently purchased from a particular retailer probably possesses these vital characteristics: The person knows the outlet and is apparently satisfied with the selection, brands, prices, and service it offers.

Another important factor in selling to current customers is the fact that the store should incur comparatively little expense in selling the person additional goods or services. The big expense in the form of advertising and other promotions traditionally involved in getting the consumer's initial order does *not* have to be spent again if the telephone is used to get him or her into the store repeatedly.

As you will see in this section, there are many ways to approach a recent buyer. It is not simply a matter of asking "What do you need today?" or "How can I help you?" Here are some of the much more effective approaches being used in leading retail operations today.

## SCRIPT 7.1a: INVITATION TO A SPECIAL STORE EVENT

Extensive tests conducted by a major furniture rental chain showed that telephone calls to customers get *three times* better sales results than direct mail does. Not surprisingly, the more personal feeling of a phone call gets much better response than a mailer, even when that mailer is personalized to some extent.

As consumers, we *do* routinely receive various kinds of mailed announcements, and we routinely disregard the vast majority of those pieces. But a call is a different story entirely.

A dramatic example of this difference is a special store event such as the showing of new lines. You might ignore a mailed invitation to attend a showing, but the following phone call hits much harder. It is used by the furniture rental firm.

*Telemarketer:* [Makes contact with the individual who is the customer of record and gives full name, name of company and location of showroom.] *Because you're a preferred customer of ours, we'd like to have you join us at a special showing on April 10 between 7:00 P.M. and 10:00 P.M.*

*You'll have an advance look at some of the most exciting new sofa and chair combinations and bedroom suites to be introduced in years. All new styles are set up in completely coordinated room groups, including accessories and wall treatments. Our staff of interior designers did all the planning, so you'll get lots of decorating ideas.*

*We'll have refreshments and entertainment. This is really a special gala for our best customers. We'd love to have you bring guests along, too. Can we expect you?*

While there is no mention of renting new pieces that may be of interest to guests, that is of course the underlying purpose of a showing like this. The firm found that attendance *and* new rentals increased when the event is described strictly as an introduction to new styles. Salespeople are present in force at the showing and are trained to cultivate new rental business as customers browse.

A closely related call follows.

### SCRIPT 7.1b: ANNOUNCING A NEW LINE

An east coast furniture retailer calls *every* old customer who has been inactive for one year. Rather than using a special showing, the store describes a new line as a pretext for renewing the relationship.

Store management recognized the fact that there had been little loyalty among furniture buyers. Most customers did not hesitate to switch dealers if convenient to do so. Management felt that a call to inactive accounts would help reverse that negative trend.

To make this particular call hit a bit harder, a customer's past purchases are briefly reviewed. The telephone approach is based on apparent gaps in the previous selection. For example, if old invoices don't show the purchase of dining-room or dinette items, the telemarketer might reasonably assume that the individual still needs those pieces. If, in the course of talking to the customer it turns out that this is an incorrect assumption, other areas of possible need are explored.

This firm's call usually takes shape this way:

| | |
|---|---|
| ***Telemarketer:*** | [Makes contact with the individual who is the customer of record and gives full name, name of company, and location of showroom.] *We recently purchased a line of dining-room furniture that I think you'll find attractive, beautifully constructed, and priced right; and we'll give you a trade on your old pieces—no matter what they look like or how old they may be.* |
| | *Is that an area you might be interested in?* |

If yes, the telemarketer continues to interest customer in a dining-room purchase, then sets in-store appointment. If no, explore other possibilities. For example:

| | |
|---|---|
| ***Telemarketer:*** | *In reviewing your past purchases, I noticed that you didn't include lighting fixtures such as table or floor lamps or hanging lamps. We can show you a number of styles that would go perfectly with the items you selected last year.* |
| | *What kind of new lamps do you feel you need now?* |

If all product appeals fail, the telemarketer attempts to sell payment terms:

> *Whatever you feel you need, we can offer you very generous payment terms—and quick credit approval—because you're an established customer. Would that be helpful to you now?*

Regardless of customer response, calls of this nature are made *at least* on a yearly basis, or more frequently if at all possible. The store claims a 50 percent improvement in customer loyalty, and repeat business is up dramatically. The cost of calling is easily absorbed in the added profits generated by this program.

One other excellent pretext is used by a retail carpeting dealer in a north central U.S. city.

## SCRIPT 7.1c: ANNOUNCING A NEW DEPARTMENT

Companies that aggressively use the telephone to increase sales find that almost *any* plausible pretext can be used to start a constructive dialogue with valuable old customers and new prospects as well. Rejection is higher than normal only when the call sounds to the customer like an obvious "pitch" to come in and buy something. Good telemarketing has to be subtle and must lead with a feature that benefits the consumer.

The carpet retailer uses the following dialogue to regain past customers:

| | |
|---|---|
| *Telemarketer:* | [Makes contact with the individual who is the customer of record and gives full name, name of company, and location of showroom.] *Since you bought carpeting here last February, we've set up a professional decorating staff that consults with our customers at no charge.* |
| | *Even though our customers have always been happy with their selections, we felt that experts specially trained in color and texture would help us get better results.* |
| | *Are you thinking about floor coverings for any rooms in your house you didn't do before?* |

If yes, a home appointment is set up with the decorator. If no, commercial applications are explored and referrals are sought.

Outside of home-furnishing stores, there are many possibilities for introducing new departments or added retail capabilities to customers. For example:

- A department store can describe the addition of a makeup expert in their cosmetics department.
- A shoe store can offer special advice on the correct sports shoes for certain activities.
- A real estate firm can provide special guidance on income property and other types of land speculation.

Almost *every* retailer has abundant opportunity to use the telephone for getting new orders from old customers.

One of the most common publicity events for a retailer is the opening of a new location.

## SCRIPT 7.1d: ANNOUNCING A NEW
## LOCATION AND GRAND OPENING

The president of a small but expanding chain of appliance stores realizes that distant customers are especially vulnerable to more convenient competitors. This company opens a new outlet every six months on average. A few weeks prior to an opening, all old customers in the vicinity of the new store are contacted by phone and invited to attend the grand opening of that location.

Here's the dialogue favored by the caller:

> *Telemarketer:*    [Makes contact with the individual who is the customer of record and gives full name, name of company, and location of the new showroom.] *We've got great news for you. On June 10, we're opening a brand new store at the Madison Shopping Center. It's being stocked with a tremendous selection of appliances and accessories, TV sets, and stereo equipment.*
>
> *Our grand opening celebration runs from June 10 to June 20, and you'll receive special discounts on anything you buy. But it'll be fun even if you* don't *make a purchase.*
>
> *I'll see to it that your account is moved there because it will be much more convenient for you. Is that okay with you?*
>
> *Can you break away to visit us during the grand opening? The new store manager, Thom Morgan, would love to meet you.*

As mentioned earlier, the important principle is *the call itself*. Such a calling program should not necessarily be measured by immediate sales numbers. The increased long-term customer loyalty is the key to contacting past buyers.

For old customers who prove difficult to reach, the following letter is used by the appliance retailer.

### *LETTER 7.1: ANNOUNCEMENT TO PREFERRED CUSTOMERS*

This letter is sent to customers who are hard to reach by telephone. It can also be modified to work as a follow-up letter to people who *were* successfully reached by phone.

Dear Mr. Jensen:

We have *great news* for our preferred customers in Montclair and Fairway.

Kraft's is opening a new appliance showroom in the Madison Shopping Center on June 10. Our grand-opening celebration starts on June 10 and continues until June 20. Please stop by to say hello, and *don't forget to bring a friend!*

This spacious new store will give our valued customers on the north side new convenience, enormous selection, and free parking. And for ten days, you'll receive big special discounts on *anything* you purchase.

Your account has been moved to the new store, so purchasing can be quicker and easier than ever. Just introduce yourself to Thom Morgan, our new manager. He'll be delighted to meet you whether you make a purchase or not.

We look forward to seeing you at the grand opening!

Sincerely,

Jack Irving

An old, established department store in the rural midwest has a telemarketer contact almost *every* customer, regardless of when a purchase was made. There is really no other motive for this call other than to make sure the customer is satisfied.

## SCRIPT 7.2a: GOODWILL BUILDING

Top managers of this thriving store base their business philosophy on this belief: "By doing everything we can to keep our customers satisfied, we will assure sales growth and customer loyalty. The only way we can make sure of that customer satisfaction is to talk to our shoppers as often as possible and *ask* them if everything is okay."

As if to reinforce a desire to take selling out of their telemarketing program, this store will only hire callers with no prior selling experience. If a customer happens to ask the caller about items in the store, that customer is promised a call-back from a clerk. But business is *not* to be conducted during this contact.

> *Telemarketer:* [Makes contact with individual who is the customer of record and gives full name and name of company.] *I'm calling on behalf of the store to make sure you are entirely satisfied with your new shoes. Is everything okay?*

That initial question will generally evoke a brief response such as "Fine" or "We're very satisfied." The caller presses on:

> *Are you waited on promptly and politely when you shop here?*

Again, usually an affirmative answer.

> *Do you usually find what you're looking for?*

In some instances, customers *will* suggest product ideas. Comments are taken seriously by the telemarketer, and noted and passed on to the appropriate department buyers. If a new product is added as a result of a customer suggestion, that consumer receives a thank-you letter from the store president.

The final question is

> *Has the quality of our products been satisfactory?*

Here, complaints *do* come up from time to time. No matter how long ago the purchase was made, a return for credit or an exchange is offered. Some merchants would cringe at the concept of opening a door to complaints that seem closed and forgotten. But the managers of this store see these old problems as dormant irritations that might some day fester and cause bad feelings.

When customers are difficult to reach, a letter is sent that covers the same ground as the call we just went over.

### LETTER 7.2: SATISFACTION ASSURANCE

True, a letter does not provide the strong personal touch of a telephone call, but it is a reasonable substitute when certain customers are tough to catch at home. The department store uses this letter as a backup to the call in Script 7.2a:

Dear Mrs. O'Hare:

Just a note to make sure that you are completely satisfied with your dealings at Singer's. We are especially anxious to know about these important areas of our performance:

*Service.* Are we responsive and courteous when you need something in the store?

*Selection.* Do you feel you have a wide range of choices when you look for a needed item?

*Quality.* Are all purchases of good value? Do they hold up well?

Since you are important to us, we want to be certain that your shopping experience at Singer's is as good as it can possibly be.

If I can be of any help, please call me directly at 471-2600.

Sincerely,

Kent Ellison

In keeping with their exceptional concern for the preservation of good will, this store also takes extra steps when delivery is for some reason delayed.

### SCRIPT 7.2b: REPORTING ON DELIVERY DELAYS

About one-fourth of the orders sold by the rural department store are delivered to purchasers by two store-operated trucks. Punctuality is a form of religion for the reason that most consumers are employed. Due to that fact, many people are taking time off work to wait at home for delivery. A seriously late truck can easily create an extremely angry customer.

On the evening before the scheduled delivery day, the customer receives a call from the shipping department. The call conveys a delivery time, supposedly accurate to within one hour. During the course of the day, if the drivers see that the stop will not be made at the estimated time, this call is placed to the waiting customer:

| | |
|---|---|
| *Driver:* | [Makes contact with individual who is the customer of record, or the person designated to receive delivery. Introduces self by name and company name.] *We're running about 40 minutes behind our scheduled delivery time. We realize that this may be a serious inconvenience to you, and we apologize for that.* |

> *Should we plan on delivering your order later today, or would you prefer to reschedule for another day?*

In some instances, the offer to reschedule is welcomed by the customer since other time commitments may exist. A store that seems indifferent to scheduled times can incur the wrath of consumers. The preceding call is one more ingredient in an outstanding system of customer satisfaction for this remarkable retailer.

On occasion, even satisfied customers do not pay their bills on a timely basis. As sensitive to their clientele as this store is, they still have to deal with collections now and then.

## SCRIPT 7.3: COLLECTION CALL

Collection problems rank high on the list of causes that contribute to breaks between sellers and buyers. Even in the most common case, that of a consumer temporarily unable to meet an obligation, there may still be embarrassment that can get in the way of a normalized relationship after the problem has been rectified. With the embarrassment factor in mind, a store's objective in a collection problem should be to proceed cautiously in order to *avoid* putting the customer in a humiliating position.

This call, used by the department store as an initial reminder call, is set up to review recent purchases.

*Accounting Clerk:*   [Makes contact with the individual who is the customer of record and gives full name and title, and name of company.] *If you have just a couple of minutes, I'd like to go over your past several purchases to make sure our records are correct. First of all, have you been satisfied with all of the things you bought?*

When satisfaction is determined, caller proceeds to assure that no unrecorded returns and credits exist:

> *During the past several months, have you returned any items?*
>
> *Have we failed to deliver any items you purchased?*

Caller now reviews the last several charges made by the customer. Most important, the current account balance is verified. Caller says:

> *So we have a present account balance of $102.32. Does that agree with your records?*

Customers will almost always agree. The caller signs off here. There is no attempt to bring up the past due status. In most instances, the customer will take the first step and acknowledge the lateness, then promise a payment. A majority of late accounts are brought up to date as a result of this contact.

More and more retailers are going beyond calling their customers. They are reaching out to turn cold prospects into valued customers. In the next section, we'll look at some of the strategies they use.

## COLD CALLS TO RETAIL PROSPECTS

In the first section of this chapter, we covered scripts used to turn retail customers and leads into new buyers. That category includes any individual who *already* knows of a certain store because he or she bought something there, or at least contacted the outlet for some reason.

At this point, we'll look at cold prospecting for retail prospects. These are consumers who may know nothing at all about a particular store but fit one or more of the following categories:

- They may live near a given retail outlet, so it would be convenient for them to shop at that store.
- They may be established buyers of a certain kind of product or service. A rented or purchased prospect list would provide, for example, names of recent truck renters.
- They might fit into a certain economic class that would qualify them to make various kinds of purchases. A case in point is a high-income family that would be much more inclined to build a new swimming pool than would a young couple living in an apartment complex.

All of the above characteristics are no more than basic qualifications. When a retailer can identify a group of consumers that appears to fit a description of what its "typical" customer looks like, that store is in a position to do some effective cold prospecting by telephone.

Spending time and cash on telemarketing to consumers taken at random from a telephone directory is the most difficult kind of prospecting since *nothing* is known about these consumers. The rejection rate in such a program is usually enormous.

The following scripts, used successfully by a sports store, are specifically targeted to cold prospects.

### SCRIPT 7.4a: INVITATION TO OPEN AN ACCOUNT

An enterprising sports-store owner obtains the names of young professional people who reside within a ten-mile radius of his store. He knows that a large number of these upwardly mobile people are active in various sports and can be expected to have enough income for leisure-time spending.

When a member of this group can be induced to open an account, purchases will probably follow. Therefore, the telemarketer's objective is to "sell" an open account at the store.

*Step 1: Basic Qualification.*

| | |
|---|---|
| *Telemarketer:* | [Contacts person on list. Introduces self by giving full name, name of store, and location. Then asks] *Do you take part in any sports?* |

If yes, find out which ones. Then go to step 2. If no, prompt prospect by naming the following activities (which prospect may not initially associate with sports).

- Workouts, such as aerobics
- Jogging or walking
- Swimming
- Camping

If one activity is identified by the prospect, go to step 2. If there is apparently *no* interest in any sports, including those on the above list, ask whether anyone else in the household is involved in sports. If not, caller goes to Script 7.4b.

*Step 2: Brief Capabilities Statement.*

> *At your convenience, we'd love to have you check out our selection of tennis equipment.*

Caller now provides a partial list of items the store carries in the prospect's preferred activity, then continues with:

*Step 3: Close.*

> *We'd like to invite you to open a charge account in our store. You seem to be just the kind of active person who would really enjoy shopping here.*
>
> *Whether you buy anything or not doesn't matter. When you are ready, you'll have the convenience of charging your selections.*
>
> *You'll also be kept up to date on sales and special events like sports clinics, trips, and so forth. We always have something exciting going on.*
>
> *Can we arrange to meet in the store tomorrow at 5:00 P.M., or would 7:00 be better for you?*

An average of 42 new accounts are opened every month through a part-time telemarketing program. About half of these develop into productive accounts.

When the telemarketer is unable to get an expression of interest in a certain spot during step 1 of the above cold call, the following dialogue is used by the sports-store caller.

## SCRIPT 7.4b: INVITATION TO VISIT STORE

As soon as the telemarketer finds out that the prospect is not particularly committed to any one sports activity that would draw him or her into the store, a *general* invitation to visit the store is extended. To illustrate this, we'll start in step 1 of Script 7.4a:

| *Telemarketer:* | *Do you take part in any sports?* |
|---|---|
| *Prospect:* | *No, I'm just too busy right now.* |
| *Telemarketer:* | *Do you work out, jog, swim, or go camping?* |
| *Prospect:* | *No.* |
| *Telemarketer:* | *When it's convenient for you, I think you'd enjoy seeing our sportswear department. Even if you can't be involved in sports right now, some of the clothing is fabulous for casual wear.* |
| | *You'll like our shoe department, too. We have a large assortment of shoes just for good looks and comfort.* |
| | *Would you like to stop in and take a look?* |
| *Prospect:* | *When I get a chance, I'll do that.* |

Telemarketer signs off. When the store has a special sale scheduled, this dialogue is added to the end of Script 7.4b:

### SCRIPT 7.4c: INFORM ABOUT SCHEDULED SALE EVENT

To add considerable punch to any invitation to visit, a special sale is described. We'll take it from the end of Script 7.4b.

| *Telemarketer:* | *And you'll like our shoe department, too. We have a huge assortment of shoes just for good looks and comfort.* |
|---|---|
| | *Best of all, almost everything in the store is on sale until March 12. To give you an example of the values we're offering right now, we have a Petersen warmup outfit reduced from $90 to $62, and $75 leather walking shoes at $39.* |
| | *Now is absolutely the best time to get acquainted.* |

When certain prospects are difficult to reach by phone, a letter gets results for the sports store.

### LETTER 7.3: NEW-CUSTOMER RECRUITMENT

This letter is used for hard-to-reach prospects and on occasion is modified to *precede* the telephone contact. This particular version sells the concept of opening an account:

Dear Mr. Kravitz:

Active sports lovers like you need the quality and values offered by Harmon's.

Whether your interest is speeding down the slopes or walking when you get an extra moment, you'll find the equipment and clothes you need *right here*. The only thing left to offer you is a new level of *convenience*. Here's our answer to that:

STOP IN AND OPEN A CHARGE ACCOUNT AT HARMON'S IN A MATTER OF *MINUTES.* Just show us a current major credit card and you'll have INSTANT charge privileges.

Take advantage of America's best sports brands and most striking sportswear styles *now.* You deserve it!

Visit Harmon's or call 832–9400 and ask for Mark.

Very truly yours,

Mark Henderson


When this letter is mailed to prospects *before* the call, the last paragraph is changed to:


Visit Harmon's or call 832–9400 for fast action. Or wait and we'll be in touch with you by telephone to answer your questions.


One of the most sadly neglected areas of telemarketing is the handling of call-ins. We'll look at this important category of calls now.


## INBOUND CALLS FROM CUSTOMERS AND PROSPECTS


Stores attract calls from consumers for a multitude of reasons. Here are a few of the leading reasons for calls from potential shoppers, whether they have done business at a particular store in the past or not:


- To get information on store hours.
- To get a price.
- To check on the availability of a desired product.


Every time the phone rings in a retail operation, it's an opportunity for that store to get one step closer to a sale.

While many retailers are doing a better job today on incoming calls than they did just a few years ago, there is still plenty of room for improvement. *Any* retailer can quickly enhance its handling of inbound calls by taking this simple measure: Make sure that every employee who takes calls understands how important *all* incoming calls are. Employees have to realize that the person who takes a call from outside bears the burden of establishing the store's image. Effective handling of a call can start a profitable relationship, and poor handling can wreck it on the spot.

There is no faster way to give retail employees the right tools than to supply them sample scripts like the ones in this section. The innovative approaches that follow are used by busy retailers to solve problems, build customer trust, and increase store sales.

## SCRIPT 7.5a: BUILDING EXTRA GOODWILL
## IN EVERY INFORMATION REQUEST

In testing various routines for taking incoming information requests, a fabric store discovered this fascinating tactic: In the opinion of store managers, when a prospect or customer calls to ask a question, it isn't quite enough to simply answer it, then promptly sign off. The store's image for service can be enormously magnified if the store employee who takes the call goes a bit further. The following script illustrates this concept.

| | |
|---|---|
| *Store employee:* | [Introduces self by store name (or department name if call has been transferred) and personal name.] *May I help you?* |
| *Caller:* | [States question. For example] *How late are you open tonight?* |
| *Store employee:* | *We're open until 9:00 P.M. this evening.* [Employee then goes directly into the extra step.] *Can I give you directions on finding the store or on how to locate the department you want?* |
| *Caller:* | *No thanks, I think we'll be okay.* |
| *Store employee:* | *Good, we look forward to seeing you later.* |

Therefore, the simple procedure of answering the caller's question, then *expressing the desire to assist by providing directions*, conveys a strong concern for service. An employee's questions can pertain to where to park around the store, which route to take to see the downtown Christmas lights, or *any* added help that clearly demonstrates the store's genuine interest in the caller.

This alternative approach is designed to promote specials:

## SCRIPT 7.5b: INTRODUCING SPECIALS TO CALL-INS

Newspaper and broadcast advertising are vital to the economic health of most retailers. The leading objective of media spending is to get the word out to consumers. The message that usually gets the most action from shoppers is information about sale items.

Since legitimate special sales generally stir up extra buying, it certainly makes sense to tell people who call in about lowered prices. That's exactly what a busy yarn shop does every time the phone rings.

| | |
|---|---|
| *Store employee:* | [Introduces by store name (or department name if call has been transferred) and personal name.] *May I help you?* |
| *Caller:* | [States question.] |
| *Store employee:* | [Responds to question appropriately, then says] *While you're in the store later, you might want to take a look at our imported knitting yarns. That entire selection has been* |

*reduced 25 percent for two days. So your timing is perfect if you have any knitting projects planned.*

Internal tracking shows that an average of 23 customers a day are informed about specials when they call to ask various questions. About half of them will actually purchase the special announced by phone. This is very likely business that would not have developed unless an employee took that moment to describe the sale.

Call-in orders from active customers are an important profit area for a west coast music store.

## SCRIPT 7.5c: GETTING TELEPHONE ADD-ON ORDERS FROM CUSTOMERS

On a monthly basis, this music store sends a bulletin to all active customers. The bulletin announces sale items and new products. About four percent of mailer recipients call the downtown store to order anything from guitar strings to trombones.

Through a little gentle urging, the telemarketer who takes the incoming orders is able to increase the average sale by almost 20 percent. In dollars, that translates to *over $5,000 per month* in extra business. Here's the store's method: In every product category, one low-cost, *high-impulse* product is identified and slightly reduced in price. For example, if the phone order is for a cymbal, the telemarketer is prepared to offer a deal on drumsticks. The offer is presented this way:

> *Telemarketer:* [Takes customer's order for one of the items in the monthly mailed bulletin. Then says] *Let me mention something that might be interesting to you. We put our best quality drumstick sets on sale after the bulletin was mailed to you, and you may find the value too good to pass up.*
>
> *Our regular $9 sticks are reduced to only $7.50 until our stock is sold out.*
>
> *I can include a set with your order and just add it to your account. Okay?*

This easy sale takes a few seconds, but adds tremendous profits to the store's bottom line.

Some very astute retailers turn customer grievances into sales.

## SCRIPT 7.6: TURNING COMPLAINTS INTO NEW BUSINESS

A women's clothing store in a New England city gets big-plus business as a direct result of complaints. Whether an unhappy customer visits or calls the store to complain, employees are trained to turn the situation around to the store's advantage. This program is based on the following theory, which is proving to be correct: Almost any consumer who experiences a problem that is *promptly rectified* by the store is *especially* open to buy additional merchandise.

A typical case would be one encountered in a call to complain about the quality of a recently purchased garment:

*Customer:*        [Complains about the workmanship of a clothing item.]

*Employee:*        *That's terrible! I hope this hasn't seriously inconvenienced you. Please bring it in at your earliest opportunity and ask for me. I'll do whatever it takes to get the situation squared away for you.*

This response differs considerably from the way all too many retailers react to complaints. Unfortunately, many store personnel—including owners and managers—become defensive, or at least grudgingly offer to work toward satisfaction for the suffering customer.

When the customer of the preceding dialogue later enters the store and the employee's attitude is *still* one of unreserved eagerness to make things right, the customer will make a *new purchase* at this retail store about 20 percent of the time.

In order to carry customer satisfaction to the ultimate level, this clothing store follows up every old complaint with this brief note:

### LETTER 7.4:   GENERAL FOLLOW-UP TO CALL-IN COMPLAINT

Dear Ms. Young:

We are pleased that the recent problem we caused you has been taken care of to your complete satisfaction. If there are still unresolved difficulties that we are not aware of, please call me as soon as possible at 532–9191.

Quality and value in every clothing and jewelry purchase you make here is of the utmost importance to each employee at Wall's.

We hope that we have earned your trust and that you will remain a valued customer for many years.

Very truly yours,

Nancy Sikeston

Next, a section devoted to carefully developed telephone approaches for selling educational programs to consumers.

## SELLING EDUCATIONAL PROGRAMS BY TELEPHONE

Schools that sell training programs to consumers are pioneers in telemarketing; for many years prior to the wide use of telephone selling in industry, schools were using the phone to create enrollments. In these proprietary schools, a wide range of short courses is offered to aspiring consumers of all ages. These people are not inclined to undertake lengthy and expensive college programs of up to four years.

This application for the phone fits in the retail chapter for two reasons:

- The selling situation for a school is actually that of a service sold directly to a consumer; it is essentially identical to the task handled by a store.

- Almost every script and letter in this section can be modified and used by a store that sells a service.

Each example presented on the following pages is part of an integrated student recruitment program used by a large private school organization operating nationally. Admissions representatives in each school use these scripts and letters to set appointments.

### SCRIPT 7.7a: ANSWERING AN AD RESPONSE

Most prospects are lured to the schools by printed advertising. Ads promise a booklet about paramedical careers such as:

- Medical secretarial
- Medical assistance
- Medical receptionist

On receipt of an inquiry, the responsible admissions representative mails the booklet, then follows up by telephone later the same day, if possible. This is the approach used:

*Telemarketer:*          [Introduces self to the person who answers the phone. If it is not the prospect, gives name only. If this individual asks what call is in reference to, say you are affiliated with the school, then add] *I'm calling about some information she requested.*

[When prospect comes to phone, give *full* introduction, then say] *I'm calling to let you know that we received your inquiry this morning, and the brochure you requested, the one about medical support careers, is being mailed to you right now. You should get it in a day or two.*

*If I may ask, how did you become interested in the medical field?*

Telemarketer proceeds to ask questions about:

- Educational background
- Family situation
- Present employment
- Time availability
- Any other areas that would have a bearing on the prospect's ability to pursue a training program.

When qualifications have been checked out, proceed to give *two* reasons for a school appointment. The first reason is so the school can determine the ability of prospect to handle such a program:

> *Mary, the first thing we should do is determine whether or not you can enroll in the Pratt School. A visit would serve two very important purposes: One is to make absolutely sure that this field is a good choice for you.*

The second reason follows without pause:

> *Another thing we'll accomplish by having you come in is to show you what it's like on the inside of a medical office. The school is set up just like a busy practice, so you can make a judgment on how you'd like that environment.*

Telemarketer sets appointment by offering a choice of times:

> *Can you make it at 4:00 this afternoon, or would 6:30 work out better?*

While *most* people who inquire will be called promptly, some will be hard to reach for one reason or another. Therefore, the following cover letter accompanies the brochure. It invites a call even though the admissions rep will probably call before the prospect gets the letter.

### LETTER 7.5: COVER LETTER TO NEW INQUIRY

Dear Ms. Martin:

Enclosed is the career information you requested, as well as some other information about the Pratt School that I thought you might find interesting. Look these things over carefully, since they might open the door to a whole new life for you.

If you still have questions after looking over this material, or if I can help in any way, please give me a call during school hours, or drop me a note.

Before you make any decisions regarding your future, please consider accepting the school's invitation to visit for an interview and tour. That may be the most significant step you could take right now.

My phone number is 768–3410. I'll be happy to do what I can.

Sincerely,

Frank Wilson

Past graduates, public school teachers, and others refer potential students to the schools. The next call is designed for that prospect.

## SCRIPT 7.7b: INITIAL CALL TO A REFERRAL

This call is modified as needed to fit the situation. For example, the opening would change if the prospect were referred by an employer of paramedical personnel. Also, the dialogue would obviously be modified when dealing with a mature adult seeking training.

| | |
|---|---|
| *Telemarketer:* | [Gets prospect on the line, then says] *Hello, Mr. Adams? This is Frank Wilson at the Pratt School. Your friend Mary Martin suggested that we provide information to you about careers in medical support fields.* |
| *Prospect:* | *Oh, she did mention that recently.* |
| *Telemarketer:* | *She told me that she feels there's a great future for people in paramedical careers, and apparently she sees you in that field. Have you given the idea much thought?* |
| *Prospect:* | *I've wanted to do medical work for a couple of years, but my folks would like for me to attend college, so that's probably what I'll do in September.* |
| *Telemarketer:* | *To study for a career in the medical field?* |
| *Prospect:* | *Well, no. Just general courses for a couple of years.* |
| *Telemarketer:* | *Have you ever had the benefit of an interview to find out what's involved in the medical field—and whether or not you'd fit into it in some role?* |
| *Prospect:* | *No. I haven't had interviews like that since early in my senior year, and that was pretty general.* |
| *Telemarketer:* | *Can I make a suggestion? Let's get together here at the school so we can find out exactly how you might fit into a paramedical career. Also, when you see the school you'll get a solid picture of what it's like for people who work in the field. Does that make sense to you?* |
| *Prospect:* | *Yes, it does.* |

Ads in classified telephone directories, bulletins in high schools, and other lead generators create incoming-call activity. The next dialogue covers the inbound inquiry.

## SCRIPT 7.7c: HANDLING AN INQUIRY CALL

Depending on the circumstances that trigger a call-in, the dialogue might be altered somewhat. Two principles that do *not* change in this script are the following:

- A brochure is *always* mailed, since the ad promises it.
- A prospect's name, address, and phone number are captured early in the call so that a follow-up is possible later.

| | |
|---|---|
| *Prospect:* | *Hello, I'd like to get some information about the courses you offer.* |
| *Telemarketer:* | *I'll be happy to help you in any way I can. May I ask how you heard of the Pratt School?* |
| *Prospect:* | *I saw your ad.* |
| *Telemarketer:* | *Okay. Which of the programs are you most interested in?* |
| *Prospect:* | *[Identifies program of most interest.]* |
| *Telemarketer:* | *Fine, I'll get our booklet into the mail this afternoon. I'll include class schedules, tuition information, student loan information, and a description of entrance requirements.* |
| | *Can you give me the correct spelling of your name?* |

Telemarketer proceeds to get address information and makes certain of correct spelling. NOTE: It is especially important for the telemarketer to secure this data early in the call—*before* an attempt is made to set the appointment.

| | |
|---|---|
| *Telemarketer:* | *How long have you been interested in a medical support career?* |
| *Prospect:* | *I'm thinking about lots of different types of training right now; I have been since I graduated high school last June.* |
| *Telemarketer:* | *Are you working now?* |
| *Prospect:* | *I sell cosmetics at a department store. I'm tired of that and want to get into more challenging work.* |
| *Telemarketer:* | *Can you tell me what other fields you are considering?* |
| *Prospect:* | *I'm looking at secretarial training and general college courses.* |
| *Telemarketer:* | *Well, a medical environment is usually quite fast-paced, and it's a good idea to find out right away whether you really want to be in a demanding position like the ones we can prepare you for.* |
| | *By having you visit the school for about an hour, we can get an idea about your chances in a medical career. In addition, you'll see what you'd encounter if you worked in a medical office. In my opinion, that would help you decide.* |

Telemarketer then offers alternative appointment times.

If the prospect insists on reading the requested brochures first, express appreciation for calling. Clear a time for a call-back to answer any questions that might arise.

### SCRIPT 7.7d: FOLLOW-UP CALL TO A NO-SHOW

About 40 percent of scheduled school appointments fail to arrive for their interviews. As a result, the admissions rep faces a major task in recontacting these people the same day, or at least within 24 hours after the appointment was missed.

In this call, it is vital to avoid blaming a prospect for wasting time. Feelings of guilt must be eliminated at all costs. This call should be made no later than *one day after the scheduled appointment:*

| | |
|---|---|
| *Telemarketer:* | *Hello Mary, this is Frank Wilson of the Pratt School. I'm sorry we couldn't get together when we planned. Your situation sounded so promising that I was really looking forward to trying to help you.* |
| *Prospect:* | *Something came up and I couldn't make it.* |

If, at this point, the prospect offers a sincere reason for not showing up, the telemarketer can quickly name a new appointment time. That would make the following dialogue unnecessary.

| | |
|---|---|
| *Telemarketer:* | *I understand how those things come up. Have you thought of any new questions since we spoke on Tuesday?* |
| *Prospect:* | *No.* |
| *Telemarketer:* | *Okay, let's set a new time that we're sure is convenient. How about Saturday at 10:00 A.M., or would noon work better for you?* |
| *Prospect:* | *I think 10:00 will be good.* |
| *Telemarketer:* | *Good! If any emergencies or last-minute developments come up, please call me. Let me give you my office phone number again.* |

Telemarketer gives prospect phone number and complete information about the scheduled day and time. Also, it helps to repeat the address of the office and directions on how to find it.

Again, in this approach there is *no blame,* hard feelings, or accusations of unreliability. By asking whether any new questions have come up, the telemarketer is subtly attempting to find out whether objections have developed that might keep the prospect from coming in.

### SCRIPT 7.7e: FOLLOW-UP ON A MISSED APPOINTMENT ATTEMPT

This call is made no more than *three days* after *failing to set an appointment* on the initial telephone call. It is assumed that an information package was sent to the prospect the same day as that first contact.

| | |
|---|---|
| *Telemarketer:* | *Hello Jim, this is Dave Lawton from the Bennettville School. I trust you have received the information I mailed.* |
| *Prospect:* | *Yes, thank you. I got it yesterday.* |
| *Telemarketer:* | *Did you find it interesting?* |
| *Prospect:* | *Yes.* |

| | |
|---|---|
| *Telemarketer:* | *Have any further questions come up?* |
| *Prospect:* | *No, I really can't think of any.* |
| *Telemarketer:* | *Well, as I think I mentioned when we spoke before, your background seems to be good enough to make a paramedical career a definite possibility. But there's no way to be absolutely sure until we know more about you.* |
| | *Can we get together at the school on Thursday at 6:00 P.M., or would 7:00 be better?* |
| *Prospect:* | *I think I'll have to consider this a little more before I come in for an interview. I'm not quite ready yet.* |
| *Telemarketer:* | *Jim, have you had a chance to discuss school with your family?* |
| *Prospect:* | *Yes, we've talked about training. My parents want to see me get into a good field, but my father thinks I should work for one more year.* |
| *Telemarketer:* | *If you don't mind my asking, have you saved anything for your education?* |
| *Prospect:* | *A little, but not enough to pay for college or your program.* |
| *Telemarketer:* | *Jim, I think we may be putting the cart before the horse. The first thing you should do is find out if you're qualified for a paramedical career. Another vital factor is, which field do you have the strongest aptitude for?* |
| | *If we do find out that medicine is a good choice, there are ways to get financial help. We may be able to assist you in getting a student loan.* |
| | *Let's get you and your parents in here for an interview tomorrow at either 5:30 P.M. or 7:30. Which is better for you?* |

The next letter helps in certain missed appointment situations.

## LETTER 7.6:  LETTER FOR A MISSED APPOINTMENT ATTEMPT

When an admissions rep's backlog of calls prevents quick telephone follow-up to missed appointments, this letter can fill the time gap until a call *can* be made. On occasion it does attract a call from the prospect.

Dear Mr. Arnold:

I hope I was of help to you on the phone last Monday. You know, the best way to really find out what the school and activities are like, and to learn whether a paramedical career is really in your best interests, is to visit the school.

I've enjoyed talking to you, and it would be ideal for both you and the school to have *all* the facts before any decisions are made on an issue that is so important to your happiness and well-being.

Please call me for an appointment so that we can explore the possibilities of a paramedical career. My number is 724–3900.

Sincerely,

Maria Morrison

When a prospect *can't* be called, here's one possible answer:

### LETTER 7.7:   FOLLOW-UP TO A "NO-PHONE"

Increasingly, people do not list their telephone numbers. Some 30 percent of the leads received by the schools are no-phones. This follow-up letter is the key to dealing with this group of prospects.

Dear Mrs. Baxter:

I hope you received the booklet I sent you a few days ago and that it answered most of your questions about the Barrington School and the career training programs we offer.

What you should do now is arrange an appointment for an interview here at the school. By going carefully into your career needs and future goals, we may be able to find out where you will find the most satisfaction. By seeing the school, you will have a chance to feel exactly what it's like to be part of a medical team.

Touring the school and discussing your future would be very helpful to you. Please call me at 323–7100 to arrange an appointment for a day and time convenient to you and your parents.

Sincerely,

Kim Foreman

Here's another tool for use with no-phones:

### LETTER 7.8:   FOLLOW-UP TO A "NO-PHONE"
### WHO FAILS TO KEEP APPOINTMENT

Dear Ms. Kenton:

I'm sorry you couldn't make it to the school as we planned, but I'm sure something important must have come up. Won't you please contact me so we can set another time? My number is 743–8100.

I'm looking forward to actually meeting you and being able to talk with you about the possibilities of a paramedical career and how it would shape your future.

Sincerely,

Susan Dolan

## REFINING RETAIL TELEPHONE SCRIPTS

Use the following checklist to make sure you consider the most important elements involved in calling, or taking calls from, retail customers and prospects.

After you go through the checklist, use the following worksheets: For cold-calls to retail customers or prospects, use Form 1.3, Cold-Call Dialogue Worksheet. For incoming calls, use Form 9.4, Inbound Dialogue Worksheet.

---

### FORM 7.1: RETAIL TELEPHONE SALES CHECKLIST

1. Can you utilize your present floor salespeople to make calls?

   ____ Yes     ____ No

2. If *not*, work out a plan for hiring outside assistance:

   _____

   _____

   _____

   _____

   _____

   _____

3. If you *can* allocate some of your employee time to calling, make sure of the following elements:

   • Work out definite blocks of time daily when calling will be done.

   • Set up performance standards in terms of minimum calls per hour, weekly sales results, and other pertinent areas.

   • Make sure all salespeople have a basic tracking system to keep follow-ups straight.

4. Determine the focus of your initial telemarketing program by targeting one of these categories:

   • Existing customers

   • New prospects

5. For the category you selected in 4, can you compile a list for your callers to use?

   ____ Yes     ____ No

6. Can you identify any special store events that you can use as the core of a telemarketing presentation?

   ____ Yes     ____ No

   If so, list here:

   _____

   _____

   _____

_____

_____

_____

7. If not, describe the appeal you plan to use in your program:

_____

_____

_____

_____

_____

_____

8. If it makes sense to establish a special commission and/or bonus plan for telemarketing, how will it work?

_____

_____

_____

_____

_____

_____

9. For *incoming calls,* have you set up a procedure to make sure that calls are efficiently forwarded to the right people in your organization?

____ Yes      ____ No

10. Do you have safeguards that will help prevent keeping people on hold for excessive lengths of time or prevent calls from being lost while on hold?

____ Yes      ____ No

11. Do you have a form for documenting inbound calls so they can be followed up on a timely basis?

____ Yes      ____ No

12. Are specific people in your company responsible for resolving complaints and calling customers back?

____ Yes      ____ No

# Chapter 8

# AN ARSENAL OF VALUABLE FOLLOW-UP CALLS

One of America's most successful business-to-business telemarketers is not especially gifted in sales strategies and does not possess remarkable verbal skills. In fact, this person is relatively inexperienced in the business world. The attitude that brings extraordinary success in this instance is tenacity: This telemarketer will *never* let go once he detects even a faint glimmer of interest or need. No matter how negative a prospect may be, if that one ray of possibility is present, this caller will make 3, 12, 30 contacts until the sale is won, or the prospect's patience is at an end. *Whatever* it takes to get the job done, this persistent person will do.

Remember, only one telephone call can be labeled as an initial contact. All the calls that follow—no matter how many—are follow-ups. By a huge margin, more sales are closed on follow-up than on initial calls. Therefore, when astute telemarketing managers recruit telemarketers, they look for the following attributes: (1) Rather than the brilliant flair that can knock prospects off their feet, wise managers look for a sense of organization that will help assure a continuing and systematic effort in maintaining a call-back schedule. (2) Instead of the high-strung prima donna, they prefer an individual who can absorb sometimes harsh rejection and recontact prospects who had cut them short.

Follow-ups assume an enormously important role because of various situations that can afflict a prospect. Here are a few:

- Simple procrastination is one that *every* seller encounters.
- A slow decision process is also common.
- Competition will often delay a yes or no answer.
- An elusive buyer can easily create the need for repeated contact attempts.

In each of these cases, failure to stay in touch will usually cause the transaction to fall apart. To the buyer, when you are out of sight, you are indeed out of mind!

This chapter covers the most important types of follow-up calls.

## WHEN FOLLOW-UP IS NEEDED MOST

Firms that have solidly planned sales programs take the time to work out a definite follow-up routine for certain typical sales situations. Figure 8.1 suggests four circumstances that would require formalized follow-up strategies.

1. When an initial call results in a field sales appointment. If the sale *is* closed, the seller should have a follow-up system that assures order fulfillment and service.

   *A definite schedule* is needed. This schedule dictates what kind of contacts should be made and at what intervals.

2. When an initial call results in a field sales appointment. If the sale is *not* closed, *a definite schedule* is needed to obtain that sale.

3. When the initial call fails to get the appointment, *a definite schedule* must be created to *set* that appointment.

4. When a telemarketer is unable to reach the targeted decision maker, further attempts are made according to *a definite schedule.*

### FIGURE 8.1: WHEN FOLLOW-UP PAYS OFF

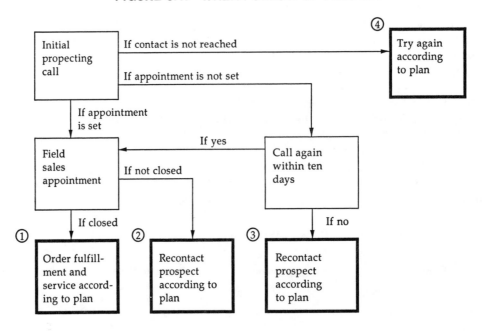

# SECOND ATTEMPTS TO REACH A CONTACT

In recent years, as telemarketing reached superstardom as a salesmaker, buyers have learned more about making themselves scarce. To counteract that trend, today's most productive callers have perfected techniques for reaching targeted contacts on the second, third, or fourth try.

Simply calling and asking for the buyer time after time isn't enough. A tough screen will never grow tired of turning down that kind of timid telemarketer. But a caller who shows firmness and conviction along with persistence is the one who is most likely to get results.

When firmness is carefully combined with politeness, very few prospects will be offended. A majority of them will respect the dedication of an approach like that. One excellent caller sums it up this way: "I'll stop calling to reach an elusive buyer *only* when an executive in the company tells me to stop. That has only happened about half a dozen times over the past couple of years."

This telemarketer is polite to screens, but flatly refuses to let them control his income. In the nicest way possible he insists that his story be presented to the responsible people in the company. He gets his way far more often than not.

In this case, no script is used in the true sense of the word. But the telemarketer *does* have a certain attitude that works for him. The following dialogue attempts to illustrate that attitude.

### SCRIPT 8.1a: USING SPECIAL TACTICS TO CATCH ELUSIVE DECISION MAKERS

*Elusive* can have several different meanings. An executive may be extremely busy and therefore genuinely hard to corner. Another might be accessible enough but avoids virtually all calls from outside. Both types are elusive in the eyes of a telemarketer.

A primary question for any caller is this: No matter what the reason is for a prospect's elusiveness, how many attempts are made to reach a buyer by telephone before special tactics are used? Informal surveys of telemarketers show that an average of three calls is the answer. When a receptionist or screen refuses to put the caller through to the contact on three successive occasions, the *fourth* attempt should employ special tactics from the telemarketer.

*Note:* Whenever possible, later call-backs of *all* kinds should be made at mutually agreeable times. The first time a screen claims that a buyer is not available, the telemarketer finds out the best day and time to call again. This enormously increases the chance of getting through on the next try.

Typically, a stronger follow-up approach might sound like this:

| | |
|---|---|
| *Telemarketer:* | [Again introduces self to receptionist or screen. Asks for targeted contact. If a screen reports that contact is still not available and the caller feels that much more can be done by the screen to reach the buyer, he or she says] *I understand that you are only trying to do your job, but all I'm asking you for is the chance to run this idea past Mr. Gould.* |

> *This is the third time I've called. I don't want to take any more of your time, and I don't want to feel as though I'm wasting* my *time.*
>
> *All I'm asking for is Mr. Gould's opinion of this or direct word from him* that he doesn't want to talk to me. Do you agree that's fair?

While the screen will sometimes plead inability to do any better, this approach will succeed in finally getting the buyer's attention. After three or four failed tries, there is not much to lose.

When the *screen* appears to be the barricade between seller and buyer, the next strategy may help.

### SCRIPT 8.1b: HANDLING AN ESPECIALLY TOUGH SCREEN

Business-to-business telemarketers largely agree that sometimes screens can take themselves too seriously. They are assigned the task of stopping the calls that are not worthwhile to their company; but, in time, a few of these people start to become tyrannical. The following changes begin to occur in the screening process:

- Instead of impartially and accurately passing a worthy seller's message to the decision maker, who will then decide whether or not to grant an appointment, the screen will make judgments based on his or her *personal* feelings about the merits of a product or service. Since most screens are really not qualified to act as buyers, an injustice can easily be done to legitimate vendors.
- Screens have been known to respond favorably to flattery. In this case, the offer itself is of little consequence. The personality of the telemarketer assumes major and distorted importance.

A serious caller, one who is not interested in playing games, might be at a terrific disadvantage.

By recognizing that the aforementioned phenomena may be taking place in a screen who repeatedly rejects an audience with the buyer, telemarketers are much better prepared to achieve their objective on the third or fourth follow-up call. One caller does it this way:

| | |
|---|---|
| *Telemarketer:* | [Again introduces self to receptionist or screen. Asks for targeted contact. If screen reports that contact is still not available and caller suspects that the problem is a breakdown in rapport, he or she says] *Can I ask you about something that's been bothering me?* |
| *Screen:* | [Will usually agree to hear what the telemarketer has to say.] |
| *Telemarketer:* | *I don't know if I'm imagining this, but I get the feeling that I'm not exactly a hit with you. I try to be as pleasant as I can* |

> *because I realize that* you're *under pressure just like every-body else is.*
>
> *Mainly, I try to do a good job, and to do that, it's extremely important for me to get my message across to certain people in a company like yours.*
>
> *If you and I do* have *a problem, I'd like to know how we can resolve it so I can get on with what I'm supposed to do. Can we talk about it?*

If a relationship problem *does* exist, this approach should bring it to the surface so it can be fixed. On the other hand, if the screen denies harboring any prejudice toward the caller, he or she may try harder to get the suffering telemarketer through to the buyer in order to avoid any appearance of bad feelings.

A firm approach can also be effective when used in seeking the *real* buyer.

## SCRIPT 8.1c: FINDING A HIDDEN BUYER

When a telemarketer contacts larger companies, the correct identification of the right buyer can be a first-class challenge. In fact, one of the ways a decision maker can hide is by telling company call takers to steer hopeful sellers to assistants. These assistants can *sound* like buyers. On occasion they may come complete with impressive titles, and they might be trained to ask the kinds of questions a vendor would expect from a buyer.

While talking to an assistant may be the *only* way to present a product or service to certain firms, the most determined telemarketers will hold out as long as they can for the top person. They do this by letting the screen or assistant know that they *are aware* of the real buyer's existence.

It can be handled this way:

> *Telemarketer:*    [Again introduces self to receptionist, screen, or buyer's assistant.] *I want you to know how much I appreciate the help you've given me since I first called. I really feel that progress has been made, but I have one more request to make that I hope we can work out.*
>
> *After the conversations I've had with your people, I'm confident we're all in a position to go a step further at this point.*
>
> *I wonder if we can set up a meeting with the person who makes the final decision so that the purchase can be considered. Who would that be?*

More often than not, this presumptive dialogue will *at least* expose a hidden buyer—if indeed one exists. If there *is* no behind-the-scenes purchasing authority, this approach can still be beneficial since it might get purchase approval moving in the right direction.

One of the most prevalent follow-up calls is the second contact to a prospect who did not agree to an appointment on the initial try.

## SECOND ATTEMPT TO SET AN APPOINTMENT

A marketing manager of an electronics company said it takes the firm's telemarketers an average of 2.2 contacts to actually set the appointment. Remember, these are *discussions* with a decision maker, not simply tries to get in touch with the right person.

This strongly suggests the following significant facts:

- A *worthwhile* appointment usually requires some degree of trust building. This may be nothing more than two people getting to know each other. There are no magic words exchanged, just growing familiarity.
- The phenomenon of achieving a major goal on the initial call is probably not realistic. Immediate closes may occur more often in consumer telemarketing, but in business-to-business calling, a fast close is a rare thing indeed. For that reason, *most* legitimate firms plan on making at least two calls to a buyer before real progress is made.

When a telemarketer is unable to set the appointment or close on the initial call, a number of reasons for the failure can usually be named. The following section provides one follow-up call for each of the most commonly heard reasons.

### SCRIPT 8.2a: CALLING BACK AN UNRESPONSIVE CONTACT

Anybody who has ever sold can recall prospects who appeared to be bored or preoccupied, yet these people choose to remain involved in the discussion with a caller. The end result is a telemarketer who doesn't feel progress is being made, but is convinced that a follow-up is required since the buyer *is* still on the line. In this particular case, the follow-up is made about one week after the inconclusive first call. This call-back was set up at the end of the initial contact.

> *Telemarketer:* [Reintroduces self, then recaps the offer. The purpose of this is to refamiliarize the prospect with the new product or service. The lead-in sounds like this] *When we talked last Wednesday, I explained how our phone system would help you in two important ways.*

Caller goes on to briefly summarize the two most prominent advantages.

The next step is an attempt by the telemarketer to move this prospect away from the unresponsive mode that has so far prevailed:

> *If you could have anything you wanted in a new phone system, with no limits whatsoever, how would you describe it?*

That open-ended question *may* get a revealing statement that describes a system similar to the one being sold by the caller.

In addition to that open-ended question, the telemarketer can use some closed questions that ask for a yes or no response. The response can then be further probed. For example:

| | |
|---|---|
| *Telemarketer:* | *Is a call-monitoring capability important to you at this point?* |
| *Prospect:* | *Yes, it's something we have to have now.* |
| *Telemarketer:* | *Can you describe some of the most prominent uses you have for monitoring?* |

Again, the previously unresponsive prospect is drawn into the discussion when the caller mixes open-ended and closed questions.

If this difficult buyer *remains* noncommittal, the best strategy is to close assumptively. This, in effect, makes the appointment *for* the prospect. For example:

| | |
|---|---|
| *Telemarketer:* | *Let's set up a time for you to meet with Terry O'Connell, our rep in your area. I'll have him over to see you at 4:00 P.M. next Thursday.* |

That kind of close *is* successful in a large percentage of cases involving an unresponsive but apparently interested prospect.

A prospect who professes to have little or no interest in a telemarketer's offer can occasionally be turned around through a well-handled follow-up call.

### SCRIPT 8.2b: "NOT INTERESTED"

A large percentage of call-backs are met with the prospect's expression of no interest. While the buyer may have appeared to be mildly involved at the time of the initial call, the follow-up runs into a brick wall.

When a telemarketer gives up at this point, valuable sales are *almost certainly* being thrown away! While it is true that a comparatively small number of these "no-interest" responses will actually be saved, that group *can* represent a hefty chunk of extra profit over a period of time.

This call is placed about one week after the initial contact:

| | |
|---|---|
| *Telemarketer:* | [Reintroduces self, then recaps the offer. The purpose is to refamiliarize the prospect with the new product or service.] |
| *Prospect:* | *I'm afraid we'll have to pass on that now. I'll keep your information on file and get back to you when we're ready.* |
| *Telemarketer:* | *We appreciate your keeping us in mind. Can you tell me what circumstances prevent you from going ahead?* |
| *Prospect:* | *We discussed the options open to us and none of them would give us exactly what we need.* |

While the precise language will of course differ, the point is this: The prospect's first response was completely noncommittal: ". . . we'll have to pass on that now." By probing, a little more information came out: "We discussed the options . . ."

By *continuing* the probing, this may occur:

> *Telemarketer:*        *If I may ask, exactly what do you need?*

When this question is successful at revealing some specific prospect needs, the caller is in a position to address the problems perceived by the buyer. To give up at the first sign of a change of heart is to abandon any hope of gaining new sales.

Dealing with a prospect who suddenly sounds too busy to talk is our next follow-up call.

## SCRIPT 8.2c: RUSHING TO END THE CALL

When the targeted prospect is recontacted and claims that a meeting is waiting, other calls are on hold, or some similar time crunch exists, some telemarketers assume that the person is using this rush act as a way of avoiding a decision.

In some cases the buyer *may* be under genuine pressure to get off the line, but because the caller has no way of knowing which cases are real and which are not, all such situations should receive decisive action by the telemarketer. Professional callers agree that the best strategy in a rush situation is to quickly get a commitment from the prospect to continue the conversation a bit later. Trying to keep the person on the line is risky. It shows contempt for the prospect's rushed condition—regardless of whether it's real or not.

Getting a quick commitment can sound like this:

> *Telemarketer:*        [Reintroduces self, then immediately encounters a situation in which prospect is clearly rushed and claims that other urgent business prevents a discussion at this time.]
>
> *Prospect:*            [Prospect may also say] *I'll be in touch with you as soon as things settle down.*
>
> *Telemarketer:*        *Okay. Have any of your requirements changed since we spoke on Monday?*
>
> *Prospect:*            *Not really.*
>
> *Telemarketer:*        *Then I'll assume we're still on track. My time is clear at 4:00 this afternoon. I'll call back then.*

When the prospect persists in putting off a follow-up conversation, the telemarketer has to come up with "important" new information. For example:

> *Prospect:*            *I'll be tied up for the rest of the day. As I said before, why don't I get back to you when I'm ready.*
>
> *Telemarketer:*        *No problem, except that I have some information that I feel will be important to you. I know you're busy, but I'd hate to see this slip away.*

It will be the telemarketer's task to come up with some kind of significant item that will fulfill the promise. There is little danger that the prospect would say "I'll take an extra moment. Tell me about the new information *now*." If that *does* occur and the caller is not ready with a new fact he or she can say "This might take a while. Let's wait until your time looks better."

Procrastination is easily the toughest problem that confronts telemarketers.

### SCRIPT 8.2d: FOUR APPROACHES FOR RECONTACTING A PROCRASTINATOR

There is no *one* way to successfully deal with a procrastinator since the root causes of stalling can vary. Here are four of the most frequently occurring root causes:

- Fear of making a bad choice of products or services.
- Worry about the ability to pay for the purchase.
- Failure to understand various details about the purchase or about the operational characteristics of the item.
- A lack of trust in the seller.

When a telemarketer is pursuing substantial business from an especially stubborn buyer, a very intelligent course of action would be to cover each root cause as successive follow-up calls are made. At some point, either the caller will prevail or the buyer's refusal to budge will win out.

To illustrate the array of attacks on a procrastinator, each root cause is shown here starting with the fear of making a bad choice.

*Telemarketer:*     [After reintroduction, prospect indicates that a decision has still not been made. Telemarketer will cover root cause number one.] *I'm not sure I told you about some of our customers in the same business you're in. Their needs are almost exactly like yours in every detail, and the TX paging system is working perfectly for them. I'm amazed that you and other managers saw the same advantages.*

*There's every reason to expect that your experience with the system would be as successful as theirs. If you think it would help, I can put you directly in touch with a couple of our users.*

Dialogue that can effectively combat worry about the ability to pay for the purchase is now provided.

*Telemarketer:*     *When we talked earlier I failed to carefully cover the costs involved in a purchase of our system and the immediate savings that would come to you.*

*Before I get into that, can you tell me if you're budgeted for a new system?*

Whether yes or no, caller then asks:

> *Out of curiosity, about how much did you expect to pay for a system like this?*

Having the above information, the telemarketer can now go into detail about payment plans, leasing, or other available programs that might help dispel financial apprehensions.

Failure to understand various details about the purchase or the product can't be effectively represented in a dialogue guide. The precise level of prospect comprehension has to be assured through probing. A telemarketer can never assume that a prospect understands everything about the product or service. Facts have to be meticulously reviewed, then repeated if necessary.

A lack of trust in the seller can easily come about when the vendor is not a nationally known firm, is not headquartered near the prospect's company, or is a very small organization.

> *Telemarketer:*      *After we talked last, it occurred to me that you really don't know anything about the Mann Company.*
>
> *We're not exactly a household word because our policy is to remain small and heavily oriented to quality. We've seen the compromises our big competitors make, and that isn't the way we want to operate.*
>
> *One thing that will prove we do a better job is the amount of service you'll get when you have our paging system installed.*

An astute telemarketer will rapidly come to grips with the fact that inevitably a higher number of follow-up calls will be made to a procrastinator. And since it isn't really feasible to cover too much ground in one call, the telemarketer can nicely deal with one root cause in each follow-up until the breakthrough is achieved.

Many seasoned telemarketers are certain that it is good strategy to essentially ignore a prospect's *first* excuse not to buy. This interesting method is covered now.

## SCRIPT 8.2e: DEALING WITH A NEBULOUS EXCUSE

If a prospect gives the telemarketer a flimsy excuse to avoid a commitment, that excuse will probably vanish *if* the caller chooses not to deal with it. That's the belief of a good many high-income telephone people who often apply this concept.

In this strategy, the caller will simply *acknowledge* the excuse, then quickly sidestep it and go on to a different topic. In a majority of cases, the excuse is not repeated. If it *is* brought up again by the prospect, the telemarketer will realize it has substance in the mind of the buyer and will then attempt to resolve it.

> *Prospect:*      *It really sounds good, but we've only looked at a couple of other systems. We'll review a bunch of others before a decision is made.*

*Telemarketer:*           *Makes sense. You were talking about training before. Can you tell me what you feel your people would need?*

"Makes sense" is the caller's acknowledgment. The prospect's statement about doing more shopping can't be *completely* ignored since that would amount to clear disrespect. Immediately after the acknowledgment, the telemarketer goes to a constructive topic, then heads for a close.

Again, if the prospect *repeats* the excuse, it definitely demands the caller's attention. Our next group of follow-up calls and letters are used after successful closes.

## FOLLOWING UP RECENT CLOSES

There are no figures available that accurately show how many sales fall apart immediately after a deal is closed. These factors can conspire to change a recent buyer's mind:

- Competitors can offer a lower price than the figure already agreed on.

- Delivery or installation, or both, are not provided according to customer expectations or vendor promises.

- For one reason or another, the buyer feels forgotten: "Once we sign on the dotted line, we're no longer as important as we were when we inquired," in the words of a manager.

Each of these gremlins that haunt new sales can be controlled by diligent follow-up. When the lines of communication with a new customer are kept open, the problems that usually kill sales become mere annoyances that don't materially affect the relationship between seller and buyer.

For a majority of companies, if the rate of cancelled orders could be reduced by one third to one half, volume and profits would improve dramatically. Most firms *could* slash cancellations by instituting a follow-up program that utilizes calls like the ones covered in this section.

### FORM 8.1:   CHECKLIST FOR VERIFYING FULFILLMENT OF SERVICES

In a midwestern computer store, new customers are routinely called by a company representative one day after making a major purchase. This call is *not* intended to obtain add-on business (although it does accomplish that rather often). Its purpose is to solidify the relationship between customer and store. Calling is done by a part-time employee who carefully follows this straightforward checklist:

Customer name: _____   Date: _____

Address: _____

City: _____   State: _____   Zip: _____

Telephone: Work (___) _____ Home (___) _____

Date of purchase: _____ Items purchased:

_____

_____

_____

_____

Please ask the following questions:

1. Did you find everything you were looking for?

   ___ Yes    ___ No

2. Were store employees courteous and knowledgeable?

   ___ Yes    ___ No

3. Are purchased items operating properly?

   ___ Yes    ___ No

4. Were all necessary parts provided?

   ___ Yes    ___ No

5. Do you understand operation of items?

   ___ Yes    ___ No

6. How can we assist you now? _____

   _____

   _____

Intensive training is provided by the store to assure a completely pleasant approach by the caller. If "no" responses are recorded, it is *not* the caller's function to deal with the problems. Checklists are turned over to store management and further follow-up is done immediately from that higher level.

This program is used for buyers who purchase items of $150 or more in value. This keeps the number of daily calls at reasonable levels.

An auto dealership in the same city also uses a follow-up call, but no checklist is followed.

### SCRIPT 8.3: OPEN-ENDED SERVICE ASSURANCE CALL

*Every* buyer of a new or used vehicle is contacted by this dealer within 48 hours of delivery. This program is unusual in that the follow-up calls are made by the telemarketer, instead of by the salesperson who handled the transaction.

By staying away from a structured checklist, the caller opens the door to *any* comment the customer wishes to make. Responses range from service needs to a drafty showroom. Positive remarks just about equal complaints. The point is, customers are *heard*, and they feel that the dealer is really concerned.

This very simple approach is used:

*Telemarketer:*     [Introduces self by giving full name and dealership name. Describes nature of call] *As you probably know, we take great pride in our service. Part of our program for excellent service is to find out exactly how you are doing. Is everything okay so far?*

Many auto-dealership managers maintain that this kind of open invitation to comment might open the floodgates and load a company down with more problems than it could handle.

In fact, nearly *all* of the complaints received are legitimate and would eventually require attention from the dealer. About 75 percent of the called customers are completely satisfied. Virtually all of them are delighted with the follow-up and tend to become repeat buyers of service and vehicles.

When the number of customers sold by a vendor prevents personal telephone contact, a letter can help do the job. This one is used by another auto dealer.

### LETTER 8.1:  OFFER OF ASSISTANCE

Dear Mrs. Phillips:

We are indeed proud to have you as a customer of McHugh Motors. Our job now is to make sure your new car gives you years of pride and reliability.

On behalf of everybody at the dealership, my responsibility is to see that your needs are promptly and efficiently taken care of—regardless of how large or small those requirements are.

Please call 331–4200 and ask for me during all dealership hours. I'm waiting to serve you when the time comes.

Sincerely,

Seth Kimball

Businesses that ignore the service needs of recent buyers may very well have fewer headaches and a lower volume of problems. But there is no question that they also face far less customer loyalty. Whether these firms choose to uncover the problems or not, *customer grievances still exist.*

An office-supply company uses a system called TelaServ to get recent buyers into an automatic purchasing mode for their small office needs. Here it is.

### LETTER 8.2:  USING THE "WANT LIST" TO GET AUTOMATIC REORDERS

This store sells too many small orders to make telephone follow-up a viable approach. They use TelaServ to set customers up for repeat business. This letter, with the accompanying order form, is sent out immediately after an individual makes a purchase in the store.

When a recent buyer mails the "want list" back to the store, it indicates what kind of small office items are needed, and the quantities normally consumed. The store then contacts the customer and computerizes the data. Now the customer can be contacted about the needed products at preplanned intervals. No thought has to be given to paper-clip supplies.

This system is notably effective in keeping competitors under control since the customer is enjoying a high level of convenience. Also, larger office needs tend to be purchased from the TelaServ dealer since the store is already performing reliably.

Here's the cover letter used by a TelaServ store:

Dear Customer:

Associated Office Supplies would like to thank you for your recent order, and we invite you to take part in our unique TelaServ program.

The enclosed package fully explains TelaServ. It's an innovative service that offers you an extremely convenient way to keep your office-supply inventory completely up to date. With TelaServ, *we call you* when it's time to order office supplies. It's FAST . . . it's CONVENIENT . . . and best of all, it's *FREE!*

Associated has been serving businesses such as yours for over twenty years. We offer one of the most complete selections of office products, printing services, equipment, and furniture in the entire Johnson County area.

Please take a moment to look over the TelaServ package. It explains how easy it is to keep your office supplies in stock *all the time.*

If you have any questions, or you need one of our sales representatives to help you with your major office needs, call me at 236–4100.

Sincerely,

Ben Biddle

This letter is sent with the TelaServ "want list," which shows 58 small, disposable, office-supply items. A sample of this form follows:

TELEASERV WANT LIST

| *Quantity Wanted* | *Description of Item* |
|---|---|
| _____ | Paper clips |
| _____ | Pens |
| _____ | Pencils |
| _____ | Punch (3-hole adjustable) |

Closes that *are* cancelled can be turned around. The following scripts are designed for that purpose.

## FOLLOWING UP RECENT CANCELLATIONS

A company selling products or services of substantial dollar value can't lightly dismiss cancelled orders. Aside from the basic problem of losing major business, these serious factors must also be considered:

- Will the defecting buyer be lost forever? And will that buyer tell other potential customers about the switch? Long-term damage might be considerable.
- *Why* did the buyer change vendors right after a commitment was made? If the reason isn't determined, the losing firm could suffer the same fate time after time.

In some firms that receive more than an average number of cancellations, it is not unusual for the managers to avoid looking at these questions. They accept cancellations as incidents that are part of the perils of doing business. They don't accept responsibility for these losses, but attribute them to outside forces that can't be conveniently or economically neutralized.

On the other side of the coin, companies that *do* take bold action on cancellations benefit tremendously. One industrial consulting firm recovers about 30 percent of the clients who announce their intention to use a rival group.

Equally important, the company can take comfort in the fact that no bad feelings linger when the prospect does go elsewhere. Also, the company doesn't often make the same mistake twice, because they try to find out *why* the buyer switched.

Here are the methods used to get better results from cancelled orders:

## SCRIPT 8.4a: REESTABLISHING GOODWILL
## AFTER A CANCELLATION

One of the most difficult tasks facing a seller is to remain upbeat after feeling the sting of a cancellation. To keep smiling even after it's certain that the buyer has purchased elsewhere is tough.

A kitchen remodeling firm has a policy of making sure that goodwill prevails whenever a project is cancelled. This call is placed after all negotiations have taken place and any possibility of saving the sale is exhausted.

> *Telemarketer:*        [Reintroduces self and company, then says] *Like everybody else here, I'm really sorry that we won't be handling your kitchen remodeling. I just want you to know that all of us send our good wishes, and we appreciate having had the chance to serve you.*
>
> *If there's anything we can do for you in the future, please remember us.*

If the reason for cancellation has not been established during prior discussions, the telemarketer can make a smooth transition into asking for the reason.

## SCRIPT 8.4b: GETTING THE REASON WHY YOU MISSED

As mentioned earlier, unless a seller knows *why* cancellations occur, he or she is destined to repeat the error. The same kitchen contractor seeks the reason, then documents it by using the Lost Sale Report (Form 8.2) that follows this dialogue.

To illustrate the flow of this script, we'll begin with the final paragraph in Script 8.4a:

> *Telemarketer:*　　　*If there's anything we can do for you in the future, please remember us.*
>
> 　　　　　　　　　*Before I let you go, I wonder if I could ask you just one question that's extremely important to us.*

Most consumers will consent.

> 　　　　　　　　　*We're always looking for ways to do a better job, and we can't accomplish that unless we know why things go wrong. I'd like to know where we went wrong in the process of bidding on your project.*

Invariably, the consumer's response will require probing by the telemarketer in order to get a complete and lucid story.

When the story is complete, the following form is completed by the telemarketer and given to management. By analyzing all lost sales, measures can be taken to improve operations.

---

### FORM 8.2:   LOST-SALE REPORT

Customer's name: _____ Date: _____

Address: _____

City: _____ State: _____ Zip: _____

Telephone: _____ Contact name: _____

Telemarketer's name: _____

Field sales representative's name: _____

Description of order: _____

_____

_____

Dollar value: $_____ Scheduled start date: _____

Date of cancellation: _____ Reason for cancellation: _____

_____

_____

_____

_____

---

Describe follow-up plan: _____

_____

_____

_____

Internal changes to be made: _____

_____

_____

_____

Comments: _____

_____

_____

_____

_____

_____

## SCRIPT 8.4c: OPENING FUTURE OPPORTUNITIES

When the telemarketer has been successful in reestablishing goodwill, it can pay to go a step further in trying to assure that future business will not be lost. In the case of the kitchen contractor, a consumer will probably not be in the market for the same kind of services in the near future, *but can refer business* to the firm.

Immediately after the caller has recorded the reason why the customer has purchased elsewhere, this dialogue is used:

> **Telemarketer:**     *I want to assure you that we* will *make changes based on your comments.*

IMPORTANT: A telemarketer may want to tell the consumer that names will not be mentioned when criticisms of certain employees are involved. A lost customer may want to remain anonymous.

> *Whenever an error is made, we take time to look at it, then take steps to fix it. That's how we get better at what we do.*
>
> *If you know somebody who needs the kind of work we do, I can guarantee you that their experience will be completely positive when they deal with us. I would personally see to it. So we'd deeply appreciate another chance from you.*

A relatively small number of lost sales make telephone follow-up a practical measure for the kitchen contractor. When a company faces much heavier customer loss, a letter can be a much more viable solution. Here's one used by a high-volume furniture retailer in dealing with order cancellations.

*LETTER 8.3: "THANKS FOR LETTING US SERVE YOU"*

Dear Mr. Collins:

*Thanks for letting us serve you!*

We are honored that you have selected your home furnishings at Bartlett's over the past several years.

Our sole objective has always been to bring you the very best values in fine furniture and accessories and to provide the kind of service that would make your buying experience exciting and trouble free.

Over the years, we believe we have achieved that goal. But sometimes we slip—as we did during your recent visit. When an error of that kind causes problems, we vow to do everything we can to make it right again.

If your trust in Bartlett's is damaged, please let me know. You have my pledge that the problem will be addressed on a priority basis.

In any event, you have the best wishes of every Bartlett's employee. We all hope to see you again. We'll do a better job!

Sincerely,

Nancy Lopez

When the *specific* reason for a cancellation is known, the letter is modified to cover that situation. When the cancelled order is sizable, telephone contacts are used by store management.

Leads are expensive. And when they are neglected, they rapidly lose value. The next section provides tools for salvaging leads that were not followed up on a timely basis.

## BRINGING "DEAD" LEADS BACK TO LIFE

Studies have proved that sales leads decline rapidly in interest. One expert claims that a person who inquires about a product or service loses about 10 percent of his interest each week from the date the inquiry was initiated. Therefore, according to that marketer, a lead potentially goes to waste in about three months if it isn't followed up.

Still, many companies let boxes of leads languish on a shelf for months, then, almost as an afterthought, they put a telemarketer on the task of converting them into sales or qualified prospects. Other organizations simply can't get to the task of follow-up despite their best efforts.

This situation will not quickly change as long as some firms can generate bundles of leads at trade shows, from "bingo cards" in publications, and through other means. For certain companies, the supply of leads usually outruns the company's ability to follow them up.

Scripts in this section are used by firms that often have to play catch-up with their on-hand supply of inquiries.

## SCRIPT 8.5: REVIVING COMMUNICATIONS
## WITH NEGLECTED LEADS

A certain percentage of leads will buy within a few weeks of generating an inquiry. But a much larger share will not take action until an effective seller enters the picture. While the interest level of the inquirer may be losing strength, many of them *can* be revived.

An interesting approach is used by a test equipment company that is periodically inundated with trade-show leads. By *gradually* reestablishing communications with these old leads, nearly 22 percent are eventually converted to solid field appointments.

| | |
|---|---|
| *Telemarketer:* | [Asks for executive identified on the lead card. Introduces self and company, then reestablishes background of the prospect's interest by saying] *We met you at the New Horizons trade show in Atlanta last February. We're the people who make heat-sensing equipment. The product you apparently liked was a hand-held model.* |

*NOTE:* Interest in a specific model was indicated on the lead card. If not, the caller should review the product line in order to try to pinpoint the area of highest interest.

> *That unit is perfect for checking heat levels in hard-to-reach places. Have you added any equipment like that recently?*

Thus, the prospect is reminded of the machine's precise function. The telemarketer also probed to find out whether a purchase has been made from a competitor during the time that has elapsed since the trade show.

| | |
|---|---|
| *Prospect:* | *We have some heat sensors built into machines, but hand-held units seem to be a good idea. They'd let us look at areas in the plant we can't easily get to.* |

Now the caller will attempt to turn the delay in follow-up into an advantage.

| | |
|---|---|
| *Telemarketer:* | *Your patience is appreciated. We were overwhelmed with orders at the show and that took us by surprise. Now we're in a position to work with you on possible applications.* |

At this point, the telemarketer will explore characteristics of the prospect's plant. Other qualifications, such as purchase timeframe, are also covered. When qualifying is complete, the caller closes:

| | |
|---|---|
| *Telemarketer:* | *It would be interesting to see how the hand-held sensor actually operates in your plant. I think you'll be impressed.* |
| | *Let me have Kate Jacobs, our western region rep, call you to set up a meeting time.* |

In some instances the task of catching up on lead follow-up is so staggering it makes good sense to send a letter as an interim measure. This one is used by the same test equipment firm when the numbers are enormous.

### LETTER 8.4: "WE BLEW IT"

Dear Mr. Harrison:

Thanks for visiting our display at the New Horizons trade show. Your interest in our model 280D heat sensor is appreciated. A fact sheet on that unit is enclosed.

Tech Magazine rated our heat sensors as the best available in terms of value and efficiency. As for our ability to keep up with demand, frankly we blew it this time. In order to maintain our usual high quality-standards, we fell behind.

The good news is that we're catching up and will soon be able to devote our undivided attention to your needs. Our field representative will be in touch with you. At that time you can set up a demonstration at your facility to see how our heat sensors can work in your plant.

In the meantime, if any questions come up, please call me directly at (414) 921–7200.

Again, your patience is appreciated. We are certain you'll find the wait worthwhile.

Sincerely,

Harvey Edwards

When an inquirer *has* already taken action on purchasing elsewhere, this next approach can be effective.

### SCRIPT 8.6a: SATISFIED WITH PRESENT SUPPLIER

When a prospect professes complete satisfaction with one particular supplier, some telemarketers see it as a fatal blow to their chances of making headway. In reality, the following situation likely exists: The prospect regards a current supplier as *adequate* in most respects but sees the task of switching to another vendor as a hassle that should be avoided. The telemarketer has to make the process of change as easy as possible for the buyer. Only then will there be a chance of success.

There are really very few buyer/seller relationships that are so perfectly formed that they can't be changed. Some that *are* difficult for a new supplier to penetrate are in high-tech or heavy-industry areas where tooling and techniques can be highly specialized and exceedingly tough for a new source to duplicate.

This follow-up call is utilized by a leasing company when their telemarketer is informed that the commitment went to a competitive leasing firm:

| | |
|---|---|
| *Telemarketer:* | [Reaches individual who generated the inquiry. Reintroduces self and company, then delivers a recap design to remind prospect about the offer, as presented during the initial contact] *Last week we talked about fleet leasing. We're the company that has a service center on Broad Street. We agreed to talk today so we could set up a meeting to discuss a new program we recently introduced.* |

| | |
|---|---|
| *Contact:* | *I remember our talk. Since then, we've decided to go with another leasing company.* |
| *Telemarketer:* | *Have you finalized a deal with them?* |
| *Contact:* | *Based on information we've seen so far, our choice looks final. They're offering everything we consider important, so we'd like to move forward.* |
| *Telemarketer:* | *You don't really know what we can do for you, and it would be a shame if you went with the second-best contract. Frankly, I don't think we're second best.* |
| | *I can help you make sure—and not take any extra time. If you could have somebody in your company tell me exactly what your top priorities are, I'll provide answers within two hours. That way there won't be any question about who can do a better job for you. I feel that our new program makes everything else in leasing today obsolete. The benefits to you are tremendous.* |

Most sales *are* lost when buyers fail to take a careful look at competitive offers.

A mystery occurs whenever a buyer generates an inquiry, then later on tells the caller there is "no need" for the product or service. The leasing firm uses this script to deal with that situation.

## SCRIPT 8.6b: "WE DON'T HAVE A NEED RIGHT NOW"

When a telemarketer follows up and hears this prospect response, he or she knows it's one of the toughest situations to contend with. This excuse is generally used to conceal some other problem. If the caller is to succeed in getting closer to a sale, the prospect's real motive has to be identified through *probing*.

Remember, in this case the buyer did inquire. You can safely assume that not many businesspeople waste their time inquiring about things they don't need. While *some* may want information to satisfy their curiosity or to research a product or service, this number is comparatively small. Furthermore, this person was contacted once before and said nothing that indicated a lack of interest.

Probing can go in many different directions. Here's just one example documented by the leasing firm:

| | |
|---|---|
| *Telemarketer:* | [Reaches individual who generated the inquiry. Reintroduces self and company, then delivers a recap designed to remind prospect about the offer, as presented during the initial contact.] |
| *Contact:* | *I appreciate your call, but we don't have a need right now. We'll get back to you later.* |

To give up and end the call here is all too common. By politely pressing for answers, the situation can be dramatically improved.

| Telemarketer: | *I'm surprised. The impression you gave me last week was that you were on the verge of leasing some vehicles. Did something develop to change that?* |
|---|---|
| Contact: | *Well, we're going to make some changes in the structure of our outside rep organization, and we don't know how many cars to lease. This is a very uncertain time.* |

At least the caller now has a defined problem to solve, and that's a lot better than simply accepting the nebulous ". . . we'll get back to you later." Probing ability is, without a doubt, the strongest attribute a telemarketer can possess.

## REFINING FOLLOW-UP CALLS

Use this section to make sure you have follow-up calls ready for every situation that exists for both prospects and customers. Refer to Illustration 8.1 at the beginning of this chapter. It pinpoints the areas where follow-up is especially important.

First, identify each type of follow-up call you will have occasion to make. Use Form 8.3: LIST OF FOLLOW-UP CALLS for that purpose.

Next, review the Form 8.4: FOLLOW-UP CALL CHECKLIST to make sure of every important detail in the follow-up procedure.

Then use a Form 8.5: FOLLOW-UP DIALOGUE WORKSHEET to work out the dialogue for each follow-up call you listed in Form 8.3. Make as many copies of the worksheets as you need.

---

### FORM 8.3:   LIST OF FOLLOW-UP CALLS

Follow-up call number 1, to _____

Timing of call: _____

Follow-up call number 2, to _____

Timing of call: _____

Follow-up call number 3, to _____

Timing of call: _____

Follow-up call number 4, to _____

Timing of call: _____

Follow-up call number 5, to _____

Timing of call: _____

Follow-up call number 6, to _____

Timing of call: _____

Follow-up call number 7, to _____
Timing of call: _____

Follow-up call number 8, to _____
Timing of call: _____

_____

_____

### FORM 8.4: FOLLOW-UP CALL CHECKLIST

*After a telephone close, or after a successful field sales appointment:*

1. Do you have a *definite* policy for calling the new customer?

    ____ Yes    ____ No

2. If so, have you worked out the precise timing of this call?

    ____ Yes    ____ No

3. Is a certain individual in your company designated to make this call?

    ____ Yes    ____ No

4. Check the items that should be covered in this follow-up call:

    ____ Description of guarantee terms

    ____ Payment information

    ____ Delivery information

    ____ Description of support services

    ____ Check on performance of product or service

    ____ Provide operational instructions

    ____ Add-on sale attempt

    ____ Other: _____

5. Ideally, what would the outcome of this call be?

    _____

    _____

*If an unsuccessful presentation was made by phone or in the field:*

6. Do you have a *policy* for calling the prospect?

    ____ Yes    ____ No

7. If so, have you worked out the precise timing of the call?

\_\_\_\_ Yes      \_\_\_\_ No

8. Is a certain individual in your company designated to make this call?

\_\_\_\_ Yes      \_\_\_\_ No

9. If reason for the missed close is *not* known, will follow-up call be designed to find out?

\_\_\_\_ Yes      \_\_\_\_ No

10. If reason for missed close *is* known, will follow-up call convey a remedy?

\_\_\_\_ Yes      \_\_\_\_ No

11. Will the objective of this follow-up call be—

\_\_\_\_ To close by phone

\_\_\_\_ To set a new field appointment

\_\_\_\_ To set up another call

\_\_\_\_ Other: _____

*If targeted contact has not yet been reached:*

12. Do you have a *policy* for calling the prospect?

\_\_\_\_ Yes      \_\_\_\_ No

13. If so, have you worked out the precise timing of the call?

\_\_\_\_ Yes      \_\_\_\_ No

14. Is a certain individual in your company designated to make this call?

\_\_\_\_ Yes      \_\_\_\_ No

15. Has the best possible approach been used to work with the screen?

\_\_\_\_ Yes      \_\_\_\_ No

16. Has the telemarketer determined the best times to reach the contact?

\_\_\_\_ Yes      \_\_\_\_ No

17. If deemed advisable, is caller being sufficiently firm with tough screens?

\_\_\_\_ Yes      \_\_\_\_ No

18. Is a *clear and compelling* story being related to screens?

\_\_\_\_ Yes      \_\_\_\_ No

---

### FORM 8.5: FOLLOW-UP DIALOGUE WORKSHEETS

Now make as many copies of these worksheets as you need, then work out the dialogue for each call you listed in Form 8.3.

a) Reintroduction: _____

_____

_____

_____

_____

b) Brief recap of initial conversation (as reminder to prospect): _____

_____

_____

_____

_____

_____

_____

_____

c) Ask for desired action and/or make desired statements: _____

_____

_____

_____

_____

_____

_____

_____

d) If applicable, set up next contact: _____

_____

_____

_____

_____

_____

# Chapter 9

# SUCCESSFULLY FIELDING
# INBOUND TELEPHONE INQUIRIES

A great number of companies have started to use more effective strategies to convert inbound inquiry calls into low-cost sales. These same firms are working harder to build goodwill during routine information call-ins from both prospects and customers.

One of America's most successful marketing strategists recently said this to a group of business owners:

> In my opinion, inbound telemarketing is where the big money is being made today in the most aggressive companies. Here's why:
>
> If you receive *any kind* of calls from prospects and customers, you *already have* everything you need to dramatically increase your sales. It doesn't cost a dime extra to make more high-profit dollars flow in.
>
> Each and every inbound inquiry call has *a definite and substantial cash value to you.* Depending on a company's product, that value can range from as little as $20 to $2,500 or more per call, depending on the product. Even service requests and complaint calls can be turned into add-on sales and enhanced loyalty.
>
> Companies have to work out strategies to make it happen. Inside employees need call-handling skills, plus simple systems to transfer calls correctly so follow-up is made in cases where it's needed.

This executive operates a medical-supply distributorship. Every time a call comes in for a price quotation, for billing information, for service, or even with a complaint, his inside staff has the know-how to turn that prospect or customer into a sale or at least into a potential buyer who thinks more highly of the distributorship.

Effective inbound telemarketing works equally well for retailers, service firms, manufacturers, wholesalers, or *any* kind of business—in virtually any industry. It comes down to this: If you receive *any* kind of calls from the outside, the material in this section can make a measurable difference to you very quickly.

# THE VITAL "FRONT END" OF TAKING CALLS

Most calls that come into a business fall into one of these categories:

- If it's a sales inquiry, you can assume that the prospect is at a comparatively high level of interest. When a potential buyer takes aggressive action by calling a seller, he or she is probably ready to make a commitment.

- When a customer calls to request service or information, the issue may not seem important to the supplier but could be critically important to the caller. Again, the person has taken action, and action is often driven by urgency.

In either an inbound sales call or an inbound service call, the prospect or customer feels much better when call takers try to find out how to deal with the situation. Therefore, the *front end* of the call-handling routine *must* be handled correctly and professionally.

Components that must be included in taking an inbound call are

- Find out exactly *what* is on the caller's mind. Qualifying is thorough and has to be done early in the conversation.

- Find out *who* the caller is and *where* the person can be reached so follow-up can be made.

To illustrate these points, a complete inbound sales inquiry is now shown.

### SCRIPT 9.1: EXAMPLE OF A TYPICAL INBOUND CALL

A furniture rental company spends a big portion of its operating budget on advertising that identifies the company as the best place in town to rent furniture. The cost of each call-in is therefore substantial.

According to tests conducted by the rental firm, a call-in will make a "go" or "no-go" decision within the first 10 to 15 seconds after the phone is answered. If the call taker is disorganized, unsure or rude, a negative judgment about the rental company will immediately follow. But a smooth, professional greeting will practically assure a favorable impression and a solid showroom appointment.

A simple six-step procedure is used by this firm to help guarantee skillful handling of incoming telephone calls.

*Step 1: Call Taker Identifies Self.*

> *Good morning, Harris Furniture Rental Company. This is Dolores Nelson, may I help you?*

*Step 2: Call Taker Gets Reason for Calling.* Write down *exactly* what the person's request is. These notes will help you or someone else in the organization later.

*Step 3: Call Taker Gets Prospect's Name and Phone Number.* Regardless of the nature of the call, identify the person and *write down* the information in case you or someone else has to follow up later. Ask:

> *Do you mind if I write down your name?*

When you have the name, ask:

> *In case I have to get back to you, can I get your phone number?*

*Step 4: Call Taker Defines Needs.* If your contact said "I'm calling about a sofa" in step 2, you still don't know whether the call is to get delivery information, a rental amount, or other facts. In step 4, you politely probe to clarify the situation. For example, start by asking:

> *Do you mind if I ask you a few questions?*

Then ask:

> *Are you a Harris customer?*

| | |
|---|---|
| **Caller:** | *No. I'm calling to find out about renting some pieces.* |
| **Call Taker:** | *How long will you need the furniture?* |
| **Caller:** | *Six months to a year.* |
| **Call Taker:** | *Have you ever visited one of our showrooms?* |
| **Caller:** | *No.* |
| **Call Taker:** | *Are you interested in renting tables, chairs, or other pieces with the sofa?* |
| **Caller:** | *Yes.* |
| **Call Taker:** | *Do you need these items right away?* |
| **Caller:** | *Soon as possible.* |
| **Call Taker:** | [Asks any other questions that will uncover the precise nature of the inquiry. Call taker writes down all prospect answers.] |

*Step 5: Call Taker Stresses Benefits of Calling Particular Company.* Deliver a *brief* statement about why your company is the leading company in the field. Emphasize

- Selection
- Service
- Style

*Step 6: Call Taker Closes for Appointment.* If prices were requested, provide price ranges, then go directly to the close. Your *sole* objective is to get this person into the showroom as quickly as possible. Some of these reasons will accomplish that:

- To see the tremendous variety of sofas available for rent.
- To get exact rental figures.
- To make sure style and colors are perfect.
- To select just the right accessories.

In many cases, a company that receives call-ins will need to transfer calls to various people in the organization. To keep callers happy, this must be done professionally.

---

### FORM 9.1: ROUTING INCOMING CALLS: WHO'S RESPONSIBLE FOR GETTING RESULTS

Inbound calls can reach a point in your company where they represent a vitally important slice of your total sales. To arrive at that stage, a firm has to be certain that the following component is in place:

Regardless of a company's size and staffing, the firm must be sure that a *qualified person* is available to take inbound calls or to follow them up as promptly as possible!

It is true that many thousands of very small firms have only the owner/operator present, and sometimes only an answering machine. But when a receptionist is available, this person should follow a definite procedure to *assure* that each call-in gets to the right person in the firm.

A security equipment company has a full-time receptionist and several departments. The routing for inbound inquiry calls is set up this way: For each type of call-in, the company has identified at least two employees who can handle the call. If the first contact is not available when a call arrives, the second normally will be.

The receptionist qualifies the caller, then finds the correct contact on the routing sheet. This company *rarely* connects a caller to the wrong department or individual.

Here is an example of the sales department routing sheet:

ROUTING SHEET

Contact 1:

Title: _____ Name: _____

Extension number: _____ Office hours: _____

Contact 2:

Title: _____ Name: _____

Extension number: _____ Office hours: _____

Contact 3:

Title: _____   Name: _____

Extension number: _____   Office hours: _____

_____

In the security company, a routing sheet is completed for each department.

In the best call-handling programs, the receptionist's opening words are carefully worked out. We'll look at some greetings now.

## SCRIPT 9.2a: GREETINGS THAT WORK

When an individual gets in touch with a company, the call taker's first words can either start things off nicely or convey an unfavorable impression. By simply giving a little thought to the greeting, a big step can be taken toward a completely successful opening.

Here's a sampling of greetings used in a variety of firms:

- "Thanks for calling George & Sons. May I help you?"
- "Austin Company. This is Barbara Jones. How can I help you?"
- "Good afternoon, Specialized Performance Company."

These simple, straightforward greetings all invite a response from the caller. None of them include gimmicks that might be construed as being in bad taste by some callers.

In smaller firms, where recorders often take calls, a somewhat different approach is needed.

## SCRIPT 9.2b: BUSINESS GREETINGS FOR ANSWERING MACHINES

A fact of life today is the presence of answering machines in day-to-day business. Even some large companies use them. For example, in the corporate headquarters of a major chain of clothing stores, an answering machine can be found in the office of every key staff employee. When the receptionist rings the extension requested by an outside caller, the machine picks up the call if the desired person is not available. On occasion, these machines are used to screen calls: The contact often monitors the greeting to find out who is calling and can cut-in if the call is wanted.

Any businessperson who places a fair number of calls in the course of a workday knows how many machine greetings are in poor taste and succeed in conveying unprofessional images. Some attempt humor. Other greetings try desperately to fill the entire 30-second message time before the "beep." Yet others are designed to try to make a small company sound big; and flop instead.

Here are a few of the most professional machine greetings:

- "Atlantis Company, this is Paul Thompson. Your call is important to me, so please leave your name and number after the signal. I'll get back to you as soon as I can."

- "Carl Biggs's office. I'm away from my desk right now. Please tell me how I can reach you and the best time to try. Thank you."
- "This is Jim Adams at Overland Ltd. Sorry I missed your call. After the beep, tell me how I can help you and leave your name, company identity, and telephone number. Thank you."

The last version does *not* promise a call-back as the other ones do and is therefore useful when a machine picks up a large number of prospecting calls.

Back to the "live" handling of inbound calls. After the greeting, key items of information about the caller must now be discovered and written down by the receptionist *and* the ultimate call taker.

## SCRIPT 9.3a: QUALIFYING THE INBOUND CALLER

Accurately qualifying people who call your company is exceedingly important for these reasons:

- While a majority of people who call in *are* reasonably precise about describing their needs, some others may *not* be altogether clear in explaining what they want.

  In larger firms, a high number of incoming calls are referred to the *wrong* departments or individuals. This wastes huge bites of time and irritates both outside inquirers *and* people in your organization who are needlessly interrupted.

- Unless qualifying is expertly done, chances are that many call-ins will never be handled the way they *should* be. That loses prospects and customers.

- When qualifying *is* accomplished, most callers are favorably impressed. They immediately get the feeling that somebody is making a genuine effort to be of help.

In companies that have the services of a full-time receptionist who transfers calls to various departments, key information will often be obtained at these two levels:

- Certain questions will be asked by the receptionist.

- Other qualifying questions will be asked by whomever the receptionist rings to handle the outside caller.

- In rare cases, a third contact may be required to ask yet other questions.

A major downfall in some companies occurs when either both contacts repeat the same questions or when neither of them bothers to ask! This happens more frequently than you may imagine in firms that don't have an organized system for taking inbound calls.

When an inbound call-handling strategy is worked out, a company defines not only what the key information questions should be, but *who is responsible* for asking them. By assigning that task to specific people, the firm is taking an important step toward constructing a well-coordinated inbound system.

Most managers agree that a receptionist should obtain only the *basic facts;* just enough data to make sure what the call is about and who in the company should handle it. The receptionist should also take information on how to get back in touch with the caller in case of an accidental disconnect.

The second contact then probes more deeply in order to start moving toward a sale or solution to a problem, as the case may be. Here's an example of how a service call might be handled:

| | |
|---|---|
| *Receptionist:* | *Good morning, Hill's Music Company. May I help you?* |
| *Outside Caller:* | *I need assistance in locating a part for your model 3W amplifier.* |

Now the receptionist has to immediately determine the identity of this caller. This helps assure that follow-up can be made in case the caller is disconnected.

| | |
|---|---|
| *Receptionist:* | *I'll be happy to try to help you. Can I get your name and number, please?* |
| *Outside Caller:* | [Provides information, and receptionist records this data.] |

At this point, the receptionist will find out whether the caller is a stocking retailer or a consumer, because different departments would be involved.

| | |
|---|---|
| *Receptionist:* | *May I ask the name of your company?* |
| *Outside Caller:* | *I purchased the unit at Frank Audio.* |
| *Receptionist:* | *Thank you. Please hold and I'll connect you.* |

If desired, the receptionist can elaborate on the call-forwarding statement. A more detailed explanation *would* provide more comfort to outside callers who may be confused about what happens next. This is covered in the next script.

| | |
|---|---|
| *Receptionist:* | [Now has caller on hold and proceeds to ring the service department. Routing sheet indicates that Herb Scott handles consumer parts requests.] |
| | *Mr. Scott, this is Carol, the receptionist. I have a call from an Alice Cone. She bought our 3W amplifier from one of our dealers and needs a part for it.* |
| *Service Rep:* | *Okay, I'll take it.* |

Call is now transferred.

*Alice? My name is Herb. I'm in charge of parts, and I'll try to help you with the part you need for your amplifier.*

Herb Scott now identifies the needed part and asks questions that will definitely establish the validity of the caller's request.

Because the receptionist effectively got key bits of information from the customer, then clearly relayed that data to the right person in the service department, the call went smoothly and professionally.

### SCRIPT 9.3b: EXPLAINING THE CALL-TRANSFER PROCEDURE TO THE OUTSIDE CALLER

In order to make sure that an outside caller understands a firm's procedure and knows who will come on the line next, the receptionist can use a statement like this:

| | |
|---|---|
| *Receptionist:* | *My name is Carol Adams. I'm the receptionist. I'm going to transfer you to Herb Scott, who works with customers on amplifier parts. Will you hold on for just a moment while I try to reach him? I'll make sure he's in his office before I leave you.* |

The receptionist should take the responsibility of assuring that no more than 20 seconds or so elapses with a caller on hold. He or she must never assume that the next contact will promptly pick up the call.

In an environment like the one we're discussing, the receptionist should use some kind of form for recording information on outside callers.

---

### FORM 9.2: DOCUMENTING THE INBOUND CALLER

A well-planned, inbound telemarketing program will work better when call-ins are formally documented. One simple form will help guarantee that proper follow-up takes place. A possible version is presented here.

---

### CONTACT FORM

Company _____ Date _____

Address _____ Source of Inquiry _____

City _____ State _____ Zip _____

Telephone ( ) _____

Contact by Priority

1 _____ 2 _____

3 _____ 4 _____

Comments _____

_____

_____

_____

_____

_____

Qualifications _____

_____

_____

_____

_____

_____

Rating _____

### Follow-Up Action Record

| Date | Talked To | Comments | Send | Appointment | Call Again | Other |
|------|-----------|----------|------|-------------|------------|-------|
|      |           |          |      |             |            |       |
|      |           |          |      |             |            |       |
|      |           |          |      |             |            |       |
|      |           |          |      |             |            |       |
|      |           |          |      |             |            |       |

A form for tracking inbound calls serves another valuable purpose, covered now.

### SCRIPT 9.4: AVOIDING THE "IT'S-FOR-YOU" SYNDROME

Many incoming calls are transferred to a second person, and that ultimate call taker hears this from the receptionist: "It's for you on line three."

Our second person has no choice but to pick up line three and start probing for basic information that was probably already given to the receptionist.

To avoid irritating call-ins, the receptionist should *fully brief* the ultimate call taker before connecting the customer or prospect. At the very least, the following data from the receptionist's contact form must be relayed to the person who will take the call:

*Receptionist:* [Rings ultimate call taker, then provides these points] *Jim, this is Pat at the main switchboard.*

*I have a call waiting on line three from a Betty Sampson. She wants information on the 600 series. Can you take care of it now?*

This brief statement covers all of the information needed to enable the call taker to get on the line and deal intelligently with the outside caller. *Most* important, the caller can't help being impressed by the firm's internal organization.

Next, we'll cover some of the special tactics used to handle inbound sales inquiries.

## TURNING INBOUND INQUIRY CALLS INTO SALES

A group of auto dealerships recently conducted extensive research on the call-handling effectiveness of their own members. The results are capsulized here:

- Receptionists often seemed annoyed that somebody would actually call and ask for information. Some of them sounded as though they were deeply involved in doing something and were rudely interrupted by the call.

- Salespeople, who in this instance were the ultimate contacts, were mostly knowledgeable and genuinely likable; but many of them obviously did not feel that a structured call-handling routine was needed. The result was an often rambling and disjointed speech to the prospect and frequent failure to systematically explore prospect needs.

- Finally, poor follow-up. Less than half of the salespeople called back on a timely basis. Many prospects would certainly have purchased elsewhere.

Salespeople who handled themselves particularly well were effective because they seemed to know exactly where they were going during the entire course of the conversation. These people were definitely *in control* of the situation.

In closely analyzing the call-handling procedures used by the better salespeople, it became apparent that three items were consistently strong in this group: the introduction, the delivery of a background story, and the needs assessment (qualifying) aspects of the inbound presentation.

The introduction and background story, as well as other key areas, are covered now.

### SCRIPT 9.5a: SPECIAL MEASURES TO GET A
### RELUCTANT CALLER'S PHONE NUMBER

If you have ever called an auto dealership to inquire about buying a vehicle, you may have discovered that most of them will go to great lengths to get your name and telephone number. A favored strategy when you call and announce your interest in a new car is for the salesperson to *immediately* say, "I'm away from my desk. Can I call you right back?" or "I'm just finishing with a customer. Give me your name and number and I'll get right back to you."

In some aggressive dealerships it is all but impossible to call and, during the course of *that* call, get the facts you seek. A call-back from the salesperson is sometimes strict policy. According to insiders, that is the only way the dealer can make sure the caller is a bona fide prospect and not a competitor. Also, it's the best way for the dealer to guarantee that the person is providing a *correct* phone number.

### SCRIPT 9.5b: HANDLING "ANONYMOUS" CALLERS

An auto shopper will usually provide a telephone number in order to get a call-back from the dealership salesperson but will sometimes refuse to supply a name. A certain percentage of inquirers in *any* industry prefer to remain unidentified.

A seller's choice is to go ahead with a presentation to this anonymous shopper or refuse to deal with the person—which is equal to cutting off your nose to spite your face, as some shy inquirers *do* eventually decide to open up, and many will make the purchase.

It makes sense to at least *try* to get a name. If that fails, proceed *without* the individual's identity. The try sounds like this at one dealership:

| | |
|---|---|
| *Salesperson:* | [After calling back a recent inquiry and introducing self.] *I understand your reluctance to tell me who you are since, unfortunately, we have a lot of high-pressure people working in this business.* |
| | *I do want to assure you though that we hold our customers in the highest respect. Nobody will ever call you if that's your wish.* |
| | *Of course, whether you decide to tell me your name or not is strictly up to you. In either case, we'll do our very best to help you find the car you're looking for.* |

This approach softens about half of the anonymous callers.

Many sellers see the introduction to an inquirer as rather mundane. They hurry through the business of explaining who they are, anxious to start selling. Here's a much better way.

### SCRIPT 9.6a: INTRODUCING YOURSELF EFFECTIVELY

An inquirer has to feel welcome before any real progress can be made by the call taker. The introduction is simply the best possible moment to make the caller feel welcome. Keys to good introductions are

- To be thorough. Convey *all* of the information the caller needs to completely identify the seller.
- To be deliberate. Slow down the tempo of this critical introduction. Rapid speech can say, "I'm in a hurry. You called at a lousy time, so tell me what

you need and make it fast." This hardly creates a hospitable selling climate, but it happens frequently.

Salespeople at the auto dealership handle introductions this way:

> **Salesperson:** *Mrs. Baker? My name is Randy Tuck. I work with truck customers here at the dealership. I'll do what I can to be of assistance to you.*

Brief and simple, but much different than the all too typical "Randy here. May I help you?" The atmosphere created by the detailed introduction is infinitely more powerful.

In dealerships that operate in communities where competition is especially stiff, a brief statement about the firm's background can help tremendously.

## SCRIPT 9.6b: DELIVERING A BRIEF, BELIEVABLE BACKGROUND STORY

There is a definite time to use a background story. The auto dealership we're looking at uses the following method:

- If a customer has *already decided* on the make of car carried by this dealer, there are strong reasons to sell the capabilities of the dealer. This will help win the battle against nearby dealers that also sell the desired make.
- When the dealer is still considering a variety of other makes, the salesperson's *first* priority is to sell the type of vehicle in the showroom. Dealer attributes can wait until later—when the shopper is more focused.

While a number of salespeople recognize the importance of telling inquirers a convincing story about the abilities of their company, far too many of them make a mess of it. The common failure is repeating this message over and over again: "We're the best . . . we sell the most . . . our prices are the lowest . . ."

To the inquirer, that speech is stale and meaningless. It may do more harm than good. But, a brief background story like this *does* work:

> **Salesperson:** [Introduces self and qualifies caller. Determines that inquirer is interested in the specific make of vehicle offered by the dealer. Then proceeds to background story] *Are you familiar with Klein Motors?*
>
> **Caller:** *Not really. I found you listed in the yellow pages.*
>
> **Salesperson:** *If you have a moment, I'll briefly fill you in.*
>
> *We've been a dealership since 1949. Our first concern has always been service. That's why people come back time after time for their car and truck needs.*

*Another interesting fact about us is our size. We're not the biggest dealership in town and have no interest in growing so big that we can't give individual attention to our customers.*

*Our prices are competitive, and I'm sure you'd find dealing with us a lot different than what you've encountered in the past at other dealerships.*

There is really no mention of "We're the best" and "We'll knock the socks off of our competitors." The above statement is credible and dignified.

A smooth transition to the close is next.

### SCRIPT 9.6c: SETTING A QUICK APPOINTMENT

Perhaps the strongest part of most inbound call routines is the close. Sellers today don't seem to be timid about asking for action. The *best* closes provide one or more reasons to visit the dealership.

| *Salesperson:* | [Goes to this close immediately after completing the background statement.] *I can show you four or five trucks that fit the description you gave me. We can check the features and options available, then have you test drive any ones you like.* |
| --- | --- |
| | *Our appraiser will be here this evening and tomorrow morning. Let's take a look at your old truck and see what we can do for you.* |
| | *Which time is most convenient for you, 6:00 P.M. today or 10:00 A.M. tomorrow?* |

Reasons for the appointment are

- To check available features and options.
- To test drive a truck.
- To get a price based on the appraised value of the prospect's present vehicle.

When salespeople close on a statement such as "Come in and we'll see if we can make a deal," it would understandably frighten many shoppers.

We'll now look at the handling of special situations that arise in handling inbound calls.

## SPECIAL STRATEGIES FOR INBOUND 800 LINES

Along with the tremendous popularity of inbound 800 service, a multitude of problems have arisen for some of the companies using the toll-free response system. In high-volume call operations, floods of responses arrive in short bursts corresponding with

TV commercials that urge consumers to call. Burst periods demand speedy but precise handling by call takers.

Another common problem is similar to one facing a disk-drive manufacturer. The firm's ads in various publications invite inquiries via an 800 number prominently displayed in the ads. In addition to receiving leads via the toll-free lines, this company also gets scores of technical questions and queries from nonbuying hobbyists, which seriously interferes with the efficient processing of inquiries from potential buyers.

In some extremely high-volume incoming-call environments, the objective is to simply capture the name and number of the caller so that thorough and qualified follow-up can be made when time permits. In other inbound programs, an order can be consummated during the initial call. One example is a magazine subscription paid for by credit card. Both of these situations require preplanned tactics that keep the system moving. Some of the most commonly used approaches are covered in the following script examples.

### SCRIPT 9.7a: OPERATING UNDER HECTIC CONDITIONS: WHAT TO TELL THE CALLER

In a typical 800 burst response mode—with calls arriving on top of each other—some things must be done differently to keep the program from caving in:

- The *introduction* must be drastically shortened. This is entirely feasible since the caller *knows* what company he or she is calling. Also, "Good morning" isn't necessary because many calls originate in other time zones.

- There is *no* need for the operator to provide a full name, since he or she will probably not be involved in the ongoing sale process.

- "Warm-up" small talk must be eliminated by the call taker and that of the outside caller kept to an absolute minimum. An operator gets right to the point, then goes on to the next call in line.

A company that sells music collections on tape and records through TV spots uses this approach:

| | |
|---|---|
| *Call Taker:* | *Music, Anne speaking. May I help you?* |
| *Caller:* | [States request.] |
| *Call Taker:* | *Thank you. Please give me your full name and mailing address.* |
| *Caller:* | [Provides information and correct spelling if required by the call taker.] |
| *Call Taker:* | *I'll need the name of the credit card you want to use, and the credit card number and expiration date.* |
| *Caller:* | [Provides.] |
| *Call Taker:* | *Thank you. Please allow three to four weeks for delivery.* |

When the purchase is more complex and requires a follow-up contact, the call taker's task is a bit different, as in this example:

## SCRIPT 9.7b: QUICK QUALIFYING ON
## HIGH-TRAFFIC INBOUND LINES

Direct mail pieces, media ads, and other types of print promotion carry 800 response numbers as often as not. The free call is provided to give a potential buyer an easy way to request information on the offered product or service.

A typical chain of events is

- An ad will trigger an information request from a potential buyer. The call taker is responsible for obtaining a name, phone number, and mailing address. Ideally, the operator will also do very fast, basic qualifying. After basic qualifying, the call taker *may* suggest that telephone follow-up will be forthcoming.

    While virtually *all* call-ins will receive a requested information packet, only the ones that look like genuine buyers will warrant later follow-up by phone.

- A sales rep calls the prospect after the information packet has been received by the prospect.

Needless to say, since inbound lines may be very busy, the call taker *must* make the qualifying both fast and right to the point. Remember, the operator will rarely be trained in the subtleties of evaluating a prospect's buying potential, so the questions will be more blunt than usual.

The disk-drive maker does it this way:

| | |
|---|---|
| *Call Taker:* | *Hartt Products Company, this is Carl. How may I help you?* |
| *Caller:* | [Requests information as promised in the ad.] |
| *Call Taker:* | [Obtains name of caller and company, telephone number, and complete mailing address, then asks these qualifying questions] *How many drives do you need now?* |

If the number needed is less than five, the caller is referred to a stocking dealer. Also, the word *now* usually flushes out the purchase timeframe.

*What types of computers will the drives be used with?*

Computer type reveals whether or not the drives produced by the firm are right for the caller.

The following step is optional, used when a prospect appears to be qualified:

| | |
|---|---|
| *Call Taker:* | *We'll get an information packet out to you this afternoon. I'll make sure that you are personally contacted by our representative in your area. We appreciate your interest in our products.* |

Now the rep will know which leads warrant follow-up and which should be scheduled first.

When outside callers request information on volume discounts or other price issues, the call taker uses this script:

### SCRIPT 9.7c: DEALING WITH PRICE REQUESTS

Most outside callers understand that the average 800 call taker probably isn't authorized to go into details such as specs or price, but some operators are still asked questions of that nature.

When a price question is asked, an ill-considered response is something like "I'm not allowed to quote prices, so you'll have to ask our salesperson when he calls you" or "I'm just too busy to quote prices now. We'll provide prices when we call you later."

A much better response is "Exact prices would depend on various factors we don't know yet, for example, how many drives you need, the capacity of the units you need, and other variables. I'll let our representative know you want that information, and we'll give it top priority."

Occasionally, an angry individual will use an 800 line to register one or more complaints. To some, calling on a free line is one small way to exact some measure of revenge. Here's an approach for coping with that dilemma.

### SCRIPT 9.7d: NEUTRALIZING AN IRATE CALLER

In a busy inbound-call operation, the last thing needed is an angry caller who insists on dominating a line while likely buyers languish on hold or suffer through repeated busy signals. A call taker *must* have the tools to do two things:

- Free the line immediately.
- Preserve the goodwill of the irate caller, who may very well have legitimate and urgent grievances.

A company may have a separate phone number that can be given to the upset caller. That would surely help in most instances. But we'll assume that the call taker has no other option but to deal with the problem without the benefit of nearby help.

| | |
|---|---|
| *Caller:* | [States problem and demands immediate attention.] |
| *Call Taker:* | *Please give me your name and telephone number.* |
| *Caller:* | [Provides.] |
| *Call Taker:* | *I have written down your name and phone number as well as the nature of your problem. I want you to know that I'm deeply concerned about this. We definitely do* not *want you to be unhappy in any way.* |
| | *I promise you we'll look into this on a priority basis. You have my word that the right person will call you back within 24 hours.* |

By far, the biggest mistake that can be made by a call taker in this position is to begin a response with some excuse like "I have nothing to do with the department that handles problems" or "Nobody's around right now who can help you." This is poor technique. Chances are, such a statement would send an already angry caller into an absolute rage.

Instead, the call taker disarms most irate callers by taking some responsibility. By saying "I'm deeply concerned," many touchy situations can be cooled off. Be sure, however, that a follow-up is made within the promised timeframe.

## REFINING INBOUND SCRIPTS

When you create a strategy for handling inbound calls, check that strategy against each item in the Form 9.3 checklist. This will give you a call routine that is complete in every detail. Use the Form 9.4 worksheet to work out dialogue for each inbound call.

### FORM 9.3:   INBOUND-CALL CHECKLIST

1. Does your receptionist have a way to determine the caller's specific area of interest?

   ____ Yes    ____ No

2. Does receptionist routinely obtain

   |  | Yes | No |
   |---|---|---|
   | • Caller's Name | ____ | ____ |
   | • Title | ____ | ____ |
   | • Company Name | ____ | ____ |
   | • Address | ____ | ____ |
   | • City, State, Zip | ____ | ____ |
   | • Phone Number | ____ | ____ |

3. Does receptionist create a record of every individual inbound inquiry?

   ____ Yes    ____ No

4. Does receptionist maintain an inbound-call log that provides a daily tally of incoming calls?

   ____ Yes    ____ No

5. Is receptionist fully briefed on current advertising and promotions?

   ____ Yes    ____ No

6. Is receptionist informed about *everyone* in the company who is qualified to handle inbound inquiries?

   ____ Yes    ____ No

7. Does your present telephone equipment permit effective handling of inbound inquiries at high volume?

____ Yes    ____ No

8. Are you entirely satisfied that inbound call takers are cordial, patient, and warm—even under peak traffic conditions?

____ Yes    ____ No

9. Are you sure that inquiry calls will not be kept on hold for excessively long periods when transferred to the next contact?

____ Yes    ____ No

10. Have you planned the routing of inbound inquiries in a way that will bring your most effective people into the call?

____ Yes    ____ No

11. Will printed information, promised in promotions, be sent to every inquirer, regardless of the outcome of a call?

____ Yes    ____ No

12. Are you satisfied that promised information can be mailed promptly (within 24 hours)?

____ Yes    ____ No

13. Are brochures, cover letters, and other mailed materials up to the best professional standards?

____ Yes    ____ No

14. Do you determine the *source* of inbound inquiries to find out which promotions are producing the best results?

____ Yes    ____ No

15. Do you have a system for following up on call-ins who do not initially agree to buy or meet with a sales representative?

____ Yes    ____ No

16. Have you set up an office schedule that assures telephone coverage during all business hours?

____ Yes    ____ No

17. Have you listed the best qualification questions to be used on inbound inquiries?

____ Yes    ____ No

18. Have you determined how those qualification questions will be divided between the receptionist and the next contact?

____ Yes    ____ No

19. Have you established an outline for a company capabilities (background) statement?

____ Yes    ____ No

20. If so, will the completed statement be brief and to the point, yet informative?

____ Yes   ____ No

---

When you can answer yes to every item on the checklist, you are ready to build language guidelines for the inbound inquiry. These refinements will *assure* outstanding results in handling a wide variety of call-ins.

---

### FORM 9.4:   INBOUND DIALOGUE WORKSHEET

Make as many copies of the worksheet as you need. You'll want one for each type of inbound call and a few extras for trying alternative approaches.

The following checklist will help you identify the call types that need strategies in your company:

- *Request for information (Inbound Inquiry).* In this case, we are dealing with a shopper who is just entering the *shopping* stage.

- *New order by telephone.* This call comes in when a company is set up to *consummate* a sale by telephone. This is a *new* customer who has an order ready and has never done business with you before.

- *Customer reorder.* An *existing* customer calls to restock inventory, extend or enlarge service.

- *Request for service.* An existing customer asks for support in using your product or service.

- *Request for billing information.* An existing customer asks for clarification on charges, terms, or some other payment aspect. If the call is a *dispute* on charges, it should be classified as a complaint.

- *Delivery information.* One more inbound contact from an existing customer. It is almost identical to the call for billing information, but may be routed differently.

- *Complaint call.* This call is from a new *or* old customer. Routing can vary from one type of complaint to another.

WORKSHEET

Type of inbound call: _____

Describe the desired outcome of this call: _____

_____

_____

_____

_____

Routing:

Contact 1:

Title: _____ Name: _____

Extension number: _____ Office hours: _____

Contact 2:

Title: _____ Name: _____

Extension number: _____ Office hours: _____

Contact 3:

Title: _____ Name: _____

Extension number: _____ Office hours: _____

Key information to be *obtained* from the outside caller:

- _____ Contact No. ____
- _____ Contact No. ____
- _____ Contact No. ____
- _____ Contact No. ____
- _____ Contact No. ____
- _____ Contact No. ____

Key information to be *given* to the outside caller:

- _____ Contact No. ____
- _____ Contact No. ____
- _____ Contact No. ____
- _____ Contact No. ____
- _____ Contact No. ____
- _____ Contact No. ____

Notes: _____

_____

_____

_____

Introduction (Greeting): _____

_____

_____

_____

Reason for call: _____

_____

_____

_____

Obtain caller identity: _____

_____

_____

_____

Explain call-transfer procedure: _____

_____

_____

_____

_____

Capabilities statement (Background): _____

_____

_____

_____

_____

_____

_____

Refer call or close: _____

_____

_____

_____

_____

_____

Notes: _____

_____

_____

_____

_____

_____

# Chapter 10

# TOTAL STRATEGIES FOR CULTIVATING MAJOR SALES RELATIONSHIPS

When a telemarketing program is powered by smart marketing, results can exceed expectations by a surprisingly wide margin. The difference between an ordinary calling program and a smart one is illustrated by the following comparison:

- One industrial laundry prospects almost every company in town by telephone. The prevailing philosophy of management is this: "There are so many potential buyers, we use a shotgun blast to bring in a flow of fresh customers. Whether we follow up the nonbuyers or not is of secondary importance as long as the new accounts keep coming."
- Management in a competing laundry sees it this way: "We decide what kind of customer we want, then we set about *finding* the prospects that fit our description. So instead of trying to sell 500 firms of all types and sizes, we lock in on the 160 or so that seem to be perfect for the way we're geared up to operate. Then we pursue that smaller group until we have their business."

A targeting strategy such as the one used by the latter firm yields two advantages: First, the selective company eventually ends up with a group of customers that spend more because they are larger firms. Also, by virtue of the selection procedure, the chosen firms use a larger number of the laundry's products and services.

Second, the targeting process results in lower sales costs since the more selective laundry isn't continually firing huge broadsides at an undefined market, as the other company does.

Targeting and market cultivation is basically a two-step process. Initially, research is done in order to identify the kind of market that makes sense to the seller. Then, once a population of prospects has been finalized, the seller sets up a cultivation program designed to get the sale, even if it takes a year or more.

This chapter gives you a fact-finding program and both short-term and long-term cultivation plans.

## CONDUCTING A MARKET SURVEY

To zero in on the most promising new markets for their telemarketing program, the industrial laundry mentioned earlier uses a three-step process:

- *Step 1* is to select a new market that *appears* to have potential. The next two steps are needed to verify the validity of that choice.
- *Step 2* is to answer some key questions about the chosen market. These questions are posed in Form 10.1, the Research Guide for New Market.
- *Step 3* is to survey a sampling of companies in the selected market. Form 10.2, Sample Questionnaire, is one example of a survey. This approach will be needed to accurately answer some of the questions in the research guide.

When the research guide is completed, a company will know how the pros of the new market balance the cons, whether there is a sufficient number of good prospects in the market, and what the dollar sales potential is for each prospect. The questionnaire will reveal additional information of critical importance to a seller.

After going through this fact-finding process, a clear decision can be made about the feasibility of the selected market.

To find out exactly what the pros and cons of a new market are, a survey works hand in hand with the research guide. This is how a highly effective survey can be accomplished:

---

### FORM 10.1: RESEARCH GUIDE FOR NEW MARKET

Describe the market you have targeted for telemarketing _____

_____

_____

_____

Why did you select this market? _____

_____

_____

_____

What products or services will be offered to this new market? _____

_____

_____

_____

What are the leading pros and cons of the market you have selected?

Pro: _____

_____

Con: _____

_____

If con, how will you deal with the problem? _____

_____

Pro: _____

_____

Con: _____

_____

If con, how will you deal with the problem? _____

_____

Pro: _____

_____

Con: _____

_____

If con, how will you deal with the problem? _____

| About how many prospects in the new market are in your effective marketing area? | | |
|---|---|---|
| | Estimated Gross Sales Per Account Per Year | Total Estimated Gross Per Year |
| Estimate the annual gross sales potential for each prospect and for the entire market. | $_____ | $_____ |
| Has a questionnaire been designed for a survey? | Yes_____ | No_____ |

Who in your company will conduct the survey? _____

Comments _____

_____

_____

_____

SCRIPT 10.1a: A BRIEF BUT COMPREHENSIVE SURVEY

Good surveys are completely nonthreatening to the business owners and managers who are expected to answer questions. The call from a surveyor should include these characteristics:

- Early on, a caller should make it clear that the purpose of the contact is *not* to sell anything.

- It should be explained to call recipients that their answers will remain confidential. Opinions will *not* be attributed to any specific individuals and will be stated only as numerical statistics.

- Questionnaires *must* be kept brief.

- Good answers can come from middle-level managers in a surveyed firm. It doesn't require the president's input.

Whether or not the surveying firm is identified by the caller is a matter of choice. If *not* identified, there is always some risk in looking like a sneaky competitor fishing for data. In that case, the door will sometimes close abruptly. Since a surveying firm is probably *not* well known in a new market, the company name won't mean anything to call recipients anyway.

This is the script used by the industrial laundry to survey medium-sized firms in new markets:

*Surveyor:*          [Gets the general manager on the line, introduces self, then says] *McNeil & Sons is interested in finding out how manufacturers control dust in their plants.*

*We'd really appreciate your answers to a few brief questions. We'll make the survey available to you at no charge when it's completed—and I think you'll find it interesting and useful.*

Surveyor proceeds to questionnaire.

---

**FORM 10.2:  SAMPLE QUESTIONNAIRE**

Name of company: _____ Date: _____

Address: _____

City: _____ State: _____ Zip: _____

Telephone: (___) _____ Ext.: _____

Contact name: _____ Title: _____

Subject of survey: _____

Name of caller: _____

    1. Does your company use:

        ____ Treated dust-mops and handles?

        ____ Cotton-pile mats?

        ____ Nylon mats?

_____ Wet-mops?

_____ Other: _____

2. Do you have special requirements for controlling dust in your work facility?

_____ Yes     _____ No     _____ Unknown

3. If special requirements do exist, what are they?

_____

_____

_____

_____

4. Who in your company is responsible for buying dust-control products and services?

Name: _____ Title: _____

5. Can you estimate how much money your company spends per year on these products?  $ _____

6. Do you currently use a service to assist you with the dust-control problem?

_____ Yes     _____ No     _____ Unknown

7. If an outside service is used, are you satisfied with the results?

_____ Yes     _____ No     _____ Unknown

8. Would your key executives be interested in attending a free two-hour seminar on dust control?

_____ Yes     _____ No     _____ Unknown

9. Any other observations about dust control? _____

_____

_____

_____

_____

_____

_____

10. Notes: _____

_____

_____

_____

At the completion of the survey, caller says:

> *I appreciate the time you provided. I'll see to it that a survey recap is mailed to your attention as soon as the study is concluded.*

In addition to a formal survey of the type we just looked at, the industrial laundry also uses incidental intelligence-gathering to collect valuable market data.

### SCRIPT 10.1b: GATHERING SMALLER PARCELS OF MARKET DATA

Telemarketers are exposed to more information about the market than anybody else in a company. Even outside sales reps don't talk to as many people as the caller does. Because the long-range success of any company depends largely on accurately reading market trends, a callers' ability to pick up information can be most important.

Intelligence-gathering can be done on a chance basis—from *general* observations jotted down by the telemarketer during routine sales contacts. Or it can be preplanned, whereby the telemarketer asks prospects certain definite questions during presentations.

A preplanned approach has the advantage of giving a company information on the precise areas it feels are vital. If management wants market data on pricing trends, a little extra probing can be done on how prospects feel about prices and what they think about the direction of future pricing policies.

The thing to avoid in gathering intelligence is clogging up the sales presentation with lots of questions. True, the answers may reveal good data, but heavy questioning might detract from the objective of getting new business. *Selling must remain the highest priority.*

To keep intelligence-gathering from interfering with effective telephone selling, try to keep fact-finding questions down to two or three. If the answers don't come up during the normal course of conversation with a prospect, save your small group of questions for the end of the call—after the presentation is completed.

Some intelligence-gathering questions that may be useful are

- "How do you feel Franklin Company's prices compare to ours?"
- "In your opinion, how does the 900 sprayer do against ours in performance?"
- "On a scale of one to ten, where would you rate our service and support?"
- "Are Delano & Sons' reps good at keeping in touch with you? Are they technically well versed?"
- "Is MarketMasters an easy firm to do business with?"
- "If I may ask, how has your relationship with Durham Company worked out?"
- "What do you think the Wiley people will be doing with their line next summer?"
- "If you could have anything you asked for in a low-end sprayer, what features would it include?"
- "What do you like the most about dealing with us? And what do you like least?"

When about 50 prospects and customers have responded to some of these questions, management can have reasonable faith in the answers and will be better poised to devise sales and marketing strategy based on the responses.

A few hours spent in determining the viability of a new market *will* pay. It can help save a major loss of time and cash by uncovering hidden pitfalls inherent in certain markets, and on the positive side, it can get you started in promising new directions.

When a new market *is* decided on, the selling company sets up a business cultivation plan that fits the situation. We'll look at the possibilities now.

## THE SHORT-TERM CULTIVATION PROCESS

When surveys are complete, a company can much more easily pinpoint the best prospects in the selected market. Stronger prospects match up to a list of standards considered important by the selling company. Standards can be

- Number of people employed by the prospect firm. This is a pretty good measure of size and is often an easier number to get than annual sales volume.

- Geographical location of the prospect.

- Nature of the prospect's business *within* the selected market. For example, while the insurance industry may be the target market, the best prospects might be firms that specialize in fire insurance.

Other criteria established by the seller can be included.

Now that an especially attractive group of prospects is listed, the seller designs a cultivation process, otherwise known as a sales cycle, similar to the one illustrated in Table 10.1. This plan shows:

- How much total time will be given to selling a prospect. Will it be thirty days? Three years? Or some other time span?

  Usually, the length of time a company is willing to devote to cultivation is tied directly to the size of the sale. A $500 product or service may be worth three months of concerted effort. But a $150,000 sale may justify two years or more.

- Within the cycle, *what kind* of action will the seller take to get the order? Actions are generally a mix of telemarketing, direct mail, and personal visits.

- Who in the selling company will be responsible for making the scheduled contacts?

A midwestern printing company successfully uses the plan in Table 10.1 for an average $300 initial order.

---

### TABLE 10.1   THE SHORT-TERM CULTIVATION PROCESS

*Initial Contact: LETTER.*

*Objectives:* To familiarize prospect with your company and to create expectation for initial telephone prospecting call.

*Second Contact: TELEPHONE CALL.*

*Timing:* Two to four days after receipt of letter.

*Objectives:* To determine

- Prospect qualifications such as

    Buying authority

    Deadline requirements

- Jobs in progress that require quotes.
- Describe your company's capabilities.
- Set up appointment call from field sales rep.

*Third Contact: FIELD APPOINTMENT.*

*Timing:* Two to four days after initial telephone contact.

*Objective:* To specifically identify printing needs and set up quotes on those projects or to close if a job is ready and a quote can be obtained during the visit.

*Fourth Contact: VISIT OR CALL WITH QUOTE/CLOSE.*

*Timing:* Within four days after field appointment.

*Objective:* To convey quote and get commitment on the project or to set up a follow-up if close can't be achieved at time of this appointment.

*FOLLOW-UP CONTACTS.*

*Timing:* Every five days in event of a specific job or every thirty days if no specific job.

*Objective:* To close.

---

The printing company can switch prospects from this very short cycle into the long-term cultivation process covered later in this chapter. A potential customer may be slow to order but look extremely promising for some future date. That situation certainly warrants extra patience.

A simple letter is the first contact used by the printer.

### LETTER 10.1:   SIMPLE PROSPECTING LETTER

Using a letter as the initial contact has the advantage of establishing the seller's identity. In addition, it is a low-cost way to start the cultivation process. In this example, the printer has selected the financial community as the market of choice. Successful prior experience in doing work for banks helped that decision along.

Dear Financial Professional:

If you don't get around to calling us, I'll be in touch soon to introduce you to our printing and graphics services.

Leading financial institutions in the Farleysville area look to Callahan Printing when top priorities are

- Quality and precision
- Service
- Fast turnaround time
- Cost-effectiveness

We understand the requirements of financial companies. Equally important, Callahan offers firms like yours a complete range of capabilities that provide a one-stop source for printing and graphics, for example, computerized typesetting, one- to four-color printing, design, binding services, thermography, embossing, and much more.

Every valuable client project is done in our efficient plant. There is simply no other way to assure the kind of results you are counting on.

When we talk, I'll answer any questions you may have, and if you have a printing need coming up for a quote, we can also discuss that.

Looking forward to speaking with you personally.

Sincerely,

Jill I. Baxter

As you can see in the cultivation process, that letter is followed by a telephone call no later than *four days* after the letter is received by the prospect. Please notice that the caller does *not* refer to the letter! This company discovered that prospects who didn't see the letter sometimes used that as a reason to procrastinate.

Here's the first follow-up phone call.

## SCRIPT 10.2: FOLLOWING UP THE MAILER WITH THE INITIAL CALL

*Time* of follow-up is of critical importance. When too much time elapses between receipt of the letter and this initial call, the impact of a double contact may be lost. To make sure of a closely spaced one-two punch, letters are sent by first class mail instead of bulk rate. This helps ensure predictable delivery.

Also worthy of mention is this: The printer mails *only* 100 letters per week. This limited number enables the telemarketer to remain on top of the follow-up workload.

Here's the initial call script:

*Step 1: Locate Contact.* If decision maker's name is not available, ask for *buyer of printing services.*

*Step 2: Introduction and Key-Point Statement.* When identity of buyer is verified, say:

> **Telemarketer:**  *I'm Jill Baxter of Callahan Printing in Farleysville. We're full-service, quality printers specializing in the needs of financial companies like yours. If you have just a moment, I can briefly explain how we might fit in as a future resource for you.*

If no objection, continue to qualifying step.

*Step 3: Qualify.* Establish authority and scope of buyer.

> *Do you personally buy all printing and stationery?*

If not, concentrate *only* on areas of this person's responsibility. Note the areas *not* covered by your contact and follow up with the right person later.

Establish quality:

> *Do you look for better-than-average quality from your suppliers?*

This question is designed to identify a client that is willing to pay premium prices for top work.

Establish timing:

> *Are deadlines usually tight?*

Explain to prospect that rapid turnaround is possible because of Callahan's orientation to service, and to the training of company employees.

Probe for immediate need:

> *Do you have any printing or graphics needs coming up that you'd like us to quote on?*

If yes, note details. If no, go to next step.

*Step 4: Presentation.*

> *Sounds like we can deliver what you need.*
>
> *Callahan Printing has been operating since 1957. Our target is to provide a complete array of services for firms like yours. The two main areas we cover are printing and design, which includes work up to fourcolor, design, typesetting, embossing, binding, and more; and fax services and in-house communications. Clients like First National Bank use us for all of their communications needs.*

*Step 5: Clear Call from Sales Rep.*

> *[Close A] You'd probably like to see samples of what we do for other financial companies.*
>
> *Why don't I have one of our account executives call you for an appointment. Is it best to reach you in the morning or afternoon? What day is most convenient?*
>
> *Would you please mark this down? I'm Jill Baxter. My number is 942–2900 in case you need to reach me.*

If prospect does *not* agree to a call from the sales rep, go to:

> [Close B] *I can send you a brochure that covers the full range of our services. Do you mind if I check with you in a few weeks to see if we can help you?*

Now the path is established for a call from an outside sales rep.

### SCRIPT 10.3: APPOINTMENT CALL FROM THE SALES REP

Standard procedure at Callahan Printing Company is to have three outside salespeople come into the office to do their own follow-up telephone work several mornings each week. The telemarketer tries to schedule most prospecting during those hours. This often results in one of the reps being put on the line with a good prospect *immediately.* No call-back is needed.

In most other instances, the rep's call-back is made later the same day. In point of fact, the elapsed time between initial call and follow-up is almost never as much as three or four days later. Due to this efficiency, nearly *all* prospects found by the caller are successfully converted to solid appointments.

When follow-up is almost instantaneous, a prospect recalls the initial contact in detail and the rep's task is eased substantially.

Typically, the next presentation is used by the rep to set a field appointment after a prospect has been uncovered by the telemarketer:

> *Sales Rep:*      *Mrs. Anderson? I'm Phil Holmes. Jill briefed me about the printing project you have underway, and it looks like we'd be qualified to help you.*

The rep now qualifies more extensively than the telemarketer did during the initial call:

> *How many printing jobs do you have coming up?*
>
> *At what stage of completion?*
>
> *Have you received bids from other printers yet?*

Other questions that reveal the scope and nature of the project should be included here.

> *Telemarketer:*      *Based on the size of your job and on your target completion date I'd recommend we get together right away.*
>
> *As Jill probably told you, we do work for other financial institutions, and we might be able to bring you some production experience that will save steps.*
>
> *I'll need about 30 minutes with you to review the project and get other information we need to put a quote together.*
>
> *Are you free tomorrow morning at 9:00 A.M., or would 3:00 P.M. be more convenient?*

About 75 percent of all initial field visits result in requests for quotes. The quote is formulated within one day of the appointment and, on average, is conveyed to the prospect about two days after the meeting. Quotes are *always* delivered face-to-face with the prospect.

## SCRIPT 10.4: SETTING UP A SECOND APPOINTMENT TO DELIVER THE QUOTE

*Sales Rep:*                         [Gets in touch with contact and reintroduces self. Then says] *I went over your job specs with our production manager and have some numbers I think you'll find interesting. Do you have any other bids yet for comparison?*

If no, rep may set a later appointment so other bids come in. The availability of comparative quotes are usually advantageous to the reps. Whether yes or no, rep continues:

*To cover this as carefully as we should, I'll need about 20 minutes of your time.* [Rep proceeds to set appointment.]

*Note:* When a prospect presses the rep for a telephone quote, the response is

*Prices are tied to various paper qualities and the design characteristics of the brochure. I can show you those differences when we get together, and the prices will make a lot more sense than they would if I quoted them now.*

If a close is not obtained at the time the quote is delivered and it appears that some time may elapse before a decision will be made, a letter goes out right after that second field appointment.

## LETTER 10.2: POSTQUOTE FOLLOW-UP

Dear Mrs. Anderson:

I would like to express my gratitude for the time you took to discuss our bid for printing your new brochure.

It was a pleasure to review the benefits that Callahan Printing would provide for you and your organization.

Enclosed is written confirmation of our quotation. Per our agreement, I'll be in touch with you on Tuesday to find out what our next step is. Again, we look forward to working with you on this challenging project.

Sincerely,

Phil Holmes

When a close *does* result, the following brief letter is sent as soon as possible after the order is finalized:

*LETTER 10.3:   NOTE TO NEW CUSTOMER*

This brief note is a gracious touch that *is* appreciated by new customers. It's a simple but important component in any relationship-building program:

Dear Mrs. Anderson:

We are extremely pleased that you have chosen Callahan's services.

As with all of our customers, your printing orders are already receiving our utmost attention to detail. Your complete satisfaction is our top priority—and we will assure that you have it every step of the way.

Once again, we are very glad to add you to our family of valued clients. We look forward to a long and mutually beneficial relationship.

Sincerely,

Phil Holmes

All *strong* prospects that are not closed during the short-term cultivation process go into an extended follow-up program, described now.

## THE LONG-TERM ACCOUNT-CULTIVATION PROCESS

In business today, a stark reality is that a certain number of very worthwhile prospects will resist being sold to right away. Many of them may take as long as a year to sell and, of course, some will *never* become customers.

Since lots of good business will come later, a "one-shot-close" syndrome must be avoided. Too many firms ignore a prospect if the sale isn't made as a result of an early contact. The telemarketer and the reps seem to lose interest and go on to other possibilities.

At the same time, some companies maintain a strong presence to all of their "almost-sold's." They realize that a significant number of these more difficult firms *will* become buyers eventually, so they build systems to keep in touch with prospects who take longer to make decisions.

A near miss should be contacted every few months at the least. A follow-up sequence is set into motion *only* after a telemarketer or field rep asks the prospect: "Do you mind if we stay in touch?"

Very few will refuse this offer of ongoing contact. The ones who *do* decline continuing contact should be revealed as early as possible.

An architectural sign company produces and sells custom products to private firms, architects, and designers. When their short-term business cultivation program fails to get a close, the more promising prospects are automatically phased into a long-term follow-up effort.

A plan for one year of follow-up is shown in Table 10.2 on the following page.

---

### TABLE 10.2:   LONG-TERM ACCOUNT CULTIVATION ACTION PLAN

Action dictated by the following steps begin *after* these early (short-term) contacts:

- Initial prospecting letter
- Initial telephone call for appointment
- Initial field appointment
- Second follow-up phone call (or sometimes a second visit for a quote or proposal)

This series of contacts, previously described in the short-term program, usually takes two to four weeks. When there is no close as a result of this beginning process, many firms make the mistake of burying the prospect record and following up on a disorganized basis, if at all.

Our example in this section, the architectural sign company, starts its long-term follow-up about 34 days after the very first contact. Their average sales occur at about the 6-month mark. The follow-up effort is not abandoned until 18 months have passed without a sale.

LONG-TERM FOLLOW-UP SCHEDULE:

*Follow-up 1: LETTER.*
*Objective:*  To thank prospect for opportunity.
*Timing:*  14 days after the last short-term follow-up.

*Follow-up 2: TELEPHONE CALL.*
*Objective:*  Tell buyer to watch for new sign colors.
*Timing:*  70 days after follow-up 1.

*Follow-up 3: LETTER.*
*Objective:*  Send new color samples with cover note.
*Timing:*  35 days after follow-up 2.

*Follow-up 4: TELEPHONE CALL.*
*Objective:*  Check on reaction to new colors.
*Timing:*  30 days after follow-up 3.

*Follow-up 5: TELEPHONE CALL.*
*Objective:*  Go for appointment to reevaluate buying situation.
*Timing:*  80 days after follow-up 4.

*Follow-up 6: FIELD VISIT.*
*Objective:*  Reevaluate needs.
*Timing:*  16 days after follow-up 5.

*Follow-up 7: LETTER.*

*Objectives:* Thank buyer for opportunity and describe any new developments such as innovations on recent projects.

*Timing:* 14 days after follow-up 6.

*Follow-up 8: TELEPHONE CALL.*

*Objective:* Go for appointment.

*Timing:* 80 days after follow-up 7.

---

From the eighth follow-up onward, contacts by phone, mail, and personal visit are made at about 80 day intervals and continue to the 18 month mark. At that point, a *quarterly* mailer is sent indefinitely.

The first five long-term contacts are provided in the following pages.

### LETTER 10.4:   FIRST LONG-TERM CONTACT

This letter kicks off the long-term cultivation program for the architectural sign company. During the various short-term activities reviewed earlier in this chapter, it is assumed that the ground had been covered thoroughly between the rep and the potential buyer, so *new* information of great significance probably isn't available in abundance. As a consequence, the content of these later follow-ups will largely consist of new angles of *previously discussed* aspects of a sign purchase.

In fact, marketing people with the sign firm say that the message conveyed in each long-term follow-up contact isn't of critical importance. Instead, it's the process of *maintaining a strong identity* to the prospect that really counts in the cultivation effort.

The first letter starts by thanking the buyer for considering the firm's line, but it also succeeds in once again making the point about quality, which is the company's strong suit.

Dear Mr. Burns:

Your interest in Dalton's nonilluminated custom-design directories is appreciated by our entire staff. As you know, years of dedication involving careful study of materials, designs, and fabricating techniques have made possible the development of this highly distinctive line.

As you compare our product during your evaluations, please take special notice of these points in particular:

- Thinner profile
- Completely concealed hardware
- Wide selection of frame colors that will better integrate with your existing installations

As questions come up, please feel free to contact me. With your permission, I'll stay in touch to see how your design program is progressing.

Sincerely,

Geoffrey H. Brown

Very little customization is needed on this letter, so it can usually be generated rapidly from a standard word-processed format.

If there is no prospect reaction, a call is made about 70 days after the letter was sent.

## SCRIPT 10.5: SECOND LONG-TERM CONTACT

Since the architectural sign company continually introduces new design enhancements such as different frame colors and product configurations, it periodically has something new to show old prospects. Almost *any* business can come up with new information that is worthy of mention to unsold prospects.

Price modifications, entirely new products, new lettering styles, and other comparatively minor developments can also serve as the subject of the sign firm's second long-term contact.

In this case, newly introduced frame colors are the focus of the second long-term follow-up contact.

| | |
|---|---|
| *Telemarketer:* | [Reintroduces self and company to the correct contact, then asks] *Has anything new developed on your Capitol Square design project?* |

That question will usually reveal what kind of action, if any, the prospect has taken to purchase signs from a competitive source.

> *We thought you'd be interested in seeing a couple of new aluminum frame colors for the directories you looked at. They could open up some different possibilities for you. Should I arrange to get samples to you?*

*Note:* When the prospect responds affirmatively, most sellers would offer to drop the samples off in person, thus providing one more opportunity to do some face-to-face selling. For the purpose of our example, we will assume that the telemarketer feels a visit is not warranted and elects to mail the samples when they are ready.

| | |
|---|---|
| *Prospect:* | *Sure, I'd be interested in seeing them . . . although your medium bronze looked good for our needs.* |
| *Telemarketer:* | *We'll have samples ready in a few weeks. I'll make sure you get the first ones available. If you don't mind, I'll give you a call to get your reaction to them.* |

About 30 days later, the color samples are sent with this cover letter:

## LETTER 10.5:  THIRD LONG-TERM CONTACT

*Every* contact with a prospect—even if the contact is a cover letter—should *sell* to some extent. In the letter we'll look at now, it isn't enough to say "Here are the samples we promised to send." The message must go further to be effective. It says "Here are the samples. They *prove* that we're always striving to provide the best possible tools for designers and architects."

Dear Mr. Burns:

As promised when we spoke on March 12, here are two outstanding new frame colors:

- Natural anodized
- Gold anodized

Our entire line of custom-designed, nonilluminated directories can be specified in these new colors, as well as in those you have already seen.

While we are aware of the fact that bronze would perfectly fit the characteristics of your Capitol Square project, these recent additions to our line might be of interest in other phases of your current design work, or in future undertakings.

This constant addition of new selections is intended to give you an increasing range of design options, and our ability to produce completely custom signs should enable you to meet the most unusual project requirements.

Because we are most interested in your opinion of the two new frame colors, I'll call you in several weeks. In the meantime, please contact me if you have any questions.

Sincerely,

Geoffrey H. Brown


Since this mailing of samples is not expected to create an urgent demand, the follow-up call in Script 10.6 is made about 30 days later. If the samples *were* expected to stir up exceptional interest, they would be presented to the prospect in person, and the next call would be made much more quickly.

## SCRIPT 10.6: FOURTH LONG-TERM CONTACT

This telephone contact is based on the pretext of finding out how the prospect liked the new frame colors. But the underlying reason for the call is to see whether the long-term prospect has moved any closer to buying.

The telemarketer will open by asking for the buyer's opinion. Probing on purchase status follows closely:

> *Telemarketer:* [Reintroduces self and company to the correct contact, then asks] *Can I get your expert and frank opinion of the natural and gold anodized frame-color samples we sent you?*

Prospect expresses opinion, which is noted by telemarketer. Now caller probes buying status:

> *We're extremely interested in working with you on the Capitol Square project. That's going to be one of the area's outstanding building lobbies when it's completed.*
>
> *Are you at a point where the next step can be taken?*

In projects of this kind, a simple yes or no from the prospect will usually suffice. Selling skills can't overcome outside technical obstacles delaying completion of a major design project. If the next step *can't* be taken at this time, the caller schedules the next contact, which in the sign company's program is another call around 80 days down the road.

### SCRIPT 10.7: FIFTH LONG-TERM CONTACT

When months have passed since the original sales presentation, a vendor can be sure that many important facts have become obscure to the decision maker. Even when a formal proposal clearly lays out the specs, the prospect's picture of the proposition is still dim. For that reason, the sign company prescribes a *new* face-to-face presentation as the *sixth* long-term contact. Therefore, the *fifth* contact is a telephone call that will set up a visit with the prospect contact.

Because new developments in product or price may not be available, the telemarketer's pretext is a review of project specifications. This seller is more than willing to invest time in another field visit as long as the potential buyer appears to remain interested.

| | |
|---|---|
| *Telemarketer:* | [Reintroduces self and company, then says] *Bob, I understand that you're still as anxious as we are to get the directories installed in the lobby of Capitol Square, but the timetable depends on factors neither of us can control.* |
| | *While we both wait, we feel it would be extremely useful to both of us to sit down for about 20 or 30 minutes so we can go over the key details we talked about last March.* |
| | *We'll make sure that all of our original concepts are still on target in view of things that may have changed since we originally met.* |
| | *Do you feel that would be helpful to you?* |

It is conceivable that some prospects would respond, "We can do our reviewing when and if I give you the order." If the answer resembles that, the best strategy is to back off and resume the next steps in the long-range cultivation program.

When that soft-sell appointment is agreed to, the get-together may not achieve the patiently awaited close. But it *will* gain an advantage over competitors who are content to sit and wait for a call from the buyer.

In the sign company's long-term program, contacts by phone, mail, and visit continue for a total of 18 months.

## REFINING YOUR CULTIVATION PROGRAM

Your Form 10.3 Account-Cultivation Checklist will help you assure that a solid foundation is in place for both a good short-term *and* long-term cultivation program.

## FORM 10.3:   ACCOUNT-CULTIVATION CHECKLIST

*Researching a new market*

1. List a new market that seems to have potential for your product or service:

   _____

2. List four reasons why this market looks promising:

   • _____

   _____

   • _____

   _____

   _____

   • _____

   _____

   • _____

   _____

3. Have you researched this market in order to verify its potential?

   ____ Yes     ____ No

4. If *no,* describe how research will be conducted: _____

   _____

   _____

   _____

   _____

   _____

5. Who will conduct the research? _____

   _____

6. How many firms will be surveyed? _____

7. Have you prepared a questionnaire that will reveal the facts you need?

   ____ Yes    ____ No

8. Have you identified sources of prospects in the market you selected?

   ____ Yes     ____ No

9. In selecting *prime* prospects from a list of companies, what attributes will qualify a firm?

   ____ Size in terms of total employees

   ____ Size in terms of annual dollar volume

_____ Location

_____ Specific nature of its business

_____ Users of certain types of equipment

_____ Past purchasing characteristics

_____ Others: _____

_____

_____

_____

*Short-term cultivation*

10. Who in your company will be responsible for assuring that contacts are made on schedule?

_____

11. Typically, how long does it take to close a strongly qualified and interested new prospect? _____

12. How many contacts will that sale require? _____

13. Check the following contact methods you are prepared to direct at prospects:

- Telemarketing
- Direct mail
- Personal visits
- Seminars
- Trade-show contacts
- FAX transmissions
- Others: _____

_____

_____

14. List the sequence of events and timing for your short-term program:

|  | Nature of Contact | Timing |
|---|---|---|
| Contact No. _____ | _____ | _____ |
| Contact No. _____ | _____ | _____ |
| Contact No. _____ | _____ | _____ |
| Contact No. _____ | _____ | _____ |
| Contact No. _____ | _____ | _____ |
| Contact No. _____ | _____ | _____ |

15. Are standard letter formats available for all short-term and long-term contacts?

    _____ Yes    _____ No

*Long-term cultivation*

16. Based on the dollar volume of your product or service, how long a time do you feel should be invested in the long-term cultivation of a prospect?

    _____

17. How often do you think your long-term prospect should be contacted?

    _____

18. List the sequence of events and timing for your long-term program:

|  | Nature of Contact | Timing |
|---|---|---|
| Contact No. _____ | _____ | _____ |
| Contact No. _____ | _____ | _____ |
| Contact No. _____ | _____ | _____ |
| Contact No. _____ | _____ | _____ |
| Contact No. _____ | _____ | _____ |
| Contact No. _____ | _____ | _____ |
| Contact No. _____ | _____ | _____ |
| Contact No. _____ | _____ | _____ |
| Contact No. _____ | _____ | _____ |
| Contact No. _____ | _____ | _____ |
| Contact No. _____ | _____ | _____ |
| Contact No. _____ | _____ | _____ |
| Contact No. _____ | _____ | _____ |
| Contact No. _____ | _____ | _____ |
| Contact No. _____ | _____ | _____ |
| Contact No. _____ | _____ | _____ |
| Contact No. _____ | _____ | _____ |
| Contact No. _____ | _____ | _____ |
| Contact No. _____ | _____ | _____ |
| Contact No. _____ | _____ | _____ |

# Chapter 11

# OVERCOMING STALLS, OBJECTIONS, AND COMPLAINTS

A telemarketer will encounter stalls almost every time new prospects are called, while later calls, usually follow-up contacts, attract objections and complaints. Handling all of these adversities with skill and poise is absolutely necessary to success in telemarketing.

In almost every company, regardless of size or the complexity of its product or service, the total number of *legitimate* stalls and objections heard from prospects can be boiled down to ten or less in each category. Once a telemarketer gets past "Too much money," "My uncle's a distributor and I buy from him," or "We have enough inventory for the next six months," the possible objections become rare.

With a number as manageable as that, there is no reason why every telemarketer should not establish *prepared rebuttals* to every expected stall and objection. In fact, many of the best callers have as many as four answers ready for every potential obstacle.

A word about "expected objections": Every seller who devotes time to pitching a particular product or service gets more or less accustomed to a basic pattern of objections. These are the negative prospect comments that come up call after call and present few surprises to an experienced salesperson who deals with a familiar product.

Form 11.1 is a worksheet that can be used to prepare the best possible responses to stalls, objections, and complaints. In entering each common (expected) stall and objection and two matching responses on this form, you will discover that the number of potential obstacles is manageable, and the entire subject of objections less intimidating.

## REBUTTALS TO STALLS THAT COME UP DURING THE INITIAL CALL

In analyzing a large midwestern telemarketing department to find out when most objections arise and what they are about, this interesting pattern became evident: During initial calls to prospects, most objections are comparatively general and are undoubtedly intended to cut the discussion short. At this early stage, the prospect often doesn't know enough about the product or service to object to specific issues such as cost or performance. As a prospect becomes more familiar with the workings and characteristics of a product, the objections begin to shift toward competitive questions and specific operating details.

Therefore, a telemarketer who contacts new prospects needs the skills to neutralize general objections, and if a caller remains involved with prospects later in the relationship, product knowledge assumes a more prominent role.

We'll now cover an important component in the battle to master objections.

## DOCUMENTING REBUTTALS TO OBJECTIONS

An automotive parts company in the southeastern U.S. has each of its nine telemarketers jot down every prospect objection that comes up during the course of calling. At biweekly sales meetings, the telemarketers work out strong responses to the objections that haven't been encountered before.

Those objections that represent new obstacles to the callers are added to an alphabetically arranged list of objections, along with the rebuttals that were established during the meetings. The result is a desktop reference for each caller. It provides assurance that even inexperienced telemarketers can handle objections quickly and smoothly.

This form is *always* in front of each telemarketer to help this program work:

---

### FORM 11.1: OBJECTIONS AND REBUTTALS

OBJECTION: _____

_____

_____

_____

Rebuttal 1: _____

_____

_____

_____

Rebuttal 2: _____

_____

_____

_____

OBJECTION: _____

_____

_____

Rebuttal 1: _____

_____

_____

_____

Rebuttal 2: _____

_____

_____

_____

OBJECTION: _____

_____

_____

Rebuttal 1: _____

_____

_____

_____

Rebuttal 2: _____

_____

_____

_____

OBJECTION: _____

_____

_____

Rebuttal 1: _____

_____

_____

_____

Rebuttal 2: _____

_____

_____

_____

_____

_____

Make as many copies of this form as you need in order to list *all* expected objections, and some of the more interesting unexpected ones, along with appropriate rebuttals.

Remember, the prospect who is seriously looking at your offer will try to find holes in it. This process of seeking out weaknesses certainly does create objections. When those objections are skillfully fielded by the telemarketer, a happy ending is often brought about. Therefore, the best salespeople will *try* to draw out some kind of resistance in dealing with a prospect who seems *too* agreeable.

Here's an example of one entry by a business forms telemarketer:

OBJECTION: _____

_____

_____

Rebuttal 1: _____

_____

_____

_____

_____

Now we'll move on to some of the obstacles a prospect may throw in the path of a caller during initial calls.

## SCRIPT 11.1a: "DON'T KNOW YOUR COMPANY"

"I never heard of you people, and that's a problem for me since I can buy from sources I'm familiar with." Three main categories of companies will encounter that comment from prospects. They are

- Start-up firms
- Established companies that have not enjoyed heavy exposure in the market they are working
- Almost any organization trying to open new markets and/or new territories

To some telemarketers, that declaration from a prospect can be devastating. They reason it this way: "What chance do I have to get the sale if I'm forced to fight for my very identity 15 seconds into the call? What real chance do I have to get past this brick wall?"

While that obstacle may indeed create a need to build credibility with the prospect over a period of time, *every* telemarketer must respond strongly to such a challenge. An aggressive rebuttal usually accomplishes two desired objectives:

- It conveys complete confidence that the vendor *will* perform as well as anyone else—and perhaps better than most, while a tentative response from the caller helps support the prospect's doubt in the seller's credentials.
- Caller confidence can subtly and indirectly say, "I'm astounded you haven't heard of us! Those who are paying attention in this industry know what we're doing for our clients."

Here's a rebuttal for "Don't know your company" used by a supplier of eyewear. In this example, the caller is contacting prospects in a foreign market for the first time:

| | |
|---|---|
| *Prospect:* | *I'm not familiar with your firm. Can you send me something that provides a little background and shows who you've done business with?* |
| *Telemarketer:* | *Be happy to do that. We have a capabilities brochure that covers most of that. Let me briefly touch on a couple of points that need to be emphasized.* |
| | *In Europe, we've become the eyewear fashion leader in the three countries where we started marketing only two years ago. Customers can select frame colors and styles, and they are custom made for that person in 48 hours in the retailer's shop. Consumers* never *had service like that on high-fashion eyewear.* |
| | *We feel that this concept will sweep this nation—just as it's now doing overseas. This thing is really hot, and the retailers who get regional sales rights should do very well.* |
| | *I can show you some of the figures being generated in England, and I think you'll want to share in the popularity of this product.* |

This rebuttal tends to sweep away "I've never heard of you." It makes the offer too big and important for such a petty protest.

In a large number of calls, the telemarketer is able to proceed directly to an appointment *despite* the earlier promise to mail a capabilities brochure.

Another objection that can often be described as a dive for cover in the face of a sales attempt is next.

## SCRIPT 11.1b: "NOT INTERESTED"

Perhaps the most futile exercise known to any caller is attempting to sell something to an individual who is *genuinely* not interested in the offer. Trouble is, the seller has no way of rapidly finding out whether

- The prospect really *is* open to buy, but is professing no interest as a way to get away from real or imagined sales pressure.
- The prospect is not in the least interested but is unable to be more emphatic and is too polite to simply hang up.

To disregard the prospect's declaration and barge ahead with a presentation is the most blatant kind of high pressure. It is certain to offend most prospects who say "No thanks, not today." The answer, according to marketing strategists in the eyewear firm, is to use a system of probing. Here's how the system works: To effectively disarm the prospect, *acknowledge* the "not interested" declaration; a prospect will probably not become defensive if that comment isn't challenged by the telemarketer.

Next, *clarify* the "not interested" verdict. Exactly *what* is the prospect referring to? The product? The timing of the call? Some bad feeling about the vendor?

Finally, solve the problem. It often sounds like this:

*Prospect:*            *I appreciate your call, but we're not interested right now.*

At this point the caller will acknowledge the prospect's comment, then attempt to find out whether the stall is based on the product specifically or conditions generally. If the contact is not familiar with the product, the situation is far easier to deal with.

| | |
|---|---|
| *Telemarketer:* | *I understand. If I may ask, how did you become familiar with our line?* |
| *Prospect:* | *I'm not familiar with it. We're just not open to buy anything at the present time.* |
| *Telemarketer:* | *If I can take just a moment of your time, let me describe something that might be valuable to you later:* |
| | *Optometrics is fashion eyewear that you or your customer can completely customize and deliver in one or two days. Frame color, prescription, and lens tint are all done in the store, constructed with high-quality modular components.* |
| | *This approach is very popular in Europe, and we're just now establishing our dealer network in the U.S.* |
| | *Do you carry anything like that?* |
| *Prospect:* | *No. Our fashion lines are the conventional ones, and we're overstocked on those.* |

The problem has been identified as a problem of overly fat inventory, and the caller now attempts to find a way around it:

> *Telemarketer:*      *Some of our retailers have had situations like yours. One good solution is to put in a starter assortment. That does two things for you: It can give you something dramatically new and appealing to your customers that should help sell your existing inventory of better frames, and it won't materially affect your inventory situation since we're not talking about a major commitment until you get back on an even keel.*

Of primary importance is this point: A telemarketer *must* avoid an argumentative attitude in handling this or any other stall. The approach has to *always* be centered on problem solving.

A prospect who uses a tight schedule as a shield is related to the one we just reviewed.

## SCRIPT 11.1c: "NO TIME"

Here again, it is entirely conceivable that your contact *is* open to buy but simply can't take time to discuss it when the call comes in. Yet, "no time" may very well be used to mask a much more serious objection that will have to be dealt with sooner or later.

By getting a definite commitment for a call-back time, hidden objections will be flushed out more often than not.

> *Prospect:*      *Sorry, I just don't have the time to discuss that now. Why don't you send out some information, and I'll get in touch if I'm interested.*
>
> *Telemarketer:*      *I'll do that this afternoon.*
>
> *I know you're extremely busy, but I have just one question before I hang up. Can we reserve a definite time today or tomorrow so I can get your opinion on an unusual line of fashion eyewear? We'll need about 20 minutes, and I feel it will turn out to be important to you.*

Some callers in this situation would desperately try to set a field appointment. It makes much more sense to set a time for a second call.

Next, the prospect who tells the caller there's no room for improvement.

## SCRIPT 11.1d: "WE'RE SATISFIED"

One telemarketing leader says this about a prospect statement that professes satisfaction with present sources: "It's a challenge to my merchandising know-how. This person is saying 'Show me how your products would give me something different.' The last thing those retailers need is one more line that fits the same general description as the ones they already have."

As before, if the prospect's "We're satisfied" statement is really an excuse to cover up other objections, more probing will be needed.

In cases where the comment proves to be sincere, the telemarketer has to use merchandising skills in order to point out how this eyewear line will do something much different than the others.

Here's how the tactic often takes form:

| | |
|---|---|
| ***Prospect:*** | *Thanks, but we're all set on fashion lines. In fact, we show more designer eyewear than any other store in the area.* |
| ***Telemarketer:*** | *Really! Which ones do you carry?* |

Which lines are stocked by the store actually doesn't matter in the least. The question is asked to give the prospect a chance to show off. This is an esteem builder.

| | |
|---|---|
| ***·Prospect:*** | [In most instances, will not hesitate to rattle off the fancy lines.] |
| ***Telemarketer:*** | *That is impressive. You're right—I haven't heard of many stores that show a range of top merchandise as extensive as that.* |
| | *Let me make just one comment before I sign off: You wouldn't have that kind of strength in your better lines unless your customers wanted special quality and appearance. They're the kind of buyers who apparently recognize something better and different.* |
| | *If you could offer fine eyewear of exceptional design—created in exactly the color they prefer—and deliver the finished product in a day or two instead of weeks later, they would certainly see that as a big breakthrough. That really is completely different from anything else on the market.* |
| | *In our initial markets, this product is outselling the standard top lines two to one.* |

Finding a strong niche for your product or service *will* help overcome the "we're satisfied" stall. That requires knowledge of competitive sources as well as clear insight into what goes on in the buyer's business.

A prospect who stalls by asking for literature is probably the most frequently encountered type.

## SCRIPT 11.1e: "SEND LITERATURE"

Telemarketing managers are in general agreement that callers who frequently cave in to literature requests are weak. To many prospects, it works this way: When a selling call comes in, and the recipient is for some reason not anxious to deal with the prospector, it is ridiculously easy to push the entire matter away by simply asking for an information packet, which almost every vendor is prepared to do.

Most decision makers understand that it may take *weeks* for the big envelope to finally arrive. And reviewing the contents could take 30 days, if it happens at all. Whether the telemarketer will follow up is pure speculation; about half the time, the transaction dies when information is mailed.

Of course there are many notable exceptions. More companies than ever before are following up more efficiently. But this fact remains: When a prospect asks for literature, it's almost always a stall. A telemarketer needs to get around that obstacle at every opportunity.

The eyewear company callers attempt to do it this way:

| | |
|---|---|
| *Prospect:* | *Sounds interesting. Why don't you send out some literature, give me a chance to go through it, and get back to me in a few weeks.* |
| *Telemarketer:* | *I'll get a package together for you today. What kind of attributes do you look for in fashion eyewear, and in the supplier?* |

This is a logical question following a request for more information.

| | |
|---|---|
| *Prospect:* | *We mainly look at materials and workmanship in frames. Our sources have to be reliable and service oriented. Not really unusual expectations.* |
| *Telemarketer:* | *Do you consider the track record of an eyewear manufacturer?* |
| *Prospect:* | *Sure, we'll base part of our decision on feedback from the retail community.* |

Now that the caller has identified the prospect's selection standards and can consider this retailer a legitimate possibility, an end run can be attempted in order to circumvent the literature request:

| | |
|---|---|
| *Telemarketer:* | *Based on what you're telling me, I'd like to suggest a face-to-face meeting in your office.* |
| | *I can much more effectively show you how we fit your criteria. For example, when you see the product, the grade of materials and the level of craftsmanship will be apparent. In addition, I can demonstrate much more clearly how we support our retailers.* |
| | *That'll take about 20 minutes. I'll bring the literature so you can review the details later, at your convenience. After we talk, that data will be much more meaningful to you.* |

It won't work every time, but this approach can improve appointment conversions for calls that run smack into literature requests.

Our final stall is unvarnished procrastination.

SCRIPT 11.1f: "I'LL THINK ABOUT IT"

If you are closing sales by telephone, this prospect response has at least a little credibility. After all, the individual is asked to make a commitment without the benefit of seeing or experiencing the product or service. That may very well invite caution.

But when the telemarketer is calling to set an appointment, "I'll think about it" has much less conviction. Think about *what?* The caller has *not* asked for a purchase decision, but is trying to arrange a face-to-face meeting. Is it really necessary to think about sitting down with a rep for 20 minutes?

The point is, those words demand probing by the telemarketer—particularly when appointments, not products, are being sold. More than any other stall, this phrase disguises other prospect anxieties. This tactic is used by the eyewear firm's callers *after* a field appointment has been rejected with the response "I'll think about it."

> *Prospect:*
>
> I'll think about it and get in touch with you if I decide to go ahead.
>
> *Telemarketer:*
>
> Of course it's very good business for you to carefully consider every aspect of becoming an Optometrics dealer. But I don't think we're yet at the stage where you can do an effective appraisal of the advantages and disadvantages.
>
> Let me quickly run through a couple of the issues that haven't yet been decided: First, you can't really pass judgment on the quality and look of this line until you hold samples in your hand. We can do that when we get together.
>
> Second, since the customization of our eyewear requires some special dealer equipment, we have to be sure that your facility would work out.
>
> Until those items are checked out, I don't think you can accurately weigh a "go" or "no-go" decision.

What this strategy amounts to is this: Gently challenge the *specifics* of what the prospect will think about. Such a challenge often succeeds in blowing that stall away.

Neutralizing the efforts of rival vendors is next.

## DEALING WITH COMPETITIVE FACTORS

Large companies considering a substantial purchase will generally get three competitive bids. In most cases, this is a matter of policy. Therefore, the sales ability of a vendor involved in a bidding situation is, to some extent, reduced in importance.

*Smaller* buyers may not be bound by necessity to collect comparative offers, but they *are* more apt to be sensitive to price. Thus, they are likely to shop around, and a difference of several dollars may influence the selection of a vendor.

As any beginning seller knows, "knocking the competition" is usually counterproductive and should be avoided at all costs. The next pages suggest ways to more constructively handle tough rivals.

SCRIPT 11.2: "WANT TO SHOP AROUND"

Over a period of years, a jewelry manufacturer has tried a variety of ways to overcome a prospect's intention to check out the offers of rival firms. It seemed that the harder a telemarketer worked to nullify that decision, the more determined a buyer became to do some comparing.

When a prospect states a desire to get the picture by talking to other suppliers and a telemarketer or rep attempts to talk the buyer out of that position, it appears to the prospect like a high-pressure sales tactic and comes uncomfortably close to knocking the competition.

Here's the successful approach by the jewelry manufacturer:

| | |
|---|---|
| *Prospect:* | *We're in the market for a strong-selling watch assortment, but right now we're looking around to see what's available. Give us a few weeks to decide.* |
| *Telemarketer:* | *We feel that's a solid way to make a decision. In fact, it makes our selling job a lot easier when buyers are open to comparing our line point-by-point against others.* |
| | *I'd like to give you four specific items to compare when you consider other sources. Can you jot them down?* |
| | *Number one, our watches are Swiss made. That still says the top in quality to most consumers.* |
| | *Two, even with our smallest sample package, you receive beautiful counter and window displays at no extra cost.* |
| | *Three, all watches come with plush presentation boxes. That makes them especially elegant gifts.* |
| | *Four, our prices run about ten percent lower than watches of comparable quality.* |
| | *Retailers who carry our line tell us that these are the points that really set us apart from the other sources. I'd like to get back in touch with you next week to find out how we come out in your comparisons.* |

Telemarketer then sets a definite call-back time.

Instead of *fighting* the prospect's decision to shop, *support* the buyer by providing a list of specific comparisons. A little research is strongly suggested to assure that the points of comparison reveal competitive weaknesses.

Dislodging deeply entrenched vendors is our next topic.

SCRIPT 11.3a: "BEEN DEALING WITH THEM FOR YEARS"

Any company that prospects for new accounts will run into many long-term relationships between buyers and sellers. When these established suppliers are performing reasonably well, they can be extremely difficult to push aside. Most often, when an old vendor *is* replaced by a newcomer, it is because prices were successfully undercut.

You don't need a special script to get a new account through deep discounts. If a firm is willing to sell at low profit margins, there's plenty of easy business out there. The trouble is, it's only a matter of time before another sharpshooter comes along and cuts yet more off the price to steal the business from the last cutter.

Getting a foot in the door by offering better service, selection, and other advantages—but holding prices to maintain healthy margins—is what we'll look at now. This is how a bedding manufacturer does it:

> *Prospect:*  *You may know that we've been a major DreamRest dealer since we opened our doors. There's really no reason for us to change.*
>
> *Telemarketer:*  *We totally respect that relationship. It's rare today to see that kind of loyalty.*
>
>    *We'd just like to point this out: Your business has grown tremendously since you started. Maybe the time has come to expand your bedding selection to accommodate a customer base that probably expects a wider variety.*
>
>    *In addition to the better choice, our line will give you quicker delivery and more generous warranty terms to customers. You'd have the best of both worlds by adding some of our best-selling numbers. They work well together in other stores, and they should do the same for you.*

Since every supplier has different strengths, it makes good sense to try to dovetail with lines already carried by a prospect. A small foothold can grow if the relationship is properly nurtured. This is a better strategy than trying to force out a line already respected by the buyer.

When the prospect throws out a challenge by claiming that the competitive line is superior, the bedding firm's caller does this:

### SCRIPT 11.3b: "THEY'RE BETTER"

Dovetailing fits in this situation, too. Why try to tear down a rival's strengths if it's easier to blend your best features with a competitor's most prominent attributes?

The bedding firm handles it this way:

> *Prospect:*  *Frankly, we think the Thomas Bedding line is superior to yours.*
>
> *Telemarketer:*  *Can you tell me what aspects of their line you feel are better?*
>
> *Prospect:*  *They provide a selection of special fabrics that give us great step-up opportunities. We don't feel we'd have that with your products.*
>
>    *Another thing is that you just don't have anything to compare with Thomas's quilted mattresses.*

|  |  |
|---|---|
| *Telemarketer:* | *I couldn't agree more. They've done a terrific job with luxury fabrics and with their higher-priced quilted line. We're* definitely *not competing with them in those areas.* |
|  | *What I envision is a situation where we provide strength in the areas where you need it. For example: Instead of trying to match Thomas's fabric selection, we can offer your customers a tremendous selection of* standard *fabrics, for those who like that price range.* |
|  | *Our standard line would beautifully complement Thomas's quilted numbers. That's our strongest seller, and it fills a void in your present line-up.* |

Regardless of specific competitive strengths, there are almost always offsetting strengths in your product or service that would *enhance* a prospect's position, not *fight* with it.

Sometimes it may be necessary for you to get the facts during your first call, then do a little work to figure out where the dovetailing can be done.

Size of a competitor can also cause headaches.

### SCRIPT 11.3c: "THEY'RE BIGGER"

To some buyers, the sheer bulk of a vendor company is a comforting factor. While that feeling may be unwarranted in terms of how the company actually performs, it *is* an issue that has to be handled from time to time by smaller firms.

In this example, a computer maintenance company handles the "bigger is better" problem:

|  |  |
|---|---|
| *Prospect:* | *We feel that Taylor Company is large enough to better provide the range of services we need.* |

Rather than accepting that general statement, the caller will attempt to pin the prospect down to definite cases:

|  |  |
|---|---|
| *Telemarketer:* | *Can you describe the specific areas where you feel they are particularly strong?* |

As often as not, the answer will be short of substance:

|  |  |
|---|---|
| *Prospect:* | *They just have the resources and people that a small company lacks. We're concerned about facilities and experience.* |
| *Telemarketer:* | *They have done a good job over the years; there's no taking that away from them. But I'd like to briefly explain how a smaller company like us competes on even terms.* |
|  | *The old saying, "We're number two, so we have to work harder" is absolutely true in our case. We did a survey of* |

*service users last year to find out where the hot spots are. One of our findings was that the smaller service outfits responded about 20 percent faster than the major firms.*

*In addition, customer satisfaction was consistently higher with small firms, and our charges averaged about 10 percent less.*

*The large service companies were able to do some on-site repairs that we couldn't do, but those occurred rarely and little time or expense was saved overall.*

*We'll do a better job for you just because we have to move faster.*

In cases where it fits, the telemarketer will use the *prospect* as an example of how smaller organizations have to be more responsive.

### SCRIPT 11.3d: "REMEMBER WHEN *YOU* WERE JUST STARTING OUT?"

*Prospect:*      *We feel that The Ardsley Group is large enough to provide the range of services we need.*

*Telemarketer:*      *When your firm was just starting to grow, you probably faced the same situation. I'll bet you hustled more in order to compete with bigger competitors, and you probably ended up doing a better job for your clients. That is exactly what's happening with us. Our customers tell us we're faster and more thorough than the larger service companies. We can do the same things for you.*

When a company charges more for its products or services, they need to be ready to justify their position.

### SCRIPT 11.3e: "THEY'RE CHEAPER"

Almost everybody in the business world understands that higher prices usually reflect better quality or superior service. The world is too competitive to permit the long-term survival of a firm that charges more but offers the same as rivals, or less.

Still, prospects need to be reminded about this phenomenon. Here's how a company in custom auto finishing does it:

*Prospect:*      *That's a lot more money than I'd have to pay at other shops.*

*Telemarketer:*      *I understand that. But it's important for you to compare apples to apples.*

*Remember, we're talking about three hand-rubbed coats of custom paint over special primer. What we do simply can't be compared in any way to the work done by ordinary shops.*

> *Their work is usually okay, but it's strictly a matter of what kind of investment you want to make in a valuable piece of property like your car. If "satisfactory" is okay, you should try to save money. But if "excellent" is what you demand, then we're your best choice.*

Now we'll cover the handling of complaints that come from both prospects and customers.

## HANDLING COMPLAINTS

Complaints usually pop up later in a sales relationship—*after* goods are delivered or services are rendered. During the process of cultivating a prospect, there isn't much for the prospect to complain about.

Complaints represent a rare opportunity for the vendor. If handled with grace and efficiency, a bad situation can be radically turned around to solidify a sales relationship. Notable examples are some department store organizations that will go to any lengths to assure customer satisfaction. They enjoy an astounding level of buyer loyalty solely by virtue of their complaint-handling skills.

At the other extreme, poorly fielded complaints will chase customers away with alarming speed, and the negative reputation spreads very rapidly.

### SCRIPT 11.4a:  ADMITTING YOU DIDN'T HANDLE IT WELL

An office coffee service operating in a large southern U.S. city encounters a wide range of complaints in serving some 250 commercial customers.

With the intense pressure of fighting hungry competitors and clogged city traffic, the coffee service still manages to retain over 80 percent of its customers for an average of 3.6 years—a very good record in that rugged industry. The reason, according to management, is special emphasis on handling customer complaints.

*All* complaint calls receive basically the same opening statement from reps and telemarketers. It's covered next.

A major key to the success of this particular approach is to first *accept responsibility for the failure.* This is done *before* the specific complaint is addressed. Doing this completely eliminates any temptation for the coffee service representative to become defensive in the face of sometimes withering criticism. This immediate and unconditional admission of responsibility also succeeds in defusing an often hot customer:

| | |
|---|---|
| *Prospect:* | [Describes problem. In this instance, the complaint was "Your quality control is terrible. The unit you people just delivered won't heat up." A defective brewer ruined the coffee break of 30 employees, and that's serious business.] |
| *Rep:* | [Pauses for a moment after customer has finished talking, then says] *That was really a major breakdown in our* |

> *system. There is absolutely no excuse for letting a bad ma-*
> *chine go out to a customer. I want to apologize to you on*
> *behalf of everybody in this company.*

From this point, the rep pledges to help resolve the problem.

### SCRIPT 11.4b: TAKING PERSONAL RESPONSIBILITY
### FOR MAKING THINGS RIGHT

Managers of the coffee company are certain that *this* step of the complaint-handling procedure makes the big difference in saving customers. The company representative, whether that person is an outside seller or an inside telemarketer, accepts the burden of fixing the problem.

This is a refreshing contrast to the typical pass-the-buck game played in so many firms that wrestle with complaints. And it *is* appreciated by most agitated customers.

> *Rep:*
>
> *I know we can't undo the inconvenience you've gone through,*
> *but at least we can do everything possible starting right now.*
>
> *I'm accepting full responsibility for finding out what went*
> *wrong on our end to let that brewer out. But more important,*
> *I want to make it top priority to make things right for you.*

In addition to providing that assurance of finding out how the slip-up occurred, the representative will come up with some way to try to compensate the customer for the discomfort.

### SCRIPT 11.4c: OFFERING A LITTLE COMPENSATION TO
### HELP SMOOTH OUT RUFFLED FEELINGS

As the rep correctly stated, there is really no way to undo the inconvenience. The problem with many complaint responses is that nobody seems to care. An irate customer may be feeling deep frustration and even anger, but most of the people in the offending firm are as tranquil as can be; they often seem to be indifferent to the snafu and to the emotions of the customer.

When some special arrangement is made, as happens in the next dialogue, the customer *does* feel that the complaint-handler is sharing the grief to some extent. And that's the magic key to calming down an upset buyer.

> *Rep:*
>
> *While I work on finding out what went wrong, I'd like to at*
> *least partially make an adjustment for your discomfort. I'll*
> *send out a box of extra coffee packets at no charge. You'll get*
> *it with your next scheduled delivery.*

This customer, perhaps on the verge of changing coffee services only moments earlier, now must feel that *extra* care is being given to his or her needs. *More* important, a clearly identified individual in the coffee company is obviously deeply concerned and committed to getting things back on track.

These promises of the representative are *not* merely idle chatter; extra attention *will* be given to the injured customer until management is certain the relationship is fixed and back to normal. Free coffee will cost less than $15, but the positive impact is worth far more than that. This strategy does save customers in an industry with customer turnover that often reaches astronomical percentages.

In a firm, such as the coffee service company, that employs 30 people, finding the correct person to handle a complaint is relatively easy. But in sprawling corporations it can present a challenge.

### SCRIPT 11.5: REFERRING COMPLAINTS TO THE RIGHT PEOPLE

Some of the most frustrated customers are created when they get lost in an organizational jungle where nobody wants the aggravation. Consumers spend long periods of time on hold and are occasionally cut off altogether. Sometimes promises to solve their problem are made and promptly forgotten by nameless company representatives.

In all fairness, many of these companies are well intentioned but haven't invested time to work out a system for channeling complaint and service calls. The receptionist should know how to qualify a caller in order to accurately transfer the customer to the appropriate department or inside staff member.

Although an inbound complaint call was covered in the chapter on inbound telemarketing, it makes sense to now look at the procedure used by a multidepartment industrial supply company. The receptionist's routine is designed to:

- Obtain information on the nature of the complaint.
- Pinpoint exactly *who* in the company should get the call.
- Assure the customer that the problem *will* be taken care of.

| | |
|---|---|
| *Customer:* | *We received a paint shipment from you and it looks like we got the wrong product.* |
| *Receptionist:* | [Starts by getting name of caller and company as well as the telephone number in case of a disconnect during the call transfer.] |

The receptionist's next move is to clarify the situation. The customer's statement *could* be interpreted as meaning either (1) "You made an error in shipping the wrong paint" or (2) "We goofed because we ordered the wrong paint."

| | |
|---|---|
| *Receptionist:* | *You didn't receive the same paint you ordered. Is that right?* |
| *Customer:* | *That's correct.* |
| *Receptionist:* | *Can you describe what you received? There's a type number on the bottom of the red label.* [Receptionist notes number given by customer.] *What use is the paint intended for?* |
| *Customer:* | *A steel bridge.* |

Now the receptionist knows that this call should be transferred to the firm's structural-supply division. Also known is the type of paint received in error. Receptionist now says:

> *Receptionist:*        *We'll start getting that situation squared away for you right now. Please hold on while I ring the person who can help us.*

Receptionist now rings the general manager of the structural-supply division and briefs him or her:

> *Receptionist:*        *I have Joseph Compton of the Oakville Highway Department on line three.*
>
> *He ordered paint for a bridge and we shipped number 62YP, which he believes is in error. Can you take the call?*

With this briefing, the manager can get on the line and do the following:

- Greet the customer by name.
- *Immediately* summarize the problem, which spares the customer from going through it again.

The impression to a customer is pure professionalism, and all it takes is a little preplanning so that the receptionist knows precisely where a complaint call goes. In setting up such a simple but effective system, try to keep the receptionist's time down to a minimum, since other calls continue to come in. In this case, about 40 seconds are needed to get the basic qualifying done.

In each complaint situation, a follow-up letter is sent to the customer.

### LETTER 11.1: COMPLAINT FOLLOW-UP

Some astute managers feel that apologizing can be carried too far. This letter gets away from begging forgiveness and goes more in the direction of declaring how valuable the customer is.

Dear Mrs. Alberti:

As promised, we have set up special quality-control measures that will guarantee you the kind of service you have always expected from Reeves Coffee Service.

We want you to know that our entire staff values your patronage and loyalty. Every conceivable step will be taken now and in the future to enhance the quality of your coffee service. We *know* how important it is to you.

Please contact me personally for any request you may have. I'll be in touch soon to make sure everything is going smoothly.

Sincerely,

Bruce T. Wagner

When the incredibly steep cost of acquiring a new customer is considered, the wisdom of protecting *existing* clients becomes apparent. In some firms, frantic prospecting barely succeeds in keeping pace with the loss of old customers who leave due to poor handling of customer complaints.

## HOW CLARIFYING CAN CUT THROUGH STALLS AND OBJECTIONS

Telemarketers working for a contract office furniture company succeed in getting past about 60 percent of the stalls and objections they encounter simply by asking prospects to provide more details about their objections. In the process of trying to more fully explain themselves, people very often talk themselves out of a problem they perceived only moments earlier.

One of the callers analyzes the phenomenon this way: "When I ask a prospect to tell me more about a problem they just brought up, the person starts to cool off almost as soon as he begins talking. By the end of the statement, lots of them realize that their objection really isn't valid, and they get off the subject."

This script illustrates how it works:

### SCRIPT 11.6a: ASKING FOR MORE DETAIL ABOUT THE OBJECTION

Here are some of the questions used by the telemarketers to request clarification. As soon as one is asked, the telemarketer waits in silence for the response:

- "Oh? Why?"
- "Can you tell us more about that?"
- "Why do you say that?"
- "I'm unclear about what you mean. Can you describe that again so I can make sure we're on the same wavelength?"

If the prospect does *not* abandon the original objection, the telemarketer has to immediately get to work on solving the problem, whatever it happens to be. The caller's next tactic is a response that includes both an acknowledgment *and* a proposed solution to the problem. It may sound like this:

| | |
|---|---|
| *Telemarketer:* | *I completely understand your concern, especially since you have never used matching loveseats before.* |
| | *We can either go back to the blue sofa and chair you liked so much or see how the loveseats work out. If you feel the loveseats are too much for that room after a few weeks, we can switch for you. But I personally think you'll like them.* |

Some telemarketers prefer to *paraphrase* an objection as a way of clarifying:

### SCRIPT 11.6b: "PLAYING BACK" AN OBJECTION TO ASSURE CLARITY

Several of the telemarketers in the contract furniture company get better results by taking a prospect's objection and putting it into their own words, then asking the prospect if that version accurately sums up the problem. For example:

| | |
|---|---|
| *Prospect:* | *I just think the room is too small for what we're trying to do.* |
| *Telemarketer:* | *You feel that a pair of loveseats may be too much for the room. Is that right?* |
| *Prospect:* | *Well . . . I guess that is a lot of bulk for a small area, isn't it?* |
| *Telemarketer:* | *We want you to be completely satisfied with every selection you make. My job is to work with you to make sure it goes smoothly.* |
| | *We can either go back to the blue sofa and chair you liked so much, or see how the loveseats work. If you feel the loveseats are too much after a few weeks, we can switch for you.* |

Yet another variation of this clarification strategy is to play the objection back to the prospect in a slightly different form. It works this way:

### SCRIPT 11.6c: TAKING THE SHARP EDGES OFF AN OBJECTION

One advantage in paraphrasing an objection as a way to achieve clarification is that the telemarketer can play back the objection in a *much milder form;* some of the sting can be taken out of the prospect's words. In fact, the very meaning of the statement can be changed. When this softer version comes back to the prospect, he or she will often realize that it just isn't a fatally serious issue.

To illustrate, the contract furniture prospect registers a price protest. The telemarketer restates the objection but manages to give it a slightly modified meaning, one that can more easily be solved so the sale can be closed.

| | |
|---|---|
| *Prospect:* | *Those loveseats are too expensive.* |
| *Telemarketer:* | *If I understand you correctly, you're saying you don't feel you can afford two pieces like the loveseats right now. Is that right?* |

The original objection, "Those loveseats are too expensive," might have really meant "Those pieces are overpriced." But through a softened playback, the caller managed to turn the situation into a budget snag which can be handled easily enough.

In dealing with the more costly high-fashion furnishings, price objections often arise. As a result, the contract furniture company has started to test *preempts* as a way to avoid objections.

## SCRIPT 11.7: STOPPING OBJECTIONS BEFORE THEY COME UP

When a certain objection comes up in an extremely high number of telephone contacts, the time has come to devise a radical strategy to control it. One such strategy is the *preempt.*

In preempting, the caller is *the first one* to bring up the problem area: Rather than waiting for the prospect to protest, the *caller* airs out the topic—but in a positive way. This often succeeds in preventing an objection. At the minimum, it sure takes the objection's punch away.

Preempting sounds like this when used to overcome an expected price reaction:

> *Telemarketer:*          [At an early stage of the telephone presentation says] *Our position is to offer our clients better lines. We don't carry the* highest *priced merchandise on the market, but our items definitely are a healthy cut above the ordinary things you see in budget projects.*
>
> *The fact is, our prices average just 12 percent more than firms offering low to medium quality. That's a slim difference for pieces that are clearly superior and much longer lasting.*

It is hardly likely that this prospect will later say, "That's too much money." Not after the cost of better goods has been so carefully established by the telemarketer.

## REFINING YOUR STALL AND OBJECTION RESPONSES

This section provides a checklist to help you plan a strategy for dealing with stalls and objections. The following approach is recommended:

- Use the checklist to make sure you are considering every factor in combating stalls and objections.
- Use Form 11.1, Objections and Rebuttals, which appears earlier in this chapter, to list every stall and objection—along with corresponding rebuttals you feel are most effective.
- Use Form 11.3, Stall and Objection Dialogue Worksheet, to help you develop dialogue for your rebuttals.

It is extremely important to *continually update and expand* Form 11.1 so that it remains a valuable tool in supporting your telemarketing program. It will be particularly useful to *new* callers.

## FORM 11.2: STALL AND OBJECTION CHECKLIST

1. In your telemarketing operation, have you made a distinction between stalls and objections?

   ___ Yes   ___ No

2. Which of the following methods will you use to find out whether an objection is genuine or whether it is a ploy to break off the call:

   ___ Probe more deeply?

   ___ Acknowledge the objection, then continue your presentation?

   ___ Paraphrase the objection and play it back to the prospect to achieve clarification?

3. If quotes have triggered problems, have you evaluated the pros and cons of giving prices over the phone?

   ___ Yes   ___ No

4. Have you listed the stalls and objections that arise in your program in order to identify the ones that come up repeatedly?

   ___ Yes   ___ No

5. If certain objections do come up regularly, have you tried to control them through a preemptive approach?

   ___ Yes   ___ No

6. Is there any tendency for your telemarketers to argue with prospects who stall or object?

   ___ Yes   ___ No

7. After an objection has been handled successfully, does the telemarketer succeed in getting back on the presentation track?

   ___ Yes   ___ No

8. List up to ten *stalls* that seem to arise frequently in your program:

   • _____
   _____
   _____
   _____

   • _____
   _____
   _____
   _____

   • _____
   _____
   _____
   _____

- _____
  _____
  _____

- _____
  _____
  _____

- _____
  _____
  _____

- _____
  _____
  _____

- _____
  _____
  _____

- _____
  _____
  _____

- _____
  _____
  _____

9. List ten *objections* that typically come up:

- _____
  _____
  _____

- _____
  _____
  _____

- _____
  _____
  _____

- _____
  _____
  _____

- _____
  _____
  _____
  _____

- _____
  _____
  _____
  _____

- _____
  _____
  _____
  _____

- _____
  _____
  _____
  _____

- _____
  _____
  _____
  _____

- _____
  _____
  _____
  _____

10. Can you change anything about your product, service, or offer to reduce your vulnerability to stalls and/or objections?

_____ Yes      _____ No

Notes: _____
_____
_____
_____
_____
_____
_____
_____
_____
_____
_____

## FORM 11.3:   STALL AND OBJECTION DIALOGUE WORKSHEET

Use this form to work out dialogue that you feel will overcome the stalls and objections you listed in Form 11.2. Make as many copies as you need.

When you have created effective language, transfer the objection and rebuttal(s) to Form 11.1, which should be kept nearby during calls to prospects.

*Objection as it would typically be stated by prospect:*

_____

_____

_____

*Telemarketer's response*

Acknowledge prospect's statement: _____

_____

Rebuttal text: _____

_____

_____

_____

_____

_____

*Objection as it would typically be stated by prospect:*

_____

_____

_____

*Telemarketer's response*

Acknowledge prospect's statement: _____

_____

Rebuttal text: _____

_____

_____

_____

_____

_____

*Objection as it would typically be stated by prospect:*

_____

_____

_____

_____

*Telemarketer's response*

Acknowledge prospect's statement: _____

_____

Rebuttal text: _____

_____

_____

_____

_____

_____

*Objection as it would typically be stated by prospect:*

_____

_____

_____

_____

*Telemarketer's response*

Acknowledge prospect's statement: _____

_____

Rebuttal text: _____

_____

_____

_____

_____

*Objection as it would typically be stated by prospect:*

_____

_____

_____

*Telemarketer's response*

Acknowledge prospect's statement: _____

_____

Rebuttal text: _____

_____

_____

_____

_____

_____

*Objection as it would typically be stated by prospect:*

_____

_____

_____

*Telemarketer's response*

Acknowledge prospect's statement: _____

_____

Rebuttal text: _____

_____

_____

_____

_____

_____

_____

# Chapter 12

# NONSELLING SCRIPTS THAT BOOST REVENUES AND CUT COSTS

Calling new prospects and following up on leads are not the only ways to make telemarketing pay big cash dividends. Under present business conditions, there are four other vital areas that demand intensive calling efforts in order to maximize profits. They are

- *Reactivating dormant accounts.* Customers who have dropped out of an established buying pattern or have stopped purchasing altogether *must* be revived if at all possible.

- *Dealing with marginal accounts.* Small-volume buyers or geographically distant customers need to be continually serviced, but *not* through costly field visits. The phone can be your answer.

- *Handling financial matters.* Solving credit dilemmas and managing collections are expedited through intelligent use of the telephone.

- *Finding and negotiating with new suppliers.* Finding the best products, prices, and terms is done rapidly and efficiently by telephone and mail. More money is made by smart buying than by selling.

Each area can be a robust producer of *new* dollars in even the smallest company. Each can bring in revenue that is sometimes written off as a lost cause in some organizations. For example, a food-products wholesaler identified all active accounts beyond a 150-mile distance from its warehouse; too far for convenient field contact. These customers were switched from expensive field routes to telephone maintenance. Understanding the supplier's need to control costs, almost every account went along with the change. The savings come to over $90,000 per year for the wholesaler, with no significant reduction in the service it is able to give to those outlying customers.

One very strong feature in nonselling programs like those previously listed is the fact that the caller needs no sales background. Therefore, these telemarketers can be expected to work on a straight salary. Commissions are not necessary or desirable, so the impact on payroll should be minimal—and easily absorbed by the additional revenue raised through the nonselling program.

This chapter describes the key nonselling ways to boost cash inflow and cut expenses.

## REACTIVATING DORMANT ACCOUNTS

How many people make sizable and frequent purchases over a period of time, then suddenly stop—and never hear anything from the company? It happens surprisingly often. It's almost as though customers are *expected* to eventually wander off and buy elsewhere.

At the very least, one would think that the abandoned source might want to know *why* valuable business was heading to competitors. That could lead to corrective action and prevent further erosion of the buyer pool. But there is nothing but silence—except for perhaps a final invoice.

An auto parts wholesaler in a southern U.S. city refuses to ignore customer loss. Once a buying pattern is solidly established, any slip in order volume after 60 days is flagged for immediate telephone follow-up. More than half of those fading customers are saved through this quick reaction. According to the firm's general manager, about $200,000 in annual sales is preserved.

We'll look at the program used by this organization.

### SCRIPT 12.1a: REOPENING DIALOGUE WITH INACTIVE BUYERS

An occasional pharmacy customer who begins to buy elsewhere will rarely be missed, but the individual who spends several hundred dollars or more each month for some kind of product will almost certainly arouse curiosity under those circumstances. An amount like that *should* be missed—and something has to be done to try to get it back.

Losing sales is one thing, but the cost that has already been spent to *get* the customer is another matter. When one considers the investment made to obtain that first sale, it becomes clear that a firm's present accounts have to be jealously guarded. The general manager in the auto parts firm provided these figures:

- *Advertising.* Cost per customer is estimated to be $138.
- *Cost of selling.* The first order requires an effort worth about $225 in time and resources.
- *Initial administrative expense.* Steps required to ship the first order, including credit checking, computer entry, and other procedures, run approximately $150.

Therefore, at least $500 goes into a new account—whether the initial order is $150 or $5,000. The parts firm knows it typically takes almost a year to recover those costs in the case of a reasonably active customer, so if the customer decides to buy from a competitor, it isn't taken lightly.

It takes the parts wholesaler 4 months to establish a pattern whereby a customer's monthly purchases can be estimated with fair accuracy. If that monthly average slips for 2 consecutive months, action is taken within 14 days. If buying stops altogether in a given month, the response is immediate.

This call is used:

| | |
|---|---|
| *Telemarketer:* | [Establishes contact with the buyer of record in the customer organization. Opens with standard introduction, then says] *Bob, I'm calling to find out how things are going so far in your dealings with us. We want to be sure you're getting all of the merchandise, quality, and service you need.* |
| *Customer:* | *Everything is fine, thanks.* |

If the customer comes right out and says "We were closed for vacation last month" or "We're getting better prices from a different wholesaler," the caller knows the reason for the drop in purchasing and can deal with it as necessary. But when the customer's answer is vague, such as "Everything is fine," further questioning is needed. It might proceed like this:

### SCRIPT 12.1b: PROBING TO REVEAL THE PROBLEM

Some lost customers will not readily tell a former supplier why buying is now done somewhere else. They may prefer to avoid any kind of confrontation with the spurned seller, or they may have some other reason for their reticence. In such a case, a little probing will usually flush out the reason.

This probing is delicately handled and must *never* come across in this way: "We're wondering why you didn't spend your usual amount with us last month."

Callers for the parts wholesaler do it this way. We'll begin with the customer's response in Script 12.1a to maintain continuity of the dialogue:

| | |
|---|---|
| **Customer:** | *Everything is fine, thanks.* |
| **Telemarketer:** | *That's great. If you wouldn't mind, we like to ask our customers certain specific questions about how they purchase parts; it helps us improve service. Can I take another minute of your time?* |

Most customers consent, though some reluctantly. Now the following questions are asked:

| | |
|---|---|
| **Telemarketer:** | *Have we been able to provide* all *the parts you've needed?* |
| | *Has delivery always been on time, and are orders filled correctly?* |
| | *Has our billing been accurate? Any problems with amounts due or trade discounts?* |

> *If I may ask, how many wholesalers do you use in your parts buying?*

That final question is the one that usually brings any problem to the surface. A dormant or fading customer who is still operating at the same location must be buying from *someone*, and it can help if the caller discovers *who* is now getting the major portion of the buyer's business.

When the telemarketer gets a clue regarding the presence of a dominating competitive supplier, steps are taken to regain some lost ground.

## SCRIPT 12.1c: RECAPTURING LOST BUSINESS

Some wholesalers react to competitive encroachment by cutting prices. While it *is* sometimes necessary to meet or beat rival quotes in order to recapture an account, discounting may succeed only in further damaging the relationship. Here are two reasons why:

- A customer will wonder why the discounting supplier didn't offer better prices *before* a competitor forced the issue. Furthermore, the customer may feel that there is yet more leeway in the price and credibility may be compromised.

- Sophisticated buyers realize that lean margins will sooner or later translate to skimpy service and quality from a squeezed wholesaler. Even bargain hunters understand that tight margins result in minimal performance.

Thus, instead of focusing an attack on prices, this wholesaler stresses service. Price *is* addressed, but the topic is handled carefully.

We'll continue from the last part of Script 12.1b:

| | |
|---|---|
| *Telemarketer:* | *If I may ask, how many wholesalers do you use in your parts buying?* |
| *Customer:* | *We use Downtown Auto Parts, Premium, and your company for most of our needs.* |
| *Telemarketer:* | *We're in good company—they're good outfits. Do you find that all three wholesalers offer about the same selection, service, and prices?* |
| *Customer:* | *Pretty close.* |
| *Telemarketer:* | *If there isn't much difference, what are the advantages in using three or more parts suppliers?* |

That's the key question. There can be numerous customer responses to it. Here are the most prevalent customer answers, along with typical comebacks from the telemarketer:

| | |
|---|---|
| *Customer:* | *We let our department heads do their own buying, and we want them to have a choice of suppliers.* |

| Telemarketer: | Can we spend some time with each of your department heads in order to familiarize them with our products, services, and prices? |
|---|---|

By simply doing a better job of penetrating the customer company, a bigger share of its buying dollar might be captured. In the preceding case, it's a matter of more exposure to the people working behind the counters.

Our next response may be encountered in the situation that the most recently added wholesaler is apparently the least trusted:

| Customer: | We like to keep several suppliers on tap so we can do some comparing and find out who gives us the best service. |
|---|---|
| Telemarketer: | Not a bad idea, but I think we'd be better able to demonstrate our performance if you gave us more to do. For example, if you could give us a share of business about equal to what your other suppliers are handling, we'd be able to prove our efficiency to you in no uncertain terms. Also, that kind of division might provide you a better basis for comparison. |

Finally, when price appears to be a reason for falling purchases:

| Customer: | We'd like to give you more, but we find that you're a bit higher on some items. |
|---|---|
| Telemarketer: | If we could sit down and work out a fairly close estimate of how much you'd buy over the course of a year, I feel we'd be able to create some better breaks for you. |
| | One good way to do that is to give us an idea of how much you now buy from your leading supplier, and we'll base a new price schedule on that figure. |

As illustrated, instead of rushing into a discount program, the caller first tries to get a commitment from the customer.

### LETTER 12.1:  FOLLOW-UP TO SMALL DORMANT ACCOUNTS

When a company has many dormant or fading accounts that don't warrant telephone follow-up due to their small total potential, a letter like this can be used economically:

Dear Mr. Johns:

We hope that all of your past purchases at Roberts's were satisfactory in every way.

Since our records show that you haven't been in since January 15, we are concerned. Every customer, large and small, is important to us.

Please take just a moment to check off the appropriate comments and send the questionnaire back in the enclosed postage-paid envelope.

_____ You don't stock items we use. (If so, please tell us what those items are:)

_____

_____

_____

_____ Salespeople were not knowledgeable or courteous.

_____ We got a better deal somewhere else.

_____ Everything is fine. We'll see you when we're ready to buy.

Look forward to hearing from you—or better yet—*seeing* you.

Sincerely,

David O. Metzker

About 25 percent of the customers respond. When they do indicate some kind of problem, a phone call is made to try to restore buying, however small the purchases may be.

Next, how to control expenses in handling small and/or distant accounts.

## CUTTING THE COST OF DEALING WITH MARGINAL ACCOUNTS

Depending on your industry, the cost of one field visit, whether it's to sell or to service an account, costs between $75 and $450. These are *not* abstract numbers. They have been carefully and accurately calculated over a period of years by marketing experts in various fields.

Costs of that magnitude definitely restrict in-person calls. Management in hundreds of companies must decide which of their accounts will continue to receive personal attention and which will not.

Organizations generally make a distinction that looks like this:

- Large-volume customers who purchase frequently are high priority—especially if they are located close enough to the supplier to visit conveniently.

- Small-volume and/or distant accounts (those *not* convenient to visit) normally fail to qualify for in-person visits. These are *marginal* accounts.

Few companies can afford to drop their lower-volume accounts since, collectively, they can add up to a considerable piece of annual business. Some other way must be found to keep their business coming in while costly personal visits to them are curtailed or eliminated.

This section covers precisely that dilemma and how some firms are dealing with it.

### SCRIPT 12.2a: SWITCHING DISTANT CUSTOMERS TO BUYING BY TELEPHONE

A distributor of meat-processing equipment, hit extremely hard by eroding profits, arrived at this method of classifying customers: A *distant* customer would be any account that lies a distance of 200 miles or more from the warehouse. If annual sales to the customer exceed $150,000 per year, the account is exempt from this classification since continued field calls would be both needed and affordable at that level of business.

Distant customers buying under $150,000 a year would *not* be visited by sales or service representatives unless special circumstances arose. Telephone and mail were to be used exclusively with distant customers.

Implementation of the switch from field service to telephone/mail maintenance was to begin immediately and would be phased in completely over a 90-day period. The first step was this call to all distant accounts:

> *Telemarketer:* [Contacts buyer of record in customer company. Then says] *Karl, if you have a few minutes, I'd like to explain an important new program we have underway that should produce some long-range advantages for both of us.*
>
> *We feel we can make things work a lot better by servicing our outlying customers by telephone instead of by field visits.*
>
> *Let me give you some details on where we think the improvements will be.*

The telemarketer is now poised to deliver the *specific* advantages of the new program.

### SCRIPT 12.2b: STRESSING MORE FREQUENT CONTACTS

One outstanding advantage in replacing field visits with phone calls is this: The number of contacts with a customer can be boosted dramatically over what it was through personal field visits. In the case of the meat-processing firm, distant accounts received an average of one visit every five weeks, along with two telephone calls. The new phone maintenance program would assure a far greater number of contacts.

Starting from the last statement in Script 12.2, here's the caller's description of the increased communications to come:

> *Telemarketer:* *Let me give you some details on where we think the improvements will be.*
>
> *Most important is the number of times we'll be in touch with you. You're scheduled for one call per week starting next Monday. That's more than double the number of contacts we've provided you in the past.*
>
> *These will be brief, efficient contacts that are major time-savers. We'll be able to take care of your fast-developing product and service needs a lot better by talking to you more often.*

Now the telemarketer will expand on the efficiency aspect.

## SCRIPT 12.2c: POINTING OUT TIMESAVING IN
## BUYING BY TELEPHONE

Personal field visits often consume huge bites of time that busy people can ill afford; an hour or more is eaten up when 20 minutes would suffice. That point is underlined in this segment of the presentation:

> *Telemarketer:*  *We've been hearing from other customers—and you may agree—that the time taken by field visits runs way over what it should.*
>
> *It is nice to get together, but the pressure of getting everything done just doesn't permit the socializing we used to do in this business.*
>
> *So using the telephone to replace personal visits makes sense in terms of protecting your time.*

Today, most managers agree with that reasoning, and they certainly go along with the final advantage—that of keeping expenses on an even keel.

## SCRIPT 12.2d: DESCRIBING COST CONTROL IN
## BUYING BY TELEPHONE

An advantage that always draws support from managers is the positive impact the telephone can have on prices. If a supplier is able to hold the line or reduce prices as a result of cutting field visits, customers will more readily let go of personal rep appearances; but if field visits are stopped and prices *still* go up, customers may develop some resentment and start shopping for a new source.

Here's how cost control comes across in the call dialogue:

> *Telemarketer:*  *Another important advantage is keeping prices as favorable as possible. You're probably wrestling with high field costs in your business, right?*

Almost every management-level contact will concur with that observation.

> *Most of the savings we realize will go toward keeping prices stable. The annual increases we've had to make over the past few years were mostly due to increasing sales costs. We're determined to reverse that trend for the benefit of both our customers and ourselves.*
>
> *Do you see any negative side to this program?*

In truth, a certain percentage of customers in *any* industry can be expected to register displeasure at losing their personal visits from an important supplier. Of these, some will be lost as customers because they will find other sources willing to send out a rep periodically. However, the savings almost always outweigh the loss of a few accounts.

A much larger segment of distant customers will be apprehensive about losing visits but will agree to go along to see how it works. Some 25 percent will enthusiastically endorse such a program.

All distant customers who remain aboard receive a letter within ten days of the switch-over call.

### LETTER 12.2: FOLLOW-UP TO DISTANT CUSTOMERS

When a company significantly alters the way it deals with its customers, increased communications are a *must.* A customer coming to grips with new procedures has to be familiarized with the new ways of doing things. Where there *is* familiarity, there will definitely be more comfort and stability.

A letter that clearly recaps the workings of the new telephone contact system is sent about ten days after the call that originally announced the change. This is one version used by the meat-processing company:

Dear Frank:

Just a quick note to recap the things we talked about last week.

We're excited about going over to a system that will enable us to take care of your needs by telephone. While we will miss our personal visits with you, the new program will put us in touch much more frequently and provide these advantages:

- Weekly calls should put us in a better position to prevent the out-of-stock situations that occasionally came up when reordering was deferred until a rep could see you.
- We'll have much more flexibility in selecting times to talk. Field visits sometimes coincided with those sudden emergencies you have to deal with.
- Product costs should remain constant—or come down a bit—since the telephone is offering some economies that we'll pass on to you.

Since we both attend some of the same trade shows during the year, I hope we can get together on those occasions.

Please let me know if there is *anything* you need. I'll personally see that it's taken care of.

Sincerely,

John D. Ralston

Most firms that take the bold step using telephone calls to replace visits to distant accounts *will* make an exception when a face-to-face meeting with a far-away customer is absolutely necessary. Even low-volume distant accounts need to understand that a supplier's rep will make the trip if a crisis arises. Still, that willingness to visit if needed should *not* be publicized by the supplier.

Accounts that lie *within* a supplier's marketing area are marginal if they buy at very low levels. We'll now look at this category of customers.

### SCRIPT 12.3: SWITCHING LOW-VOLUME BUYERS TO TELEPHONE PURCHASING

A customer can be only a mile away from a supplier's firm but still be classified as marginal. In fact, a small manufacturer of sporting goods lists as marginal some 36 retail customers, all situated within a 10-mile radius of the company. Each retailer buys

$5,000 or less per year and therefore fits in the very small customer category, according to the firm's definition of the term.

These marginal accounts do *not* justify the attention of a field representative for the reason that this manufacturer estimates the cost of a field visit at $125 each. Since an outside rep would see each client about 14 times per year, the total cost of outside calls *for just one $5,000 account* might easily reach $1,750. It doesn't take a financial genius to figure out the devastating impact that cost would have on profits!

This particular manufacturer makes the most of inviting nearby small accounts into the factory to do their buying. The company uses a small showroom to display wares.

Outlying low-level buyers are on a telephone maintenance program that is almost identical to the system used by the meat processor described earlier in this chapter.

When dollar volume of purchases is the standard by which accounts are classified, this interesting complication comes up: Customers that spend *near* the break-off point will occasionally go over or fall under the line that separates marginal from all other accounts. Since it isn't practical to grant and rescind personal visits as an account bobs up and down, a judgment can be made every two years on these particular customers.

The call used to switch a small account to telephone maintenance is more sensitive than the one for distant accounts. A small-scale buyer is more likely to feel discriminated against than a customer who is far away. The latter can readily comprehend the reason for losing a supplier's personal coverage, but the owner of a start-up firm may feel that the big boys always get preferred treatment.

Here's the switchover call used by the sporting goods maker:

| | |
|---|---|
| *Telemarketer:* | [Contacts buyer of record. Then says] *Bob, we're starting a new ordering system that I think you'll find quicker and more convenient. If you have a couple of minutes, I'd like to give you the details.* |

If time is successfully cleared, caller proceeds:

> *We've created a separate method of processing orders from customers who mostly buy our sports apparel products. Starting right away, you'll have a "hot-line" number that goes directly to a telemarketer trained to guide you through those products.*
>
> *If you need larger equipment or have other kinds of needs that require the help of a representative, just call me and we'll get you together with the right person.*
>
> *We've been testing this system, and most customers prefer ordering by phone instead of through field visits, which are comparatively time-consuming for both customers and our reps.*

There are *no* apologies. The package is presented as a plan to facilitate ordering for customers who buy small items. Use of a "hot line"—a phone number dedicated to marginal buyers—fits beautifully into the new package and also serves a completely functional purpose; that line is manned by a person who specializes in low-ticket sporting goods.

This letter goes out about a week after the call:

### LETTER 12.3: FOLLOW-UP TO LOW-VOLUME BUYERS

Instead of dwelling on the difference between large- and small-volume buyers, this letter concentrates on the efficiencies of the new hot-line. It accompanies a packet of specially prepared materials, which are outlined in the letter:

Dear Ed:

Here's everything you need to start using the new INSTANT-ORDER program. In this envelope, you'll find:

- *Our HOT-LINE number.* It puts you in immediate contact with Nancy Mills. Her *only* job is to help you with all of your needs.
- An up-to-the-minute catalog and price list that assists you in rapidly identifying items, prices, and minimum quantities. Use the blue order forms to list your needs and keep it as a record of your purchase until you receive our computerized list, mailed right after you place an order.
- For your extra convenience, we now have a fully stocked showroom at the Eighth Avenue plant. Free parking is available at the south side of the building. Attendants are on duty at this facility during all normal business hours.

Exercise equipment and large sporting products are not listed in the catalog since orders for these items will be handled separately. Please call (912) 740–7400 for information regarding these product categories.

We're sure you'll like the speed, efficiency, and economy this new approach will bring you. Thanks for your continued loyalty. I'll be in touch soon to find out how everything is going.

Sincerely,

Cecil Kincaid

This program enabled the sporting goods manufacturer to reassign field reps. The immediate objective is increased attention to major accounts and intensified efforts to sell prospects of large-volume potential. Also important is a marked improvement in small-order profits.

Next, keeping better control of financial situations through telemarketing.

## HANDLING FINANCIAL MATTERS

Efficient collections and tactful but firm credit dealings can build extra income. Equally important, the skillful handling of financial matters *will* solidify good will in an area of customer relations that is too often damaged.

In companies with unusually heavy customer attrition due to tactless handling of collection and credit situations, managers have been known to say: "Our administrative people don't normally come in contact with customers, so it's understandable if they upset a customer now and then.

Actually, there is *no* justification for badly handled credit and collection transactions. In well-run firms, management takes the following steps to ensure that doesn't happen:

- Illustrate to *every* administrative employee the value of a customer to the company. Through understanding the cost and effort required to develop a client, the needed appreciation should be established.

- Management must give administrative people the right tools to work with. Scripts like the ones on the following pages represent a strong start toward that goal.

- Select carefully the administrative employees who will take on the responsibility of speaking to customers. In any organization, there are employees who are more adept than others at handling customers.

When customers are offended, it isn't just that individual who may be lost as a buyer. Word has a way of spreading and injury to the company can grow.

The scripts and letters that follow have been developed by a west coast publisher of local travel and restaurant guides.

### SCRIPT 12.4a: REQUESTING COD ON THE FIRST ORDER

When a recent purchaser is told that credit can't be granted on an initial order, that hopeful customer will be upset to some degree under the *best* of circumstances. If COD on the first order is company policy for *all* new accounts, the explanation is easier; but if the new purchaser is borderline for one reason or another, the situation calls for extra delicacy. The latter state of affairs is the one we'll look at.

This basic script is used by the publisher when the credit manager demands cash on (or before) delivery:

*Credit Department*
*Employee:*                    [Contacts purchaser, introduces self, then says] *We appreciate the order you placed Wednesday. We want to clear the way for delivery, so I'm calling to get some of the financial details settled.*

Now the caller verifies ordered quantities and dollar totals. This serves the purpose not only of verifying data but also of building rapport between the two individuals. Now the employee gets to the point:

*Your open account status will be completely established on the next shipment we deliver to you. The amount due on this order can either be prepaid or remitted to the carrier when the books reach you. Which way do you prefer?*

Since it has been made clear that credit *will* be extended on subsequent orders, only about half of the customers on this arrangement question the request for cash up front. On occasions when this requirement *is* challenged, the employee responds this way:

> *Like most companies, we have a complex set of requirements that sometimes seems arbitrary. I hope you don't interpret this as any lack of trust. On the contrary, we're very pleased to have you as a dealer. But whether it seems right or wrong, we have to try to live with this decision.*

When a customer like this claims that other publishers and various suppliers don't hesitate to ship initial orders on open account, it's a difficult argument to reject. The publisher's strategy is to request references.

### SCRIPT 12.4b: REQUIRE CREDIT REFERENCES

When a request for references is stated this way, it can further irritate an already agitated customer: "Can you give me some credit references?"

No matter how nicely the words are spoken, it comes across as a challenge. Distrust *is* inferred. There is no magic in simply packaging this request so it *means* the same thing, but seems a lot softer. The publisher's credit people ask this way:

| | |
|---|---|
| **Customer:** | *That doesn't make sense. I do business with other publishers, distributors, and companies of all kinds. As far as I recall, they all gave me terms on my first order.* |
| **Credit Department Employee:** | *If our credit manager knew that, it probably would make a big difference. If you could find a few minutes to select five or six of your suppliers who've been selling you various things for at least a year, I think we can work this out.* |
| | *I'd need names and phone numbers so we can get right on this for you. Can you do that conveniently?* |

When a firm is faced with too many borderline customers to call, a "need cash" letter is used.

### LETTER 12.4: NEED COD OR CASH BEFORE DELIVERY

A maker of novelty items will process an average of 30 orders per day—about 6 of them first-time buyers. Nearly all of the new buyers request billing. The number of new purchases and the comparatively low dollar volume of each order combine to make calling impractical.

This letter—which of course can be transmitted via FAX when possible—is used to take care of the problem:

Dear Mr. Danielson:

Your order for keychains and paperweights has been entered. These items are in stock and can be shipped via UPS as soon as you inform us of your payment preference.

New accounts can be opened promptly if the initial shipment is prepaid or if the new customer remits cash on delivery. Later orders can normally be shipped on open account.

As an alternative, you may prefer to provide several current trade references. This usually entails a delay of three workdays to permit checking from our end.

We know you will understand this requirement, and we hope it doesn't cause you undue inconvenience. Please let me know how to proceed.

Again, your business is very much appreciated, and we look forward to serving your needs for many years to come.

Sincerely,

Jack M. Monroe

As much care as a company takes to check credit, delinquent accounts *will* occur. The next section deals with that important topic.

## COLLECTING PAST-DUE ACCOUNTS

There are countless reasons why a customer fails to pay an invoice on time. Here are a few of the leading causes:

- To improve cash flow. The buyer may take extra time to pay to avoid cash-flow problems. Generally, this situation will delay payment up to 90 days, but rarely beyond that point. Usually this is not quite late enough to seriously risk the relationship.

- Neglect. A customer's operation is disorganized, thus, the customer has no reliable system for scheduling payments.

- Genuine financial problems. A customer is simply unable to pay outstanding invoices.

- Dispute of invoice amount or some other point of disagreement that causes the customer to withhold payment.

In three of these situations, buyers *do* have the ability to pay and probably should be retained as customers despite the aggravation they inflict on suppliers. Only one, the customer in trouble, is wisely dropped as soon as possible.

Since it is often impossible to find out exactly *why* a past-due account is slow, a certain degree of patience by the creditor is a good move. Pushing too hard too fast to collect money from a financially *healthy* customer may risk big future orders. For that reason, the novelty company uses this system for collections.

This series of timed contacts is successful in recovering 66 cents of every past-due dollar: When an account is *14 days* past due a reminder letter is sent; when *30 days* past due a first collection call is made; when *60 days* past due a second collection letter is sent; when *90 days* past due a final collection letter is mailed.

Samples of each of these four contacts are now provided.

### *LETTER 12.5:   REMINDER, 14 DAYS PAST DUE*

Sent when an account is 14 days past due, or 44 days from invoice date, this is the *gentlest* kind of reminder. When only two weeks have passed since the due date, extra care is taken to avoid offending a customer, so the words *past due* are not mentioned at this early stage:

Dear Mrs. Schuster:

Your order for binders was shipped via UPS on April 18. We trust it was received by you promptly and in good condition.

So that you can check the accuracy of your records, that shipment was billed on our invoice #265301-82 in the amount of $336. Terms, net 30 days.

If there is any discrepancy, please call or write Carla Hall in our accounting department, extension 11.

Thank you for your continued patronage.

Sincerely,

Gerry Swanson

If no response ensues, the next contact comes one month later.

## SCRIPT 12.5: COLLECTION CALL, 30 DAYS PAST DUE

Accounts that reach this degree of lateness are not overwhelming in quantity, so a brief telephone contact is feasible. Direct contact is about 50 percent more effective in getting payment than are letters, so this call often eliminates the need for subsequent letters.

*Accounting*
*Department*
*Employee:*            [Contacts the head of accounts payable in customer company. Introduces self, then says] *I'm pleased to meet you. I'm calling in regard to payment on an order we shipped to you on April 18. It was billed on May 10 in the amount of $336. Do you need our invoice number or any other information?*

All information requested by the accounts payable person in the customer company is promptly provided. If customer's response is "I'll check on it and call you back," the supplier ties down *a definite time* for that next contact.

*I'm usually all over the offices here and it may be hard to reach me. Why don't I call you again this afternoon at 4:00 P.M. Will that be enough time for you to find out about payment?*

The caller states this factually. There must be no anger or sarcasm. At the same time, the delinquent customer should get a clear message that the next conversation must produce concrete answers about the outstanding invoice.

In difficult collections, a promise to pay by a specific date is generally made by the customer and not kept. The next contact gets a bit tougher.

*LETTER 12.6:   COLLECTION, 60 DAYS PAST DUE*

By now the account has gone 90 days from invoice date without paying. Under these circumstances the supplier still isn't quite ready to burn bridges, but does turn up the volume noticeably and suggests more drastic action later.

Dear Mrs. Schuster:

We have not received payment for our invoice #265301-82 in the amount of $336. Your account is now 60 days past due.

If you are having difficulty, we will work with you if at all possible. It is urgent that you contact me by telephone before August 15 so that we can discuss this very serious matter.

If I do not hear from you or receive payment by the above-stated date, we will regretfully take appropriate action.

Sincerely,

Gerry Swanson

When no response is forthcoming, the final step is taken:

*LETTER 12.7:   FINAL NOTICE, 90 DAYS PAST DUE*

This letter is mailed *only* when the creditor company is fully prepared to take drastic action to collect. Drastic action means:

- A collection agency
- An attorney

In either case, the matter moves out of the creditor's hands and, for all practical purposes, the relationship is badly damaged.

If steps as harsh as this are *not* desired, the owed company is better off hanging on to the delinquent account and continuing to send a variety of milder letters. The point is, don't make dire threats if you have no intention of following through with them.

In the case of the novelty company, 90 days past due is the point where patience finally runs out, and the most drastic steps are taken:

Dear Mrs. Schuster:

Repeated efforts to cooperate with you have been made since last April to no avail. You have chosen to ignore our attempts to obtain payment on invoice #265301-82 in the amount of $336.

We now have no choice but to turn your account over to our attorney for possible legal action. This will be done on Friday, September 13, 19———.

This outcome is genuinely regretted since we feel everything possible was done by our organization to achieve a more agreeable outcome.

Sincerely,

Gerry Swanson

Copies of all prior collection letters as well as notes taken during any telephone calls are important elements of the documentation and are given to the collection agent.

One more extremely valuable nonselling area is establishing solid connections with potential sources of supply.

## FINDING AND NEGOTIATING WITH NEW SUPPLIERS

When a company succeeds in identifying the best sources for its needs, success comes a big step closer. One affluent wholesaler says: "We make far more money buying than we do selling. The products we select and the prices we negotiate enable us to come out on top."

Based on a random survey of 200 wholesale and retail companies, those words are absolutely true. About 15 percent of them are extremely active in searching for new sources. These same 30 organizations are among the fastest growing in the surveyed group.

A clear majority of the surveyed companies rarely purchase from sources outside of the most obvious ones. The result is often a boring selection and prices that tend to range from ordinary to high. In price-sensitive industries, this reluctance to explore can cause a gradual loss of competitive edge.

In some industries, it is a fact that there are a limited number of suppliers from which to choose; but in most businesses the opportunities to buy smarter are almost boundless. For example, a manufacturer of women's fashion items constantly searches for new fabrics and better deals on everything from thread to industrial sewing machines. The result is a never-ending inflow of exceptional values, superior quality, and innovative new looks and ideas. Through its ongoing exploration of the industry's nooks and crannies, this firm always manages to remain a step ahead of bigger competitors—and consistently undersells them.

Approaches used by this organization are deceptively simple. A very brief letter goes out to *every* potential supplier. Those who respond are called by the manufacturer in order to work out the most favorable purchase arrangements.

Here's the program used by this company:

### LETTER 12.8: REQUEST FOR SAMPLES AND PRICES

During an average week, about two clerical hours are devoted to finding the names and addresses of potential suppliers that were previously unknown to the manufacturer. These are usually found in:

- Trade publications
- Newspaper articles
- Classified telephone directories from other cities
- Observations made during routine travels
- Chamber of Commerce directories
- Industrial directories
- Trade associations

This letter is sent to every potential new supplier:

Attention:  Customer Service
                   Carolina Notion Supply

Enclosed is a photocopy of a lace applique.

We are looking for a wholesale source that can supply this item. Current needs are six thousand pieces which should cover us for approximately the next sixty to ninety days.

Do you carry this item, or would you have anything comparable to it? If not, we would appreciate your referring us to a source that might carry a similar item.

Thank you for your service.

Sincerely,

Gina Delancey


*Or:*


Dear Mr. Feinstein:

Enclosed are swatches of several fabric patterns we are using in large quantities. We would like to know whether or not you can supply these and, if so, how much they would cost per yard.

Also, we will be needing red lace and would be interested in seeing anything you might have.

If these items are not in your line, we would be grateful for any advice on who we can contact in the industry.

Thanks for your service.

Sincerely,

Gina Delancey


Such a query letter can request information about fabrics, sewing equipment, or *any* other component used by the manufacturer. If a photocopy can't effectively convey the desired design, a sample, sketch, or photograph is enclosed. A typed and hand-signed letter is used since this gets much better response than a form letter.

About one fourth of these query letters attract an answer. Half of the responding suppliers do not carry the requested item but provide valuable information on related products that may eventually be needed. The other answers are either on target, very close, or recommend another source.

Next, how this fashion manufacturer negotiates small quantities and good prices.

## SCRIPT 12.6: BUYING SMALLER QUANTITIES AT THE BEST POSSIBLE PRICES

A small company may run into problems with suppliers that prefer not to bother with lower-volume buyers. A request for 6,000 appliques may be almost meaningless to a firm that typically ships 50,000 pieces to its *smallest* customers. To compound that difficulty, lower-than-usual quantities would not often be priced competitively.

In an attempt to overcome these problems, the following call is placed as soon as a promising new source is identified:

*Buyer:*    [Contacts the individual who signed the letter of response, introduces self, then says] *The applique you provided looks like it would serve our needs for a product we're introducing in our spring line. Can you quote me on 6,000 pieces?*

While a discouraging response could be worded any number of ways, the basic message comes across this way:

*Seller:*    *We'd like very much to help you, but our minimum is 18,000 pieces. I can refer you to one of our distributors who can work with the numbers you need.*

*Buyer:*    *I understand your position. We've been through similar situations with our other major suppliers. All of them agreed to work with us on smaller initial orders than they normally like to handle, and we quickly reached and passed their minimums.*

*I think they understood that a distributor wouldn't be able to ship as fast as we need the goods since they'd have to first order from you. Plus, the extra step adds more cost than we're able to tolerate in a competitive business.*

*We really need your support now. If we can get that from you, you'll have a steady stream of business that should exceed your minimums pretty quickly.*

*I can give you the order right now.*

Some sources will adamantly refuse to deal direct, but a substantial number will recognize this fact: Here's a customer who may be too small to deal with according to arbitrary standards that were designed to exclude the smallest orders. Yet this is obviously a manufacturer who *is* going to increase order size as time goes on, so it doesn't make sense to penalize them—perhaps damaging their chances of introducing a competitively priced product.

### LETTER 12.9:   ORDER CONFIRMATION AND REQUEST FOR PAYMENT TERMS

When shipment is approved by the seller pending receipt of a written order, the fashion manufacturer mails this order confirmation, which includes references and a request for payment terms:

Dear Ms. Kramer:

Per my discussion with you by telephone, the following is our order for six thousand appliques. Please match the blue and peach with the enclosed color samples.

We would appreciate immediate shipment on your standard billing arrangements. Trade references follow; these should facilitate prompt delivery: [Four references are provided.

These include the names of contacts and telephone numbers. A bank reference is also provided.]

If you have any questions, please call me.

Again, we deeply appreciate your special consideration and look forward to a long and mutually beneficial business relationship with your company.

Sincerely,

Gina Delancey

## REFINING YOUR REVENUE-BUILDING SCRIPTS

Checklists are now provided for each of the following revenue-building and cost-cutting areas:

- Reactivating dormant accounts
- Dealing with marginal accounts
- Handling financial matters
- Finding and negotiating with new suppliers

Use the checklists to make sure your call strategy hits the most vital areas. Then use the worksheets that follow each checklist to work out the best possible dialogue.

### FORM 12.1: CHECKLIST FOR REACTIVATING DORMANT ACCOUNTS

1. Does the dollar amount of your average sale warrant a special effort to revive dormant accounts?

   ____ Yes     ____ No

2. Define a dormant account in your business:
   - Is it a *completely* inactive customer, or one that has dropped in purchase activity?

     _____

   - If you define *dormant* as buying less than previously, how *much* less, and for how long a time? _____

     _____

     _____

3. Do you have a system in your company that will accurately and quickly reveal dormant accounts?

   ____ Yes     ____ No

4. How long after a dormant account is identified will follow-up occur? _____

5. Have you designated a telemarketer to handle the task?

___ Yes     ___ No

6. If you plan to use a combination of mailings and calls to reactivate dormant accounts, outline the type of contacts you will make and their timing:

| Activity | Timing |
|----------|--------|
| _____ | _____ |
| _____ | _____ |
| _____ | _____ |
| _____ | _____ |
| _____ | _____ |

_____

_____

## FORM 12.1a:  DIALOGUE WORKSHEET FOR DORMANT ACCOUNTS

Introduction: _____

_____

_____

_____

_____

Opening question: _____

_____

_____

_____

_____

List probing questions (if customer's response to your opening question is inconclusive):

• _____

_____

• _____

_____

• _____

_____

•  _____

_____

If you can offer special incentives to reactivate customers, describe them: _____

_____

_____

_____

Notes: _____

_____

_____

_____

_____

_____

## FORM 12.2:  CHECKLIST FOR DEALING WITH MARGINAL ACCOUNTS

1. To be classified as marginal, how far from your place of business is a customer located? _____ miles

2. At what dollar volume level do you consider a customer marginal?   $_____

3. Do you now provide field visits to marginal accounts?

   ____ Yes    ____ No

4. If so, can you eliminate those visits and still provide adequate customer services?

   ____ Yes    ____ No

5. What changes in your operation will be needed to effectively replace field visits with telephone contacts?

   ____ Simplified installation of the product?

   ____ Improved telephone service and support to customers?

   ____ Better literature?

   ____ Stronger telephone selling capability?

   ____ Enhanced prospect and customer tracking system?

   ____ Other: _____

   _____

   _____

   _____

6. How often will marginal accounts be contacted by telephone? _____ times per month

7. Can you develop a showroom capability to sell your products or services from your offices?

   \_\_\_\_ Yes    \_\_\_\_ No

8. Can you take maximum advantage of a toll-free 800 line to assist marginal accounts?

   \_\_\_\_ Yes    \_\_\_\_ No

---

### FORM 12.2a: DIALOGUE WORKSHEET FOR MARGINAL ACCOUNTS

Introduction: _____

_____

_____

_____

_____

_____

Announce new program (visits to be replaced by telephone contact): _____

_____

_____

_____

_____

_____

_____

Advantage 1 (more frequent contact): _____

_____

_____

_____

_____

_____

Advantage 2 (time saving): _____

_____

_____

_____

_____

_____

_____

Advantage 3 (cost control): _____

_____

_____

_____

_____

_____

_____

Other: _____

_____

_____

_____

_____

_____

Describe details of program start-up: _____

_____

_____

_____

_____

_____

_____

Notes: _____

_____

_____

_____

_____

### FORM 12.3: CHECKLIST FOR HANDLING FINANCIAL MATTERS

1. If administrative people in your company handle credit and collection issues with customers, are those employees trained to maintain good relations?

  ____ Yes   ____ No

2. Are you set up to check credit references?

  ____ Yes   ____ No

3. Do you have a clear procedure for granting credit terms?

  ____ Yes   ____ No

4. Do you have a definite sequence of collection steps worked out?

  ____ Yes   ____ No

5. If not, create a sequence that includes letters and telephone contacts:

| Activity | Timing |
| --- | --- |
| _____ | _____ |
| _____ | _____ |
| _____ | _____ |
| _____ | _____ |
| _____ | _____ |

### FORM 12.3a: DIALOGUE WORKSHEET FOR COLLECTION CALL

Introduction: _____

_____

_____

_____

_____

Describe shipment or invoice: _____

_____

_____

_____

_____

Describe past-due status: _____

_____

_____

_____

_____

Request payment: _____

_____

_____

_____

_____

Establish a *definite* payment deadline: _____

_____

_____

_____

Notes: _____

_____

_____

_____

_____

_____

### FORM 12.4: CHECKLIST FOR FINDING AND NEGOTIATING WITH NEW SUPPLIERS

1. Identify the areas of your business in which price, quality, selection, or service depend on outside sources and can stand improvement:

   ____ Office supplies

   ____ Products you sell

   ____ Services you sell

   ____ Raw materials you use in manufacturing

   ____ Other: _____

   _____

   _____

   _____

2. For each area you checked above, list several good sources that might help you find potential new suppliers:

*Area:* _____

      *Sources:* _____

               _____

               _____

*Area:* _____

      *Sources:* _____

               _____

               _____

*Area:* _____

      *Sources:* _____

               _____

               _____

3. Have you formally listed all of the qualifications a supplier should have to best serve your purposes?

_____ Yes _____ No

4. If not, list desired qualifications here:

_____

_____

_____

5. How many queries can you comfortably send out each week? _____

_____

_____

### FORM 12.4a: WORKSHEET FOR NEW-SUPPLIER QUERY LETTER

Since a good query letter is the cutting edge for finding better sources, it is important for you to work on that aspect first.

*Letter opening*

Describe item or service needed: _____

_____

_____

_____

Can you supplement the above description with a sample, sketch, photo, or other means? _____

*Optional*

State quantity needed: _____

_____

_____

_____

*Optional*

Ask for price quote: _____

_____

_____

_____

*Optional*

Request sample: _____

_____

_____

_____

If unable to supply, ask for information on other sources that may be known to the addressee: _____

_____

_____

_____

Sign off: _____

_____

_____

_____

Notes: _____

_____

_____

_____

_____

# Chapter 13

# SCRIPTS FOR INTERVIEWING NEW TELEMARKETERS

When business owners and operators seek advice about their telemarketing programs, around 75 percent of the questions they ask are about the recruitment of callers. Whether a company is involved in a program or merely contemplating a move in that direction, attracting and selecting the right person is often the point of greatest concern.

Questions are usually about the following areas:

- Where can I find a telemarketer?

- How do I screen in order to reveal a person's strengths and also weaknesses that might obstruct success of the program?

- What can I say to an applicant that would make my business and the job I'm offering look better than all the other positions available out there?

This chapter provides many of the answers to those crucial questions. The people who created and use these interview techniques have recruited and screened thousands of callers for a variety of different industries over a period of years.

In addition to its value as a tool for finding top telemarketers, this material can also be useful when interviewing candidates for *other* positions. While desired personal attributes would obviously vary from one job to another, the *screening* process certainly applies to virtually any hiring situation an employer is apt to encounter.

## RECRUITING THE BEST POSSIBLE PEOPLE

Effective recruiters explore every potential source of people. While classified help-wanted ads are effective, they also represent only one of the many recruitment avenues available. We'll go through a list of the good sources, and some of the pros and cons of each:

- *Classified newspaper ads* are responsible for a significant percentage of the total telemarketing department hiring done nationally. Many experienced recruiters say that classified ads are not the best choice, since they are read primarily by people who are unemployed, and some of the best candidates are presently working and satisfied with their present position.

  Aside from being costly, the pulling power of classified ads is at best unpredictable. A well-constructed ad (covered later) may work one day but flop a week later.

- *Employment agencies* are not recommended as a source. While an agency can keep your schedule loaded with interviews, they probably will *not* do the kind of meticulous prescreening you need.

- *Universities and colleges* represent one of the most cost-effective recruitment sources. For example, business school undergraduates have worked out nicely as telemarketers.

  Contact the school placement office. They can either put you in direct contact with job seekers or see that you get space for an announcement on a school bulletin board. In addition, schools often publish newspapers that can carry your ad. Another possibility is a marketing internship for undergraduates.

  The first downside of this possibility is that active students may not always be able to devote their energies full-time to you and probably won't be in a position to give total commitment to the job.

  Second, inexperience will invariably be a factor to contend with. While a bright person can be trained, there is some question about the basic people-handling skills present in a very young adult. People skills are difficult to teach.

  Finally, there is the likelihood that a student or recent graduate may be interested in an interim job, but may very well have longer-term career objectives in a completely different industry.

- *Competitive companies* are definitely a choice, but can present numerous pitfalls. For example: (1) Can you afford to stir up competitors who would not hesitate to retaliate by hiring people away from you? (2) Would you be able to retrain an industry veteran in the style and approach you prefer? and (3) If the person jumped firms once, what prevents him or her from jumping again the moment something more attractive comes up?

- *Networking* has gained tremendous respect as a recruiting device in recent years. Some of the possibilities include: professional organizations, such as national clubs and management associations, and friends who know people in the job market. If you spread the word, you *will* get results.

Since a brief, punchy recruitment ad can be used in not only newspapers but also in a number of other publications, we'll take a look at some that have been effective.

## FIGURE 13.1: SAMPLE CLASSIFIED ADS

Your objective in an ad is to say a lot in very little space. Secondary goals are

- To *qualify* the job seeker to some extent. In other words, to discourage the people who really are not right for the position for one reason or another.
- To distinguish your employment offer from all the others if at all possible.

A telemarketing position can be romanticized by using a few choice words in your ad copy. But the realities should *also* be stated since they will come out eventually.

Abbreviating can save space but if carried to excess can make an ad exceedingly hard to understand. For example, "furn." for "furniture" would usually be interpreted accurately, but "rntl." for "rental" might stop some readers.

When you look for a telemarketer, come right out and *say* it's a calling job. Remember, many people *want* to work by telephone and would be attracted by that.

Here are a few more helpful suggestions:

- Be explicit about the *location* of your offices. An employee who has to fight traffic to get to work and home again is under a severe handicap.
- It usually makes sense to quote a salary range in your ad. This tends to discourage both underqualified people and the inevitable high rollers who expect very high income.
- Training has proved to be an attractive job feature. Applicants often realize that this is an investment the company is willing to make in them. It *does* have tangible value to growth-oriented people.
- Select the newspaper in your community with the *largest* Sunday help-wanted section. Sunday does generally pull best. Responses will be at a peak on Monday, then trail off as the week progresses.

  Remember, the ad you write for the newspaper classified section can also be run in university publications, trade papers, and other journals that are economical but reach potential applicants.

- Quick response to call-ins is absolutely essential. Line up interviews with your better candidates as soon as you can.

Here are sample ads. They are used by different companies, and all performed well in attracting better people:

*Telemarketing*

JOIN THE FURNITURE RENTAL LEADER

Fast-paced showroom in Salt Valley needs one exceptional person to develop residential and bus. clients. Excellent trng, benefits and pay plan. $25K first yr. easy. Definite career oppty. in a growth industry. Let's talk *today.*

Hardy Furniture, Inc.
Nancy Stout 225–8050

*Telemarketing*

RARE OPPORTUNITY FOR ONE HIGH-LEVEL PERSON

A leading building-products distributor needs an outstanding person to help us build long-term relationships with key accounts. Friendly, up-beat, low-pressure environment, but the career outlook is exciting for a bright self-starter. Grow into major responsibilities FAST! Great trng., benefits and flexible hours. Realistic $40,000/yr.

Call Mrs. Gettle 866–6256

*Telemarketing*

FOUR HOURS A DAY/$2,500 A MONTH

Rapid growth creates rare opp'ty in a fast-growing private school. We need ONE high-class telemarketer willing to learn our unique ethical approaches. Great working environment, teamwork, training, and career advancement.

Mr. France 328–2838

---

Many top recruiters feel that requesting a resume is not necessarily good practice for this reason: Someone who is *presently* employed, and is spending some time looking for a better opportunity, probably has not prepared a formal resume and thus will not be in a position to provide one. But he or she often *will* make a phone call, which is also safer.

*Tell* your other employees about your ad! If you do not inform them, the incoming calls may be misunderstood and mishandled. Script 13.1, Referring Calls from Applicants, provides dialogue for employees who field calls from ad respondents.

Some of the most productive recruiters urge companies to create a job description as the first step in searching for a new telemarketer—if such a description does not already exist. An example follows:

---

### FORM 13.1: CREATING A TELEMARKETING JOB DESCRIPTION

Sharp applicants *will* ask an interviewer questions about the position. If the job is a new one in the company, there are no prior experiences to draw from. A description will prove especially valuable in that case.

The following sample can be used as a model and modified as needed. This particular description is one for a telephone *closer*.

*JOB DESCRIPTION*
Position:   Telemarketer
Reports to:   Marketing Manager

*Tasks and Responsibilities*

1. Generating Sales Revenue
   - Call new prospects
   - Follow up and close
   - Take call-ins from customers and prospects during designated hours
   - Achieve at least 20 hours of actual calling per week
   - Attend meetings as required
   - Participate in "blitzes" and clearance-center sales
   - Achieve sales plan

2. Paperwork
   - Complete daily lead paperwork and results reports
   - Request completion of credit information by mail
   - Verify credit card or charge information
   - Receive proper signatures on agreements/amendments by mail
   - Explain long-term contracts to all interested customers
   - Request remittances for purchases
   - Record correct information on contracts and reports

3. Showroom Maintenance
   - Housekeeping (keep desks clean and organized, ashtrays clean, etc.)

4. Adhere to company policies on dress code, customer closings, and showroom procedures

5. Field Work
   - Blitzes
   - Proper handling of manager referrals
   - Achieve any field hours designated by district manager

6. Office Security in the Absence of Manager
   - Lock files and desk
   - Lock door and set alarm
   - Open offices on time

7. Showroom Records
   - File
   - Record all sales
   - Check paperwork for errors
   - Submit proper documents to marketing manager for approval

When the caller's responsibilities are listed, a recruiter is in a much better position to screen candidates. The four-step process described next is used with tremendous success to zero in on the strongest applicants.

---

### FIGURE 13.2:  AN EFFECTIVE FOUR-STEP SCREENING PROCESS

Every time a business goes through personnel turnover, many hundreds of dollars are lost. The interruption in productivity, wasted training time, paperwork processing, and recruitment efforts are all tangible expense items. The following four-step screening/ hiring system will help identify hot-spots in the relationship *before* a commitment is made by either employer or applicant:

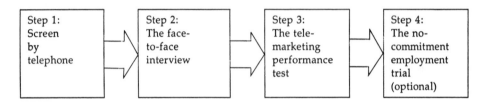

This approach was developed by a high-tech company that has extremely low caller turnover in its national telemarketing operation.

*Step 1: Screen by Telephone.* Seasoned recruiters are impressed by the *verbal abilities and listening skills* of a telemarketing applicant. They are *not* influenced by a person's physical appearance or body language since those characteristics are of little consequence in telephone work.

In order to properly appraise the strengths that help in effective telephone work, the recruiter must insist on listening to an applicant by phone *before* a personal interview takes place.

Through the five- to eight-minute conversation held in this first interview by telephone, the screener identifies the people who come across best. Some recruiters use a checklist during each call. This reminds the screener to rate each major attribute such as voice quality, listening ability, basic telephone etiquette, and others. A sample checklist is provided in Form 13.3.

Generally speaking, out of 30 responses to a classified ad, around 5 people should be impressive enough to warrant a personal interview, described right now.

*Step 2: The Face-to-Face Interview.* By the time stronger candidates actually visit your facility, you are *reasonably* certain they have what it takes to be effective on the phone. But the acid test is yet to come.

There are a number of reasons why a personal interview is important, but *none* is as vital as *setting up the telemarketing performance test*, which is the last thing done during the face-to-face interview. Here's a recommended interview process for the personal meeting:

With each candidate, go through a standard interview routine. This usually consists of:

- A get-acquainted small-talk session which helps reveal a bit more about the individual's personality and how the "chemistry" works between the two of you.

- A description of the telemarketing position. You'll show the person what the products look like or how the service works and explain what kind of customers you have. Then you'll conduct a tour of your offices.

- An explanation of compensation and benefits.

- Questions about the person's business and educational background.

*Step 3: The Telemarketing Performance Test.* If the applicant is still in contention at the end of the personal interview, the time has come to set up the all-important performance test.

Explain to your telemarketing candidate that the next step in the hiring process is a telephone sales presentation with *you* in the role of prospect or customer, whichever is appropriate to the job in question. For example, if the person is being considered for a telephone service position, then of course the performance test deals with a pertinent service topic.

You give the applicant a typed sheet that provides the basic steps of a telephone presentation. Accompanying this is a little hard data about one of your products or services. The applicant will study this so at least a rudimentary knowledge can be achieved before the call.

The candidate will call you within the next 24 hours at a designated time and will try to set an appointment with you, close an order, or solve a service problem, as the case may be. You need to specify in advance what the call objective is.

It is entirely true that the finalist probably has no prior experience in your industry—and perhaps little or none in telemarketing. That is exactly why this call will reveal how good the person's *instincts* are. Good performance will demand quick thinking and improvisation, both vital ingredients in a top telemarketer.

This performance test will invariably separate the pros from all the others. Your winner, while maybe not technically accurate, will be responsive and will try to overcome problems. All other things being equal, your final choice is the person who turns in the best telephone performance.

NOTE: When you take the role of prospect or customer, try not to make the situation overly difficult for your candidates. One mild objection from you will serve the purpose of demonstrating how well an aspiring telemarketer keeps his or her composure under fire.

The final step in this screening process gives you one more margin of protection and assurance.

*Step 4: The No-Commitment Employment Trial.* Some companies use this final screening step, some elect not to. One recruiter made this comment about the 30-day employment trial his company uses for new telemarketers:

> As good as an applicant seems to be, you'll always find out things about that person you wouldn't have dreamed of once they're aboard. No matter how carefully you interview someone and check their references, you can never think of everything. The areas you missed will come out later—and you may find them impossible to live with.
>
> Another thing is that a person may *think* they want to work in your industry but find out later it isn't really right for them. A 30-day trial gives the applicant a chance to find out if they'd be happy in your field.

The employment trial is a no-fault employment test of 14 days, 30 days, or whatever period you feel is sufficient to prove the compatibility and ability of your new telemarketer. Both parties—the employer and the employee—can unconditionally terminate the relationship at any time within that period. No reason need be given and no prior notice is required from either side. The level of compensation is the same you both agreed to during the initial interview stages, and so is the work schedule.

Since step 1, Screen by Telephone, is the tone-setter in this procedure, we'll now look at scripts for screening used by a leading calling operation.

## SCREENING APPLICANTS BY TELEPHONE

When a company and a potential new employee begin to come together, major decisions will soon be made on *both* sides. The company is preparing to devote considerable resources to an individual, and promising applicants are no doubt weighing other career possibilities, or at least other companies. A lot rides on each contact between the hiring firm and the job seeker.

There is no more crucial moment than the first call made to a company by a job candidate. That first impression is made in only a few seconds, and the initial impact is likely to endure even after other conversations have taken place between both parties.

Consider a highly qualified telemarketer who responds to a classified ad then is handled badly by someone in the hiring firm. That few seconds of negative experience may permanently damage the relationship. There are several very definite measures a firm can take to ensure a positive initial discussion:

- Prepare employees to pick up calls from applicants. This is the subject of Script 13.1.

- Have a fully organized presentation ready for screening applicants. This encompasses two areas, one of which is intelligent probing, a topic covered in the following section.

   The second area is a clear presentation of what the position is about and what the company does. This is covered in the section entitled Making Your Offer Look Bigger and Better.

- Finally, be ready to resolve the initial call in some way; either the applicant will proceed to the next step or not. But the situation should never be left in limbo.

Better applicants *know* whether or not an interviewer is prepared and may base a decision on that knowledge.

### SCRIPT 13.1: REFERRING CALLS FROM APPLICANTS

When a classified ad is running and other recruitment promotions are underway, a company must be prepared in every way to handle the expected call-ins. One vital precaution that *must* be taken is that employees must be alerted and prepared in advance of an ad, otherwise they can get drawn into conversation with respondents. One result is that inaccurate or conflicting information may be given.

These important call-ins should be *expected* by the people who pick up calls that come in. Furthermore, they should be equipped to handle them professionally.

A major retail music-store chain prefers not to have employees give applicants answers to any questions they may ask. All staff people who are likely to pick up calls are instructed to handle them this way:

| | |
|---|---|
| *Employee:* | *Good morning, Fisher Music Company. May I help you?* |
| *Applicant:* | *Hello. I'm calling about the ad in today's paper for a tele-marketing position with your company.* |
| *Employee:* | *Let me get you on the line with Jill Adams. First, can I take down your name and telephone number?* |
| *Applicant:* | *Sure. My name is Frank Kelly, and my number is 747–9419. Can you tell me how much the job pays?* |
| *Employee:* | *I'm certain Miss Adams will provide you with that informa-tion and answer any other questions you may have. Please hold for a moment and I'll let her know you're waiting to speak with her.* |

Employees are polite and helpful but simply will not impart any kind of job-related information.

Now the applicant is connected to the interviewer.

## SCRIPT 13.2a: A GUIDE FOR NARROWING THE FIELD

Since incoming call traffic will no doubt be heavy as a result of recruitment efforts, some quick decisions have to be made about the merits of applicants. The screener's objectives are

- To keep the initial call brief, but still get sufficient information to determine whether or not an applicant looks good enough to invite in for the step 2 personal interview.
- To "sell" the position to those worthy applicants who are probably talking to other companies that may be offering attractive employment packages.

An industrial-chemical company uses this format to guide their selection of tele-marketers and field representatives:

1. *A guide for screening incoming calls from applicants.*
   - Interviewer gives name, title, and, if necessary, complete company identifi-cation to candidate.
   - If this information has not been relayed by the person who picked up the call, interviewer asks for candidate's name, address, and phone number.
2. *Determining candidate's basic motivation.*
   - Why is candidate interested in this position?
   - Find out which categories fit the situation:

        Career growth

        Convenient to residence

        Long-range earnings potential

        Short-term survival income

   3. *Grade key aspects of candidate's background.*

By this stage of the conversation, the interviewer should be able to make judgments on:

        Candidate's voice quality

        Clarity of thinking and speech

        Vocabulary level

        Listening ability

        Ability to convey enthusiasm

        Ability to control conversation

Each of the above areas should be graded by the interviewer on an attribute checklist such as the Scoresheet at the end of this chapter.

   4. *Provide details about the position.*
      • Cover the following areas:

        Responsibilities

        Personal and professional growth

        Training

        Work environment

   5. *Candidate warrants further interviewer time.* Set showroom appointment for interview.

Dialogue for each section of the guide is now provided, beginning with Part 2:

## SCRIPT 13.2b: CALIBRATING MOTIVATION

In some instances, applicants who look good at first can suddenly turn sour if their motivation turns out to be thin. For example, few firms would want to invest in an individual who wants the job because it's convenient or because it would provide enough quick income to cover an overdue car payment.

    Motivation of the applicant must be probed *early* in the telephone interview. This dialogue is used by the chemical company after the introductory steps in Part 1:

    ***Interviewer:***        *Why do you think you'd like to work with us?*

In the words of this firm's personnel manager, this totally open-ended question "gives applicants enough rope to hang themselves." But if the response is guarded and does not reveal any clues about motivation, probing proceeds this way:

| | |
|---|---|
| *Applicant:* | *I like the sound of your ad. It seems like you people know what you're doing.* |
| *Interviewer:* | *We think we do. That's why we're looking for a person who is strongly motivated. So it is important for us to know two things about you.* |
| | *One, what is it that makes you want a highly responsible position? And two, what specific items in our ad caused you to call?* |

Another vague response here would serve to bring the interview to an end. Other disqualifiers would be "I only live about a mile away" or "I need the money." The interviewer is looking for *long-range* money motivation and/or career growth. A solid applicant would reply this way:

| | |
|---|---|
| *Applicant:* | *I know a little about your business, and I feel the income potential could be tremendous for the right person. If your compensation plan is good, I'd be interested. [or] I've known a few people in your industry and they've done well. I'm ready to get my teeth into a substantial career and build it for myself.* |

Now the interviewer moves to find out more about the applicant.

### SCRIPT 13.2c: EXPLORING PREVIOUS EMPLOYMENT AND EDUCATION

To qualify for a telemarketing position with your company, should a person be well-versed in your product or service? There are varying opinions on that issue. It certainly does help if you can hire a person who understands the fine points of your business, but many employers say it doesn't matter to them as long as the right attributes are present in the applicant. Some managers are even apprehensive about a telemarketer who has prior experience in the same industry. That particular situation is covered later in Script 13.2d.

Should a newly hired telemarketer have past experience in telephone or any other kind of selling? Here again there are various points of view. There are firms that maintain large calling staffs and can't spend the time on training. These firms often *insist* that an applicant have prior telephone experience. At the same time, many organizations have had notable success with inexperienced people in telemarketing positions. Once again, each firm must come to its own conclusions about the best way to go.

And what about formal education? Is it important for an individual to possess a certain level of schooling? There is no strong evidence to support the theory that education creates better revenue producers. This is another individual policy that has to be made by each hiring firm.

This segment of the interview should uncover the facts needed by a recruiter to effectively screen for previous employment and educational background. We'll start with the applicant's last statement—a response to the interviewer's question about motivation:

| *Applicant:* | *I've known a few people in your industry and they've done well. I'm ready to get my teeth into a substantial career and build it for myself.* |
| *Interviewer:* | *What kind of work have you been involved with over the past few years?* |
| *Applicant:* | *For the last four years I've worked for a company that sells limited partnerships. I was consistently in the top ten percent of their sales organization.* |
| *Interviewer:* | *Are you still with them?* |
| *Applicant:* | *Yes.* |
| *Interviewer:* | *If you were selected for this position, how soon could you break loose?* |
| *Applicant:* | *I'd like to give them two-weeks notice—but they'd probably let me go right away.* |
| *Interviewer:* | *Do you feel they'd give you a good reference?* |
| *Applicant:* | *I don't see any reason why not; we've always been on good terms.* |
| *Interviewer:* | *Why do you want to leave?* |
| *Applicant:* | *I don't feel I can go much farther here. Frankly, I'm looking for much more growth potential.* |
| *Interviewer:* | *How far have you gone with your schooling?* |
| *Applicant:* | *Two years of college and some part-time evening classes in business law.* |

When an applicant indicates prior experience with a rival industrial-chemical firm, extra probing is done:

### SCRIPT 13.2d: PROBING PRIOR EXPERIENCE IN YOUR INDUSTRY

Recruiters in this company have mixed feelings about hiring people who have past experience in the chemical industry. These applicants are not arbitrarily disqualified, but special care is taken to find out whether such a background will have a positive or negative impact on the firm if the individual is hired.

| *Interviewer:* | *What kind of work have you been involved with over the past few years?* |
| *Applicant:* | *I worked for Consolidated Chemical Company for the past couple of years. I was their second-highest producing telemarketer. I think that experience might be valuable to you.* |
| *Interviewer:* | *How come you left?* |

| *Applicant:* | *Personal reasons. The department manager and I didn't see eye to eye.* |
| *Interviewer:* | *Do you mind telling me a little about the issues you disagreed with?* |
| *Applicant:* | *The way leads were given out. New people got most of the easy stuff, and the higher producers like me were expected to develop all of our own prospects.* |
| *Interviewer:* | *Did you have a strong customer following?* |
| *Applicant:* | *I know of about 60 companies I could call for business.* |

This situation would be interpreted by the chemical company recruiter this way: The fatal disagreement might very well stem from a justified grievance. A danger signal would be if the caller appeared to be a chronic malcontent, always trying to change the system. This does not seem to be the case. The interviewer *could* have asked Would you be open to adopting our methods and leaving your other ones behind?

Since the answer to that question is almost always affirmative, many recruiters don't bother asking. On the positive side, this person demonstrates a healthy ego and also could bring a ready-made list of prospects to the job. The personal interview will help complete the picture for the recruiter.

When applicants are deemed unqualified during this initial call, the interviewer will stop the discussion at this point by saying, Thank you. As soon as we have reviewed other applicants, we'll contact you.

Then, within 48 hours a letter is sent that either rejects the applicant outright or describes a possible future opening, as the case may be. Examples of both letters are provided later.

When an applicant looks promising up to this point, the interviewer will proceed to briefly describe more about the company and the position.

## MAKING YOUR OFFER LOOK BIGGER AND BETTER

Due to heavy competition among recruiters for the best available telemarketing talent, ads are often grossly exaggerated. Misrepresentation can be rampant. Even the most sophisticated job seekers will sometimes have trouble sorting out fact from fancy when dealing with these predatory outfits.

Because of that unfortunate state of affairs, ethical recruiters face the problem of making the truth sound almost as good as fantasy. Recruiters for small firms have to put forth special efforts to describe the job and the company in the best possible light. *Any* effective interviewer who is up against that handicap must make the following points:

- The company is legitimate, ethical, reasonably substantial, and on at least a moderately fast growth track.

- Potential earnings are at an acceptable level for the applicant, and the compensation plan puts those earnings within reach.

- Job tasks are within standard parameters.
- A career track exists for a person who performs well.
- Professional growth is available by virtue of training and other learning opportunities.
- Work surroundings are set up for efficiency and comfort.

When a recruiter can *believably* establish those items as components of the job, it will look good to most intelligent applicants.

Dialogue for each point follows.

### SCRIPT 13.3a: "MERCHANDISING" THE COMPANY

Seasoned interviewers are able to effectively sell the job and company to an applicant but remain just aloof enough to keep the candidate wondering. It's a difficult balance to achieve. One top interviewer summed it up this way:

> We work on making the position sound just as good as it *can* sound. But the overall impression we try to give the applicant is, "Don't you wish *you* could qualify for this incredible opportunity?"

Here's the opening used for describing the company. Remember, this segment of the interview is *only* used when the applicant appears to be a solid possibility:

*Interviewer:*     *I'm sure you're wondering about who we are and exactly what the position entails. I'll run through some of the basics now. If you feel it's the kind of opportunity you want to pursue, we can set up an appointment for you before we hang up.*

*Barnett Company was founded in 1953. We're a fast-growing, privately owned manufacturer of specialty chemicals — mostly used in plant maintenance applications. We employ 225 people and export our products worldwide. Our strong suit is research and development; our customers see us as a highly innovative firm that emphasizes quality and safety.*

*We're therefore able to compete on even terms with much larger companies but provide better service than they can.*

Now that the size and scope of the company have been established, the interviewer proceeds to deliver a few words about potential income.

### SCRIPT 13.3b: "HOW MUCH MONEY YOU CAN EXPECT TO MAKE"

While the classified ad may have provided a range of potential income, a bright applicant will want to know how that potential income is reached. This information is important due to the pie-in-the-sky promises made by unethical recruiters.

It is *not* necessary to get into exhaustive detail about the compensation program at this stage, but a *concise summary* is needed.

From the statement about the company in Script 13.3a, the interviewer goes directly into the compensation description:

> *Interviewer:*    *The first year $30,000 to $40,000 income range mentioned in our ad is based on a guaranteed $20,000 salary plus commissions of four percent. Actually, that's conservative since we have a bonus system that should take the new telemarketer up to the top end of that range, or higher.*
>
> *We include a complete benefits program that I can review for you later.*

Having this brief explanation of the pay program early in the presentation—*before* the applicant requests it—is a good move for this reason: Unethical telemarketing operations will often avoid the topic as long as they can, and even when it does come up, an applicant may have to dig for specific numbers.

A survey of job tasks is now given to the hopeful telemarketer.

## SCRIPT 13.3c: SCOPE OF RESPONSIBILITY

During the initial call, a telemarketing applicant will seldom press for *details* about what the job entails for fear of appearing brash. It is therefore a strong plus when those specifics are presented.

> *Interviewer:*    *The person we'd like to have aboard will spend about two hours a day on new prospects and another couple of hours on follow-up contacts.*
>
> *The balance of the day is used for preparing mail-outs, updating lists, and handling other related sales support work.*
>
> *Some time each day will be needed for working with outside sales reps who will be following up on some of the leads created by telemarketing. Also, we'd want our telemarketer to attend and contribute to sales strategy meetings on a weekly basis.*
>
> *Our typical day is 8 A.M. to 5 P.M., Monday through Friday, but extra hours may be necessary on occasion.*

At about this time, the applicant will be wondering about where this job can go:

## SCRIPT 13.3d: PROFESSIONAL GROWTH

An applicant may be apprehensive about advancement when the hiring firm is small and privately owned. A vision of key jobs being filled by sons, daughters, and other relatives is a natural reaction and could discourage some job seekers.

This brief statement can eliminate concern:

*Interviewer:*      *We like to get our managers from inside the company and prefer people who come up through sales. Our founder is now retired, and his son is our chairman. Outside of that, there are no family members in active positions.*

Facts about training follow soon after the preceding statement.

## SCRIPT 13.3e: TRAINING OFFERED

A remarkably high percentage of people hired for various positions say that the employer's promise to provide training was a material factor in their decision to take the offer. Extra knowledge and proficiency often rank higher than income to many new employees.

This statement gets the point across:

*Interviewer:*      *The entire first week of employment is devoted to product familiarization. That includes intensive work on industrial applications for our products and various problems that we typically deal with in client situations.*

*That type of training is ongoing. Sessions are usually held monthly in our offices.*

*In addition, we pay for seminar attendance when topics are pertinent to what we do. There are usually three or four per year held locally by outside firms.*

*After the week of product training, we spend three days covering our business and sales procedures. We make a big investment in new employees to assure a high level of professionalism.*

Next, a little about work surroundings:

## SCRIPT 13.3f: WORK ENVIRONMENT

A good many telemarketers have been through at least one situation where they joined a firm and ran into complete bedlam. In the most drastic example, the calling area was an afterthought—a desk and chair crammed into a dark corner. A printer chattered constantly, punctuated by slamming doors and shouting. A final blow was the need to wait each time for an outside phone line.

Unfavorable facilities may be compounded by people problems. In poor environments, callers may be regarded as intruders or outsiders. That makes good performance tougher to achieve.

These words should help erase any doubts in the applicant's mind about environment:

*Interviewer:*      *We've also put a lot of thought into our telemarketing facility. It's extremely quiet and comfortable—yet accessible to other departments. The telephone system is new and should be sufficient for the next several years.*

*Most important is the fact that telemarketing is a respected operation in this company, so one of the things we need in our new person is the ability to work closely with others to maintain that esteem.*

Finally, the face-to-face session is set up with candidates who have been chosen to advance to step 2:

### SCRIPT 13.3g: SETTING UP THE PERSONAL INTERVIEW

An interviewer must guard against sounding too anxious during the conversation—and especially at this point. An applicant has to feel that the job is a plum, that competition is stiff, and that the interviewer is hard to impress. At the same time, the objective should appear to be attainable:

*Interviewer:*     *If you feel you might fit into the position based on the information I've given you so far, we can arrange to spend about an hour at our offices so you can see the operation and get more detail on the points that may not be clear to you right now.*

*We have other people to see, and I'm sure you have other interviews scheduled, so we can try to find a day and time that works for both of us.*

*Complete* telephone interviews—ones that cover both the qualifying of an applicant *and* a description of the offer—only constitute 10 to 20 percent of the total calls received in response to recruitment efforts. Therefore, the six minutes or so this call takes is usually not difficult to fit in—even when phone traffic is fairly heavy.

An interviewer must control questions from applicants. If the person is a strong candidate, questions should be deferred to the time of the personal interview if possible. This will help keep the time-per-call down and also works to keep the applicant's curiosity at a high level.

More and more interviewers are using a checklist like this to grade applicants.

---

### FORM 13.2: CALLER SCORESHEET

By using this scoresheet, you can rate the strengths of each ad respondent. Change the attributes to best fit your screening needs.

Name _____  Source of Applicant _____

Address _____  Date _____

City _____  State _____  Zip _____

Telephone (    ) _____

|                                                                          | Yes | No |
|--------------------------------------------------------------------------|-----|-----|
| 1. Definitely *wants* to sell by telephone.                              | ___ | ___ |
| 2. Genuinely people-oriented and sociable.                               | ___ | ___ |
| 3. Appears agreeable to compensation offer.                              | ___ | ___ |
| 4. Empathy and sensitivity.                                              | ___ | ___ |
| 5. Good listener. Never cuts in when other person is talking.            | ___ | ___ |
| 6. Gets to the point quickly.                                            | ___ | ___ |
| 7. Enunciates well/has good speaking voice. Projects.                    | ___ | ___ |
| 8. Above-average intelligence. Can improvise quickly.                    | ___ | ___ |
| 9. Not excessively vulnerable to rejection.                              | ___ | ___ |
| 10. Ability to punch into speech. Uses exciting language instinctively.  | ___ | ___ |
| 11. High energy level, but not overly temperamental.                     | ___ | ___ |
| 12. Organized, good work habits; uses available selling time wisely.     | ___ | ___ |
| 13. Has solid product knowledge in this or related field.                | ___ | ___ |
| 14. Willing to start work early.                                         | ___ | ___ |

**Total Score:** (Multiply each "Yes" by 7.1 for total score.)     _____

Notes: _____

_____

_____

_____

_____

_____

_____

_____

_____

_____

*LETTER 13.1:   OUTRIGHT APPLICANT REJECTION*

There are basically two kinds of rejection, one in which an individual is totally un-suited to the position; the other in which the person is not in the running but is worthy of consideration at some future time.

An outright rejection is used for the applicant who misses qualifying by a wide margin:

Dear Mr. Farmer:

Your interest in Consolidated Chemical Company is appreciated.

Our ad for a telemarketer attracted responses from a large and high-quality group of people. We were fortunate enough to connect with an individual who we feel is uniquely well suited to handle the demands of the position.

Our best wishes for your success.

Sincerely,

Richard G. Ashton

For those people who may be considered in the future, the following rejection letter is used. It is assumed that this particular applicant made it to step 2 of the screening process, the personal interview.

### LETTER 13.2: POSSIBLE FUTURE OPPORTUNITY

Dear Mrs. Warner:

Thank you for your patience during our selection process. Coming to a decision was more difficult than we ever could have imagined due to the large number of truly exceptional people who responded to our offer.

A uniquely well-qualified person was finally chosen.

Your name was high on our list. Although you will undoubtedly move on to other opportunities, we would like to consider you when another opening comes up if your circumstances permit.

So, if you desire, please keep us informed of your whereabouts.

Sincerely,

Richard G. Ashton

## REFINING YOUR APPLICANT INTERVIEWS

Use the Form 13.3 checklist to help assure that key components are included in your screening program. By doing some advance planning on how your selection process will work, the task will proceed more smoothly and will look far more professional to applicants.

When the components are worked out, use the Form 13.4 Interview Dialogue Worksheet to settle on points to include in your initial telephone discussion with those who respond to your recruitment efforts.

### FORM 13.3: INTERVIEW CHECKLIST

1. If you do *not* plan to use the four-step process described earlier in this chapter, what kind of contacts with applicants *will* you use?

   Step 1: _____

   Step 2: _____

Step 3: _____

Step 4: _____

2. List six of the most important personality characteristics you will seek in the leading candidates:

   • _____

   • _____

   • _____

   • _____

   • _____

   • _____

3. How do you feel about prior experience in your industry?

   ____ Desired      ____ Not desired

4. Is prior sales experience desirable?

   ____ Yes      ____ No

5. If so, how much experience? _____ years

6. What kind of prior education will you require? _____

   _____

7. Will you measure an applicant's motivation in terms of:

   ____ Money?

   ____ Career growth?

   ____ Both?

8. If your compensation program is established, describe it briefly here: _____

   _____

   _____

   _____

9. In describing your telemarketing position by telephone, which areas will you cover?

   ____ Company background

   ____ Compensation program

   ____ Job description

   ____ Career growth potential

   ____ Training

   ____ Environment

_____ Other: _____

_____

_____

10. Do you have scoresheets ready to use for each call?

_____ Yes     _____ No

11. Do you have rejection letters ready?

_____ Yes     _____ No

12. Have you prepared a format for conducting personal interviews with the better applicants?

_____ Yes     _____ No

_____

_____

## FORM 13.4:  INTERVIEW DIALOGUE WORKSHEET

Work out dialogue for the initial telephone interview with applicants. Use only the questions and descriptions you feel fit your situation. You may want to cover some topics later, during the face-to-face interview.

*Introduction*

Give name, title: _____

_____

_____

If necessary, get full applicant identification: _____

_____

*Qualify Applicant*

Calibrate motivation: _____

_____

_____

_____

_____

Explore employment background: _____

_____

_____

_____

If desired, further probe experience in your industry: _____

_____

_____

_____

_____

Explore educational background: _____

_____

_____

_____

_____

*Describe the Position*

Statement about the company: _____

_____

_____

_____

_____

_____

_____

_____

_____

_____

_____

Compensation program: _____

_____

_____

_____

_____

Job responsibility: _____

_____

_____

_____

_____

_____

Professional growth: _____

_____

_____

_____

_____

_____

Training offered: _____

_____

_____

_____

_____

_____

Environment: _____

_____

_____

_____

_____

Set up personal interview: _____

_____

_____

_____

_____

Notes: _____

_____

_____

_____

_____

_____

# INDEX